THE
Journey

THE
Journey

HOW TO LIVE BY FAITH
IN AN UNCERTAIN WORLD

BILLY GRAHAM

W PUBLISHING GROUP
A Division of Thomas Nelson Publishers
Since 1798

www.wpublishinggroup.com

THE JOURNEY
© 2006 Billy Graham

Published by W Publishing Group, a division of Thomas Nelson, Inc., P.O. Box 141000, Nashville, Tennessee 37214.

W Publishing Group books may be purchased in bulk for educational, business, fund-raising, or sales promotional use. For information, please e-mail SpecialMarkets@ThomasNelson.com.

All Scripture quotations, unless otherwise indicated, are taken from The Holy Bible, New International Version (NIV). Copyright © 1973, 1978, 1984, International Bible Society. Used by permission of Zondervan Bible Publishers.

Other Scripture references are from the following sources:

The New King James Version (NKJV®), copyright 1979, 1980, 1982, Thomas Nelson, Inc., Publishers.

The Holy Bible, English Standard Version (ESV), copyright © 2001 by Crossway Bibles, a division of Good News Publishers. Used by permission.

The King James Version of the Bible (KJV).

The New Century Version® (NCV), copyright © 1987, 1988, 1991 by Word Publishing, a Division of Thomas Nelson, Inc. Used by permision. All rights reserved.

Library of Congress Cataloging-in-Publication Data

Graham, Billy, 1918–
    The journey : how to live by faith in an uncertain world / by Billy Graham.
        p. cm.
    ISBN 0-8499-1832-4 (HC)
    ISBN 0-8499-9145-5 (IE)
    1. Christian life. I. Title.
    BV4501.3.G72 2006
    248.4—dc22   2005034999

Printed in the United States of America
06 07 08 09 10 RRD 9 8 7 6 5 4 3 2 1

CONTENTS

Preface / vii

SECTION ONE:
THE JOURNEY BEGINS

1. Welcome to the Journey / 3

2. The Great Designer / 13

3. The Great Design / 23

4. What Went Wrong? / 32

5. Can We Start Over? / 43

6. A New Beginning / 53

7. Can We Be Sure? / 63

8. Heading in the Right Direction / 74

SECTION TWO:
STRENGTH FOR THE JOURNEY

9. Preparing for the Long Haul / 85

10. The Unending Battle / 94

11. Our Unfailing Guide / 104

12. Keeping in Contact / 114

13. Traveling Together / 124

14. Our Constant Helper / 134

15. Strength for Each Day / 143

CONTENTS

SECTION THREE:
CHALLENGES ALONG THE WAY

16. Prone to Wander / 155

17. Confronting the Enemies Within / 165

18. Emotions That Defeat Us / 175

19. Things That Destroy / 185

20. When Life Turns Against Us / 195

21. When Others Disappoint / 205

22. Dealing with Suffering and Loss / 215

SECTION FOUR:
STAYING THE COURSE

23. One Day at a Time / 227

24. Forks in the Road / 237

25. For Better or for Worse / 247

26. Keeping the Flame Alive / 257

27. Passing the Baton / 267

28. Making an Impact / 277

29. As Life Moves On / 287

30. Our Glorious Hope / 298

A Final Word from Billy Graham / 310

Acknowledgments / 312

PREFACE

BY BILLY GRAHAM

Y OU CAN'T CHANGE THE PAST. WHATEVER HAS HAP-
pened in your life so far—both good and bad—cannot be
altered, and all the decisions and events that have made you what
you are today are indelibly inscribed in the story of your life.

But with God's help you *can* change the future—and that's what
this book is all about. The future doesn't need to be a copy of the
past, nor does God want it to be. No matter what your life has been
like so far, God wants to put your feet on a new path . . . a better
path . . . His path. And regardless of what you may have thought,
His path promises joy and peace and purpose far beyond anything
you could have imagined.

This doesn't just happen, however. An architect draws the plans for a new building—but it still has to be built. A composer writes a new piece of music—but it still has to be played. A chef devises a new recipe—but the ingredients still have to be cooked.

In the same way, God has given us a blueprint for living—but we must know what it is and then put it into action. And this can happen because God doesn't leave us to do it alone. He wants to be with us every step of the way, guiding and helping us (and even correcting us when necessary), because He loves us and wants what is best for us.

My prayer as you read this book is that God will use it to help you begin a new journey in life—the greatest, most exciting journey you could ever experience. As we'll see, it isn't always an easy journey, but even in the midst of our problems, temptations, and sorrows, life can be different. Most of all, it is a journey of hope, because it leads us to heaven.

No matter how young or old you are or what your life has been like so far, I invite you to explore this journey for yourself. May God bless you as you read this book and teach you through its pages how you, too, can live by faith in an uncertain world.

SECTION ONE

—

THE
JOURNEY
BEGINS

ONE

WELCOME TO THE JOURNEY

O LORD, . . . if you will, please grant success to the journey on which I have come.

—GENESIS 24:42

LIFE IS A JOURNEY.

Like every other journey, it has a starting point. You had no choice about it, of course, any more than you had a choice about your parents or the color of your eyes or your race or gender. But the minute you were born you embarked on a journey—the journey of life.

And like every other journey, it has an end. It may come suddenly and unexpectedly, or after years of declining health—but it *will* come, and like your birth, you'll have no choice about it. You can ignore it or laugh at it, but that won't change its inevitability. A wise poet once said that death comes equally to us all and makes us all equal when it comes.

But like every other journey, it also has a middle—and that is our real journey: those years between our birth and our death. For some it is tragically brief. For most of us, however, our life's journey will last many years, moving successively from childhood to adolescence and young adulthood, then on through the middle years to old age.

Like birth and death, this part of the journey is also inevitable. Try as we might, we can't turn back the clock or stop the relentless march of time. Years ago I never dreamed I would live well into my late eighties, but life has a way of surprising us, and none of us can predict how long our journey will last. My wife, Ruth, and I talk about it frequently, knowing that some day soon our journey through this life will be over and we will embark on another journey—one that will last forever.

Caught Up in the Present

Life is a journey—although sometimes we forget it. Life becomes so hectic, and we become so preoccupied with our immediate concerns that we don't step back and see the whole picture. For many people life is a constant struggle just to survive. Others have everything they could ever want yet remain unsatisfied and unfulfilled.

Perhaps you see your own life's journey as a series of unrelated events—some good, some bad—strung together like beads on a string. Or perhaps you feel trapped like a leaf in a rushing stream, tossed about by circumstances beyond your control. Or like many people you may never have stopped to think about the road you are traveling—never asking where you came from or why you are here or where you are going.

But God didn't intend for our journey through life to be this way. Instead, He meant for it to be filled with joy and purpose, with even the most ordinary events being part of His plan. He also wants to guide us as we make decisions and give us hope for the future. Most of all, He wants to join us on our life's journey.

What Kind of Journey?

Life is a journey—but what kind has it been so far for you?

Perhaps your journey has been marked by disappointment, sorrow, and heartache. You yearn for something different, something better in life—but lasting happiness and peace have eluded you. Or perhaps you decided years ago to spend your life pursuing excitement, pleasure, fame, or success. For a time those may have satisfied you—but eventually (if you're honest) you discovered they led only to boredom, disillusionment, emptiness, or even self-destruction.

Or you may have found yourself overwhelmed by crushing problems beyond your control: sickness, financial pressures, broken relationships, fear, guilt, loneliness, despair. Life for you has become a hopeless burden with no end in sight. Or perhaps you are one of those whose journey has been relatively free from problems yet aimless and empty, without any real purpose or direction. You may even believe in God and consider yourself a sincere Christian, and still you're discouraged and confused, overwhelmed by circumstances you don't understand and don't know how to escape. Tragically, every year thousands decide they can't bear life any longer and decide to end it. You may even have been tempted to follow them.

The words of Job in the Old Testament are just as true today as when they were written thousands of years ago: "Man is born to trouble as surely as sparks fly upward" (Job 5:7). Job knew it from personal experience, and so do we.

Can Life Be Any Different?

But must our journey always be this way? Are we destined to lurch down life's road from one pothole or detour to another?

Down inside we all sense that this was not the way life was meant to be, and we yearn for something better. We suspect there must be another way, a different path from the one we have been traveling. But why do so few people seem to find it? Why have we missed it? *Can life be any different?*

The answer to that last question is *Yes!* No matter who you are or what your life has been like so far, the rest of your life's journey *can* be different. With God's help you *can* begin again. With Him you *can* confront your problems and begin to deal with them, and you *can* avoid life's pitfalls and detours. More than that, with God's help you *can* make an impact on our world. I have experienced this in my own life, and over the years I have met countless others who have discovered it as well. So can you.

Life is a journey, but how can it become a *good* journey, a journey that is not only satisfying and challenging, but one that fulfills the purpose for which we were created? Answering that question is the reason for this book, and in the following pages I invite you to join me in discovering God's plan for this exciting journey called life.

You will only make this journey once. Why not make the most of it?

The Divine Appointment

Before we begin, however, we need to understand three great truths about our journey through life. They are like the backdrops or scenery for a play, setting the stage for everything that follows.

The first truth is very simple—but also very profound: God put you on the journey of life.

You aren't here by chance or by accident; you are here because God put you here. Long before the world was created, God knew all about you, and He planned to give you life. *From all eternity you were part of His plan.* No, you didn't have any choice about whether or not you would be born—but *God* had a choice about it, and *He chose to give you life.* He is the Creator of everything—including you. This journey is yours to travel—but God gave it to you. Never forget: God put you on the journey.

Throughout the Bible this truth made a difference in people's lives—and it will in yours as well. God told Jeremiah, "Before I formed you in the womb I knew you" (Jeremiah 1:5), and Jeremiah accepted God's call to be His prophet. The young shepherd David understood it: "All the days ordained for me were written in your book before one of them came to be" (Psalm 139:16). When David became king, he led the Jewish people to the greatest heights they had ever known.

You and I aren't here by chance or by accident; God put us on this journey called life. We came from Him, and our greatest joy will come from giving ourselves back to Him and learning to walk with Him every day until we return to Him.

We Are Not Alone

We need, however, to understand a second truth: God wants to join us on this journey.

Think about that a moment. God could have created us and then abandoned us and forgotten all about us. Many people, in fact, believe this is exactly what God must have done, or at least they act as if they do. They assume God isn't interested in them—

so why should they be interested in Him? To them God is distant, remote, unconcerned about the problems and decisions they face every day.

But this isn't true! God not only put us on this journey but He wants to join us on it, if we will only let Him. We don't need to be alone, for He is with us! The psalmist asked, "Where can I go from your Spirit? Where can I flee from your presence? If I go up to the heavens, you are there; if I make my bed in the depths, you are there" (Psalm 139:7–8).

If we understand this truth, it gives us hope—hope that our lives *can* be different, because God cares about us and wants to help us. No matter what happens, God will never abandon us if our trust is in Him. Moses declared, "The LORD himself goes before you and will be with you; he will never leave you nor forsake you" (Deuteronomy 31:8). Jesus promised, "Surely I am with you always, to the very end of the age" (Matthew 28:20). Across the centuries millions have discovered the truth of these words, and so can you.

A New Path

There is, however, a final truth we need to understand about life's journey: Not only has God put us on our journey . . . not only does He want to join us on this journey . . . but God calls us to a new journey. To put it another way, *God calls us to take a new path—the path of faith and trust in Him.*

Imagine you were hiking in the woods one day, planning to go somewhere you had never been before, and after an hour or two you came to a fork in the trail. Now, instead of having only one path you could follow, you had two. But which was the right path? Both obviously led somewhere—but where? Which would get you to your destination?

On closer inspection you saw that one path appeared much wider and easier to travel and was apparently used by more people. You were tempted to take it; after all, if most people traveled it (you reasoned), it must be the right way.

But then suppose another hiker approached. What would you do? The logical thing would be to ask him if he knew which path you ought to take to reach your destination. Without hesitation he urges you to take the second path, even if it is narrower and less traveled. Only it, he says, will take you to your destination. Are you *sure*, you ask him somewhat doubtfully? Certainly, he replies— because I made the path. In fact, I'm headed that way myself, and I'll walk with you so you won't get lost.

Which path would you choose? You probably wouldn't even hesitate; you would choose the second one. You still would be on a journey, but now you would be on a different path—the right path.

This is what God urges us to do: *to choose a new path—a different path from the one we have been on.* This path is one He has laid out for us, and He assures us that it alone leads to true life. Our journey will continue, but now we will be on the right path, even if most people don't take it. Jesus put it this way: "Enter through the narrow gate. For wide is the gate and broad is the road that leads to destruction, and many enter through it. But small is the gate and narrow the road that leads to life, and only a few find it" (Matthew 7:13–14).

Why Take It?

God invites us to change paths and take the rest of our journey with Him. In fact, He not only invites us, He *urges* us! But why should we? Why not stay on the road we already know, even if we haven't yet found the peace and security we seek? Why risk taking a new path?

Let me give you three reasons why changing to God's path is worth the risk.

First, the old path will never deliver what it promises.

Look around and ask yourself how many people are truly happy. On the surface some appear satisfied and content—but are they really? What happens to them down the road or when life turns against them?

The old path promises peace and security—but ends up in anxiety, fear, heartache, boredom, and sorrow. The old path promises freedom—but enslaves us with lust, greed, anger, and bitterness. Like the self-centered rich man in one of Jesus' parables, the old path says, "Take life easy; eat, drink and be merry." But God says, "You fool! This very night your life will be demanded from you" (Luke 12:19–20). That man chose the wrong path—and it destroyed him.

The old path promises us everything, but its promises are hollow and leave us with nothing. Why stay on it?

Promises Fulfilled

But there is a second reason to choose God's path for the rest of your journey: God's path always delivers what He promises.

Perhaps you have known people who were on that road we have labeled "God's path." (You may even be on that road yourself.) They weren't perfect; they may even have had some rough edges you didn't particularly like. But in spite of that, you detected something different about them, you sensed something was missing in your own life. When things went wrong, they had an inner peace you couldn't explain. When others were hurting or in need, they responded selflessly and with compassion. Why? Because they had discovered the secret of walking on life's path with God.

Don't misunderstand me; I'm not saying our journey will always be easy and trouble free. Those who say God always promises us prosperity and health have forgotten Jesus' warning: "In this world you will have trouble" (John 16:33). Christians aren't exempt from suffering and grief. Yet in the midst of it all, they experience "the peace of God, which transcends all understanding" (Philippians 4:7).

The Way Home

One final reason for choosing God's path is of supreme importance: It leads us home.

Whenever I am traveling, I constantly look forward to the moment when I will return home. Even if I'm very busy and preoccupied, in the back of my mind one thought is always present: "Soon I'll be going home!" Home is a place of peace and security and rest; home is where I belong. When my team and I went to Australia for six months, none of our families were with us. As time went on, we grew more and more homesick, and we talked more and more about home. We knew we were serving the Lord, and we knew missionaries and military personnel often stayed away from their homes much longer. But that didn't ease our own deep longing for home.

How much greater should be our longing for our eternal home! You and I aren't meant to live for only a few decades on this earth; *we are destined for eternity.* The Bible says this world is not our final home; we are "strangers and pilgrims on the earth" (Hebrews 11:13 NKJV). Our true home is heaven—and that is where God's path leads.

Which Way Will It Be?

You and I are on a journey; we have been on it since the day we were born, and it won't end until our time on earth is finished. But what kind of journey will it be for you?

The answer to that question is in your hands. You can't change the past, but with God's help you can change the future. He knows all about you: your strengths and weaknesses, your failures and heartaches. But He doesn't want you to be shackled by the past. Instead, *He wants to free you from your old ways and put your feet on a new path—His path.*

Jesus said, "I have come that they may have life, and have it to the full" (John 10:10). You can begin life's journey afresh by committing your life to Christ and learning to walk with Him every day. This is what this book is all about, and this is what I invite you to do.

Let the journey begin!

TWO

THE GREAT DESIGNER

O Lord, our Lord,
  how majestic is your name in all the earth!
You have set your glory
  above the heavens.

—Psalm 8:1

Y OU WILL NEVER UNDERSTAND WHO YOU ARE UNTIL
you understand who God is.

The reason is simple: God made you. You and I aren't here by chance or accident, or because of some blind natural process. We are here because God put us here, not as an afterthought or on a whim but by a deliberate act of creation.

But how can we know what God is really like? After all, people have all kinds of ideas about God—some logical, some very fanciful or even contradictory. How do we know which one is right? Or if any of them are?

How Can We Know?

Some years ago I was invited to visit the Soviet Union's famed "Academic City," one of their finest scientific research centers located near Novosibirsk in Siberia. While there I had a lively debate with one of their most distinguished scholars, the head of their anthropology department. As we talked, I asked him if he had ever found a tribe or group of people anywhere in the world that did not believe in God or in some type of higher power. After a few moments he admitted he had not. Although he claimed to be an atheist, he reluctantly agreed that belief in a divine power was universal.

Down inside we all sense there must be something—or Someone—greater than ourselves. We also sense that death must not be the end, but there must be something beyond the grave. The Bible says that God "has also set eternity in the hearts of men" (Ecclesiastes 3:11).

But what is God like? Some picture Him as a kindly old grandfather with a long white beard and a vague smile (although a bit out of touch with the times). Others see Him as a stern policeman, always ready to punish us if we get out of line. Still others conclude God must be like their own father might have been, indifferent or cold or never satisfied because we always fall short of what He demands. And some believe God is only a vague, impersonal force (somewhat like gravity or magnetism), or they conclude we can't know anything for certain about Him. Your guess about God, they say, is just as good (or bad) as mine. And some people, of course, reject the whole idea of God.

Sometimes people ask me why I urge them to believe in Jesus Christ. Isn't that narrow, they say? Don't all religions believe essentially the same thing? Isn't one just as good as another?

In reply I point out how different the world's religions actually are from each other—something they often haven't realized. Some religions believe in one God; others believe in thousands of deities. Some believe God cares about us; others contend God is indifferent to the human race. Some believe in life after death; others don't. Some believe God is the limitless, sovereign ruler of the universe; others worship man-made idols or animals or planets and stars. Some believe God is gracious and loving; others see Him as harsh and judgmental.

They can't all be right, not if we live in a logical world (which we do). But are *any* of them right? How can we know?

God Has Shown Himself

Unfortunately, most speculations about God miss one very important truth: God *wants* us to know what He is like. We don't need to guess, because *God has revealed Himself to us.*

Suppose you decided you didn't want anyone to know you existed. What would you have to do? Not only would you have to avoid any contact with other people, but you'd have to be sure you didn't leave any evidence around that you existed. You couldn't even put out your trash or turn on a light! Just the smallest trace would indicate you existed, and the more clues you left behind, the more convinced people would be that you were real.

This is somewhat the way it is with God. We know He exists because He has left clues behind for us to discover. But there is a crucial difference: *God isn't trying to hide from us.* Quite the opposite: God *wants* us to know He exists. Not only that, *He wants us to know what He is like.* In other words, He wants to communicate with us! Just as we can only know someone if they reveal themselves to us, so we can only know God if He reveals Himself to us. And He has!

Finding God's Footprints

How has God revealed Himself? One way is through the world around us, the world He created. His "footprints" are everywhere, if we will but see them.

Look up on a starry night, and you will see the majesty and power of an infinite Creator. Recently I saw a report about some new discoveries in astronomy. It stated that astronomers now believe there may be as many as 140 billion galaxies in the known universe, some more than eleven billion light-years away and each containing at least several hundred billion stars. We can't begin to imagine such distances or quantities.

Or examine a drop of water through a powerful microscope, and you will see God's concern for even the smallest detail. Inspect a newborn baby's hands and feet, and you will marvel at the intricacy of His design. Recently I read an article pointing out that our bodies contain about ten thousand *trillion* cells, each one containing a strand of our individual DNA, an unimaginable number. Or think about the way plants grow and rain falls and animals provide for their young, and you will see God's wisdom and care. Even when we look within ourselves, we detect God's handiwork. Our creativity, our inner sense of right and wrong, our ability to love and to reason—all bear witness to the fact that God created us in His image.

The Bible says God "has not left himself without testimony: He has shown kindness by giving you rain from heaven and crops in their seasons" (Acts 14:17). The Bible also says, "For since the creation of the world God's invisible qualities—his eternal power and divine nature—have been clearly seen, being understood from what has been made" (Romans 1:20). Professor Charles Townes, who won the 2005 Templeton Prize and shared the 1964 Nobel Prize in physics as coinventor of the laser, was recently quoted as saying, "The face that the universe has a beginning is a very striking thing. How do you explain that unique event without God?"

No matter where we look, we see God's footprints.

The God Who Speaks

Simply looking around us isn't enough. We need something more if we are to see God clearly. *We need Him to speak to us.*

You might learn something about me if you saw me walking down the street (you would at least conclude I exist!). You would learn even more by watching me work. But you would only discover what I was really like if we sat down and talked. The same is true with God. We need Him to speak to us—and He has!

How has He spoken? *First of all (as we will see later in more detail) God has spoken to us through a Book: the Bible.* This is why we call the Bible "God's Word," because God gave it to us and He speaks to us through it. One biblical writer put it this way: "God spoke . . . through the prophets at many times and in various ways" (Hebrews 1:1).

The Bible is actually a library of books—some long, some short—written over hundreds of years by many authors. Behind each one, however, was another Author: *the Spirit of God.* The apostle Peter wrote, "Above all, you must understand that no prophecy of Scripture came about by the prophet's own interpretation. For prophecy never had its origin in the will of man, but men spoke from God as they were carried along by the Holy Spirit" (2 Peter 1:20–21).

God has spoken to us in words we can understand, and those words are found in the Bible.

Second, God has spoken to us through a Person: Jesus Christ. Just as the Bible is God's *written* Word, so Jesus is God's *living* Word. Jesus was God in human flesh, and through Him we discover what God is really like. The Bible says, "For in Christ all the fullness of the Deity lives in bodily form" (Colossians 2:9). Do you want to know what God is like? Look at Jesus Christ, for He was God living among us. As John recorded, God "became flesh and dwelt among us, and we have seen his glory, glory as of the only Son from the Father, full of grace and truth" (John 1:14 ESV).

We *can* know what God is like because He *wants* us to know. And we can know what God is like because *He has spoken* to us — through the written Word, the Bible, and through the living Word, Jesus Christ.

But what is He like?

What Is God Like?

I will always be grateful to my mother for making me memorize these words from our church's old catechism when I was a boy: "God is a Spirit, infinite, eternal, and unchangeable in His being, wisdom, power, holiness, justice, goodness, and truth." I can't say I fully understood those words then (and even now I marvel at their depth), but over the years they have given me a rich understanding of who God is and what He is like. Admittedly we can't fully understand God. He is far greater than we are. He is infinite and we are finite. Only in heaven will we see Him in all of His fullness.

Sometimes when I was a boy my father would drive us from our home near Charlotte to the Blue Ridge Mountains. I remember seeing them through the haze in the distance, and when they first appeared, they seemed so small, while we seemed so big in our automobile. But as we got closer to the mountains, they became huge, and we became small.

The same is true with God. Sometimes we think God must be just like we are, only a little bit bigger. But that isn't an accurate picture. He is God—and we are human. God reminded the ancient Israelites, "I am God, and not man—the Holy One among you" (Hosea 11:9). Only when we understand His greatness will we understand our smallness.

But this doesn't mean we can't understand *anything* about God. We *can* know what He is like, because God has revealed Himself to us. Let me summarize *four important truths* He wants us to understand.

God Is a Spirit

The first truth God wants us to know about Himself is that He is a spirit. "God is spirit," Jesus told the Samaritan woman He met outside the village of Sychar (John 4:24). God isn't made of atoms or molecules; He isn't part of the created world. He exists instead in a wholly different realm—the realm of the spirit.

What do you think of when you hear the word "spirit"? Do you imagine some kind of wispy, ethereal being drifting around like fog? Or do frightening images come to mind, such as you might see at Halloween or in a scary film? But those miss the mark, because spirit is the opposite of material. Jesus said that "a spirit does not have flesh and bones" (Luke 24:39 NKJV).

Because He is a spirit, God isn't limited by time or space. He can be everywhere at once. He is in the midst of the largest galaxy—and the smallest atom. He is far greater than the material world (which is one reason we aren't to worship idols or nature). Because He is a spirit, He is not limited in any way. If you have been trying to limit God, don't! Don't try to confine Him to one place, or paint an imaginary picture of Him in your mind, or restrict Him to one way of doing things. Don't put limits on His power or greatness or love or wisdom. Limiting God is like looking at a mud puddle and thinking it's the ocean.

God Is a Person

Not only is God a spirit, but He also is a person—that is, He has a personality, just as we do. Every trait we attribute to ourselves can be attributed to God. A person feels, thinks, desires, and decides—and so does God. A person enters into relationships—and so does God. A person acts—and so does God. God feels; God thinks; God sympathizes; God forgives; God hopes; God decides; God acts; God judges—all because He is a person. If He weren't, why pray to Him or worship Him? God is not an impersonal force or power; He is a *person*—the most perfect person imaginable.

There is, of course, a vast difference between God's personality and ours: He is perfect, but we are not. Emotions like anger, selfishness, hatred, jealousy, and pride overwhelm us. Our personalities may even become sick or self-destructive.

But God isn't this way. He alone is perfect. Even His anger is righteous, because it is directed solely against evil. The Bible says, "His works are perfect, and all his ways are just" (Deuteronomy 32:4).

God Is Holy

Not only is God a spirit and a person, but He is also holy and righteous and pure. The Bible says, "Your eyes are too pure to look on evil; you cannot tolerate wrong" (Habakkuk 1:13).

Admittedly we have a hard time understanding this. We are weak and imperfect, and we can scarcely grasp the overwhelming perfection and holiness of God. We have become so used to sin that we can't imagine anyone being absolutely perfect. But God is! The Bible says, "God is light; in him there is no darkness at all" (1 John 1:5). Because God is holy, He never does wrong—ever. Occasionally we hear of someone who is exceptionally good and self-sacrificing—but even then, we know they aren't perfect. (If we think we are perfect, it just proves we aren't!) Only God is perfect and holy.

From one end of the Bible to the other, God reveals Himself as absolutely pure, without flaw or blemish of any kind. When Isaiah glimpsed a vision of God, he was overwhelmed by God's holiness — and his own sinfulness. He saw angels surrounding God's throne, "calling to one another: 'Holy, holy, holy is the LORD Almighty'" (Isaiah 6:3). In John's vision of heaven he saw the same truth: "Day and night they never stop saying, 'Holy, holy, holy is the Lord God Almighty, who was, and is, and is to come'" (Revelation 4:8).

Only when we understand the holiness of God will we understand the depth of our sin. God is holy, but we are not — because of that a great chasm has opened up between us and God. We stand guilty and condemned before Him, worthy only of His judgment and condemnation. Apart from Christ we have no hope of heaven, because even one sin contaminates us and makes us unfit to come into God's presence. From time to time I have visited leper colonies and tuberculosis hospitals in various parts of the world, and I have never been allowed to come close to those who were sick unless I was wearing special protective clothing. Just as someone with a contagious disease may be cut off from human contact, so the disease of sin cuts us off from God's holy presence.

Don't take the holiness of God lightly, for it is the very essence of His character.

God Is Love

If God were *only* holy, however, we would have no hope of heaven when we die and no hope of His blessing right now. But listen: *God isn't only a spirit and a person who is holy and righteous. God is also love* — and this makes all the difference. The Bible says, "God is love" (1 John 4:8). And just as His holiness is perfect, so too is His love.

The more I read the Bible, the more I realize that love is God's supreme attribute. Behind every dealing God has with us is His perfect love. It was love that made Him create us, and it was love that caused Him to send His Son to redeem us. His love pursues us and draws us to Himself, and His love will someday take us into His presence forever. "This is love: not that we loved God, but that he loved us and sent his Son as an atoning sacrifice for our sins" (1 John 4:10).

As with other aspects of His nature, we have a difficult time fully understanding God's love. For one thing, the word "love" has come to mean almost anything today. We say we "love" ice cream or the color of a car, or we say we "love" an entertainer or celebrity (although we've never met them and never will). But God's love is far deeper than this. His love is not a passing fancy or a superficial emotion; it is *a profound and unshakable commitment that seeks what is best for us*. Human love may change or fade; God's love never will. He says to us, "I have loved you with an everlasting love; I have drawn you with loving-kindness" (Jeremiah 31:3).

Don't sentimentalize God's love, however. God's love isn't a warm, fuzzy feeling that ignores sin or shuns judgment. God's holiness demands that sin be punished—but God's love has provided the way of redemption through Christ. If it weren't for God's love, we would have no hope, either in this life or in the life to come.

But there *is* hope because He loves us. He loves you!

THREE

THE GREAT DESIGN

Abraham . . . was called the friend of God.

—JAMES 2:23 NKJV

IT IS THE GREATEST DISCOVERY YOU WILL EVER MAKE: *You were created to know God and to be His friend forever.*

You and I weren't put here just to be preoccupied with ourselves—our own problems and pleasures. We weren't even put here just to make this a better world (although that has its place). If this is all there is to life, then it truly is "meaningless, a chasing after the wind" (Ecclesiastes 1:14).

But life was not meant to be this way—and the reason is *we were not made for ourselves; we were made for God.* The Great Designer had a Great Design: that we might know Him and be His friends forever.

A Perfect World

Why are we so restless? Why are we constantly searching for lasting peace and contentment yet never fully satisfied? "My friends all say I have everything anyone could ever want," one man wrote me recently, "but down inside I'm empty and restless. What's wrong with me?" Countless people could echo his cry, if they were honest.

The Bible says this happens to us for a very good reason: *We are incomplete without God.* If we leave Him out of our lives, we have an empty place in our souls, a yearning deep inside us that only God can satisfy. No matter how hard we try, if we ignore God that hollow place stays with us, and our search for lasting peace and happiness will be futile. Centuries ago St. Augustine wrote, "You have made us for Yourself, O God, and our hearts are restless until they find their rest in You."

It wasn't always this way. In the beginning, when God first created the human race, that inner restlessness and emptiness didn't exist. As we shall see more fully in the next chapter, Adam and Eve were totally content when God created them—at peace with themselves, their world, and God. Their relationship with each other was perfect, unmarred by even the slightest hint of selfishness or conflict. Their relationship with nature was perfect, unmarred by fear or insecurity or death. And their relationship with God was perfect, unmarred by guilt or disbelief.

Think of it: No sin, no sorrow, no hurt feelings, no thoughtlessness, no insensitivity—nothing tarnished the perfect world God had created for them. The Bible says, "God saw all that he had made [including Adam and Eve], and it was very good" (Genesis 1:31). Adam and Eve walked in perfect harmony with each other and with God. He supplied their every need, and they loved Him completely and without hesitation. We can barely imagine what it must have been like because our world—and our lives—are so different today.

Created in God's Image

How could their lives be so perfect? It was possible for one reason: *God deliberately created Adam and Eve to be His friends forever.* Their fellowship with God was an unbroken reality every moment of the day.

You see, Adam and Eve weren't simply physical creatures, nor were they just a superior type of animal. They were far greater than that. They were also *spiritual* beings, created with a soul or spirit that gave them the ability to know and experience God. In fact, the Bible says they were made in God's image—that is, God implanted something of Himself inside of them: "God created man in his own image, in the image of God he created him; male and female he created them" (Genesis 1:27). God gave them a unique spiritual nature.

This is also true of us. Like Adam and Eve, we not only have a body and a mind, but we also have what the Bible calls a spirit or a soul. God gave it to you; He implanted part of Himself within you. Our souls set us apart from every other living creature, and that makes us unique. It also makes us fully human.

The Value of a Soul

How important is your soul? Jesus said our souls are more valuable than all the rest of the world put together. One reason is because our souls will never die. Your body will die, but your soul (or spirit) will live forever. Your soul is so valuable that Christ was willing to give His life to redeem it. Jesus said, "What good will it be for a man if he gains the whole world, yet forfeits his soul? Or what can a man give in exchange for his soul?" (Matthew 16:26).

If we think we are only sophisticated animals, we will begin to act like sophisticated animals. But if we realize we were created in God's image and have a God-given soul, we won't live like animals. Our souls make us uniquely human, and they give dignity and value to every human life. The Bible says, "You made him a little lower than the heavenly beings and crowned him with glory and honor" (Psalm 8:5). That is why human life should never be scorned or abused or wantonly destroyed, for every person was created in God's image, no matter how young or old.

Most of all, our souls are the part of us that can experience God and have fellowship with Him. Because we have souls, *we have the capacity to know God and be His friends forever.* We were equipped by our Creator not only to live on this earth, but also to live in touch with heaven. This was the Great Design of the Great Designer.

Created out of Love

Adam and Eve, created in God's image, were different from every other creature God had made. But *why* did He create them? What motivated Him to form the human race in the first place? And why did He create *you*? The answer can be summed up in one word: "love." It was *love* that prompted God to fashion a creature after His own image and likeness and to place him in a paradise of enchanting loveliness.

As we have seen, God isn't a vague, impersonal force; God is a person—that is, He has a personality. And perhaps the most distinctive characteristic of His personality is love. His love is perfect— because God is perfect. The Bible says, "As for God, his way is perfect; the word of the LORD is flawless" (Psalm 18:30). Human love is imperfect and changeable, but God's love is perfect, never changing or growing weak.

Admittedly there is much about God's love that we will never fully understand this side of eternity. For example, how can a loving God still permit evil? Later we'll look in more depth at this difficult question, but just because we can't understand *everything* about God's love doesn't mean we can't understand *something*.

Why is God's love important at this point? It is important because it tells us why God made us: *He made us because of His love.*

On a human level we know that love needs an outlet—that is, it yearns to be expressed and shared. In a far greater way, God's love had to have an outlet. It had to be expressed, and it had to be shared. That is why God created Adam and Eve. And He created them in His image so they would have the ability to love also—to love each other and to love Him. God is love, and now this wondrous characteristic of His personality was being given to Adam and Eve. What a gift! God created Adam and Eve out of *love* and gave them the ability to love Him (and each other) in return.

Don't misunderstand this, however. God didn't make Adam and Eve because He was lonely or because He needed someone to love Him in return. This is true with human love, but it isn't true with God's love. God is complete in Himself; He lacks nothing. But His love *compelled* Him to create those first humans. His love needed to be expressed. Just as an artist has a compelling urge to create a beautiful painting, or a skilled woodworker has a compelling urge to create a fine piece of furniture, so our loving God had a compelling urge to create humanity. His love was expressed in the creation of the human race.

Made to Be God's Friends

But *why* were Adam and Eve created? And why were *we* created? Biologists speculate about *how* we came to be here, but the crucial question is *why* we came to be here. Don't miss what the Bible says about this: *God created us to have a personal relationship with Himself.* To put it another way, *He created us to be His friends.* This was the divine plan right from the beginning, when Adam and Eve were first created—and it had its origin in the love of God.

It was, however, a friendship with a difference. On a human level we usually choose friends who are similar to us—those with like interests or kindred personalities. But God and Adam were not equals. God is the sovereign Ruler of the universe, the all-powerful Creator, who not only made everything but also controls and sustains it, from the largest galaxy to the smallest glimmer of light. In addition, God is everywhere at the same time. He is also the all-knowing Lord who sees everything that happens, including every detail of our lives. The Bible says, "Nothing in all creation is hidden from God's sight. Everything is uncovered and laid bare before the eyes of him to whom we must give account" (Hebrews 4:13).

Adam was none of these. God was the Creator; Adam was the creature. God was limitless; Adam was limited. God was independent; Adam was dependent. But in spite of the vast difference between them, *God still wanted Adam and Eve to be His friends.* This was why they were created, and this was how they lived until sin entered the world and destroyed that perfect friendship. In the beginning, God was Adam's perfect friend, and Adam was God's perfect friend.

God's plan for Adam and Eve is also true for us. God has not changed and neither has His purpose. We are not here by accident; we are here because God put us here—and *He put us here so we could be His friends forever.* God *wants* you to be His friend! Once you understand this, your life will never be the same.

The Unending Search

Tragically, many people never discover this truth. They may not even think about it, or if they do, they search in all kinds of directions trying to answer the question of why they are here. They may go through life without ever realizing who they really are or why God put them here. On the outside they may be successful, well-liked, even envied by others. But down inside something is still missing, and no matter how hard they try to fill that void in their souls, it remains empty and unsatisfied.

Advertisers promise happiness and fulfillment if only we will use their product. Philosophers and self-improvement gurus promise success and inner peace if only we will buy their books or tapes. Pundits and politicians promise abundance and world peace if only we will listen to their wisdom or vote for them. Their promises, however, always fall short. We spend all our time and energy pampering our bodies and minds, but if we ignore our souls, we will end up spiritually starved and malnourished.

Some years ago I was invited to be on a television talk show with one of the most famous personalities in America. Afterward she took me aside and told of the emptiness in her life. "My beauty is gone," she said. "I am getting old, I'm living on alcohol, and I have nothing to live for."

On another occasion my wife and I were invited to have lunch with one of the wealthiest men in the world. He was seventy-five years old, and as he sat at the dining table, tears came down his cheeks. "I am the most miserable man in the world," he said. "I have everything anyone could ever want. If I want to go anywhere, I have my own yacht or private plane. If I want something, I can buy it, no matter what it costs. But down inside I'm miserable and empty."

These stories could be repeated countless times—and not just by famous or successful people. Perhaps you have sensed this emptiness in your own life. Almost every day I get letters from people who tell how they have spent their lives searching for something to fill that vacuum in their hearts. They may not have even realized it was there, but they have tried everything in their desperate search for happiness: sex, drugs, alcohol, fame, money, possessions, power, success—you name it.

Each path promised contentment and peace, but those promises turned out to be false (as they always are). Their lives were still empty, and in some cases they almost destroyed themselves in their frantic search for happiness and peace. Like a square peg in a round hole, life has never quite fit.

Some of those letters, however, go on to recount how Christ has changed their lives and how He has met their deepest inner longings. Their search has ended; the empty space in their soul has been filled. *They have discovered that they were created to know God and to be His friends forever.* So were you.

Shortly after visiting the wealthy man I mentioned above, Ruth and I met another man who preached in a small church nearby. He was vivacious and full of life, and he told us, "I don't have a penny to my name, but I'm the happiest man in the world!"

Made to Know God

God wants us to know Him—not just to know *about* Him, but to *know* Him in a personal way.

Do you see the difference? I might know *about* you; I might have heard your name; I might have seen your picture; we might even have exchanged letters or e-mails. But I couldn't really say that you and I were friends or that we had a personal relationship until we actually met and got acquainted with each other. Only then would I really *know* you.

The same is true with God. According to all the latest polls, most people believe in God. They believe He exists, and they may even have some definite ideas about Him. But for most, God is distant and fuzzy, because they only know *about* Him. They have never met Him or come to know Him in a personal way, and they can't honestly say they know He is their friend. And yet that is what He wants to be. He wants us to *know* Him.

This is a staggering truth. Think of it: The infinite, all-powerful, holy God of the universe wants to be your friend! He wants you to know Him personally and to discover what it means to walk with Him every day. He wants you to know He is with you, and He wants to have communication with you through His Word and through prayer. He wants to comfort you when you are upset or anxious and to encourage you when you are dejected or depressed. He wants to guide you when you face difficult decisions, and He even wants to correct you when you are about to do something foolish or wrong.

Human friends may fail us, but God never will. The Bible reminds us that "A man of many companions may come to ruin, but there is a friend who sticks closer than a brother" (Proverbs 18:24). That friend is God. Jesus said to His followers, "I no longer call you servants. . . . Instead, I have called you friends" (John 15:15).

God wants to be our friend, and for us to be His friends as well. But what has gone wrong? And can it ever be made right again?

FOUR

WHAT WENT WRONG?

I do not understand what I do. . . . For what I do is not the good I
want to do; no, the evil I do not want to do—this I keep on doing.
—ROMANS 7:15, 19

T HIS WORLD IS NOT THE WAY GOD MEANT IT TO BE.
When you stand by the grave of a child snatched away by
accident or illness, this is not the way God meant it to be. When
a marriage breaks down or a friendship turns sour, this is not the
way God meant it to be. When you hear of millions of children
orphaned by AIDS . . . or a terrorist bombing that kills hundreds
. . . or another devastating famine or war . . . or the booming business in Internet pornography—this is not the way God meant it
to be.

And when you go numb because the doctor tells you it's cancer . . . or watch helplessly as someone you love gets caught in the grip of alcohol or drugs or mental illness . . . or find yourself powerless to change your life—then you need to remember: *This is not the way God meant it to be.*

The Mystery of Evil

The question of why a loving and all-powerful God allows evil to exist is almost as old as the human race. Theologians and philosophers have grappled with it for centuries without finding a complete answer. Some have concluded God must not care . . . or He is too weak to do anything about it . . . or even that He doesn't exist. We live in a random universe, they say, with no rhyme or reason to it. In the midst of his agony, Job cried out, "Why is life given to a man whose way is hidden, whom God has hedged in? . . . I have no peace, no quietness; I have no rest, but only turmoil" (Job 3:23, 26).

I have asked myself hundreds of times why God allows tragedy and suffering, and I have to admit that I don't fully know the answer, even to my own satisfaction. I have had to accept by faith that even in the face of great evil, God is still sovereign, and He is still loving and merciful and compassionate. The Bible speaks of "the mystery of iniquity" (2 Thessalonians 2:7 KJV), and that's what evil is: a mystery.

God is real—but so are evil and suffering. They aren't just an illusion, nor can we banish them by thinking positive thoughts or optimistically telling ourselves everything will be all right. Evil and suffering are real, and we see them everywhere we look. Our headlines scream it; our experience confirms it; our own hearts and minds know it.

The Great Rebellion

But where did evil come from? Why do we live in a world that includes *both* good and evil?

Even if we can't understand everything about evil, the Bible does reveal something of its origin. We must begin where the Bible begins: with Adam and Eve in the Garden of Eden. In the beginning, the perfect God created a perfect world, and in it He placed two perfect human beings. Adam and Eve walked with God, and no shadow came between them. They were God's friends, and God was their friend as well.

But Adam and Eve weren't robots. They were completely free: free to choose to love God *but also free to reject Him*. If they had not been free, then their "love" for God wouldn't have been love at all, because we only truly love someone when we freely *choose* to love them. From their first moment on earth, they *chose* to love God.

But then something went radically wrong—something so devastating and so catastrophic that we are still living with its terrible consequences today. What happened was this: Adam and Eve rebelled against God. They decided they would go their own way, and although they may not have realized it at the time, *they also were rejecting God as their friend*.

It happened this way. God told Adam and Eve that everything in the Garden was theirs to enjoy, provided by Him to meet their every need. There was only one exception: the tree God called "the tree of the knowledge of good and evil." Of its fruit, God said, they must not eat. If they did, they would die.

But one day Satan (whose name means "Adversary") met them. At the dawn of creation, the Bible tells us, Satan had been one of God's angels, created by God to serve Him and do His will. But Satan was determined to take God's place. He and his angelic followers rebelled against God, and he became a powerful spiritual force whose sole goal was (and is) to oppose God's work. Jesus declared, "I saw Satan fall like lightning from heaven" (Luke 10:18)—perhaps referring to this event before the dawn of creation. Isaiah's portrait of Lucifer describes Satan's arrogance and rebellion: "How you have fallen from heaven, O morning star, son of the dawn! . . .You said in your heart, 'I will ascend to heaven; I will raise my throne above the stars of God. . . . I will make myself like the Most High'" (Isaiah 14:12-14). Lucifer, a mighty angel, became filled with pride (notice how often the word "I" or "my" occurs in these verses). As a result, he rebelled against God and tried to take God's place.

This is one of the Bible's greatest mysteries, and there is much we don't know about Satan and the origin of evil. We can barely imagine the battle that raged in the heavens when he and his followers lashed out against God. But Satan is real, and the most important truth you need to remember about him is that he is absolutely and implacably opposed to God and His people. The Bible calls him the one "who leads the whole world astray" and "the accuser of our brothers" (Revelation 12:9–10). It also labels him "a liar and the father of lies" (John 8:44), "the tempter" (1 Thessalonians 3:5), "the evil one" (1 John 3:12), and "your enemy" (1 Peter 5:8). Don't think of Satan as a harmless cartoon character with a red suit and a pitchfork. He is very clever and powerful, and his unchanging purpose is to defeat God's plans at every turn—including His plans for your life. His first victory was with Adam and Eve.

Satan told Adam and Eve that God did not tell them the truth about the forbidden tree. In fact, he asserted, God lied to them. "You will not surely die," he said. "For God knows that when you eat of it your eyes will be opened, and you will be like God" (Genesis 3:4–5).

In other words, Satan told them, God wasn't their friend after all. In effect he was saying, "Would a friend deceive you? But that's what God has done to you! That tree isn't bad (as God claims). It's good! Eat from it—and you will become like God!"

What a powerful temptation: to become like God! And in that terrible moment Adam and Eve turned their backs on God's truth and believed Satan's lie instead. They rebelled against the One who had made them, renouncing His friendship and choosing to go their own way.

This is the essence of sin: *rebellion against God*. When we sin, we reject God's Word. When we sin, we are saying we are wiser than God and our way is better than His. Scholars have pointed out that the Bible uses almost two dozen different words to describe sin, such as "missing the mark," "turning away," "falling short," "wrongdoing," "lawlessness," and "unbelief." But they all point to the same truth: Sin is rebellion against God.

What happened in Eden was a preview of what happens to us every day. Adam and Eve's decision is repeated by every generation and by every person. We all are guilty of sin, because we all choose our own way instead of God's way. If we deny we are sinners, it is because we have allowed pride to blind us—and pride is itself a sin. The Bible says, "There is no one righteous, not even one. . . . For all have sinned and fall short of the glory of God" (Romans 3:10, 23).

The Terrible Consequence

Theologians have called this primeval tragedy at the dawn of the human race "the Fall" and rightly so. From the heights of the honor and glory they had once known, Adam and Eve now fell into a pit of disgrace and shame. They became fallen creatures, living in a fallen world. In an instant they lost their innocence and came under sin's domination. As a heartbreaking symbol of this, the Bible says God drove Adam and Eve out of the Garden of Eden and set angels with a flaming sword to block its entrance (Genesis 3:23–24).

Since that fatal moment the human race has been trying to get back into that Garden without success. Try as we might, its happiness and perfection elude us. The reason is because we too are fallen creatures, living in a fallen world. Adam and Eve's sin affected not only their lives, but ours as well. The consequences of their rebellion against God have come down to us, and we share in their guilt and shame.

Some people have a hard time accepting this. Why, they ask, am I responsible for what Adam did? It's a logical question; after all, if your great-grandfather committed a crime a century ago, no one would think of taking you into court and charging you with his crime today.

But Adam was different, for he was the fountainhead of the whole human race. I remember as a boy on my father's dairy farm finding one of his cows dead beside a creek running through our property. We discovered that a textile mill some distance upstream was discharging poisonous waste into the creek, and eventually we had to fence it off to safeguard the animals. My father wasn't responsible for the pollution, but he still had to live with its consequences. In somewhat the same way, Adam's sin flows down through the ages, polluting everything in its path.

To put it another way, in the Garden of Eden Adam acted as our representative. When we send someone to Congress or Parliament, we expect them to act as our representative. In other words, we expect them to vote the way we would vote if we were actually there. And that's what Adam did: He voted the way we would have voted if we had been there. You might contend you would have acted differently—but if you are honest, you know you would have done exactly what Adam did, because you do it every day. The Bible says, "Sin entered the world through one man, . . . and in this way death came to all men, because all sinned" (Romans 5:12).

Sin's Devastation

Don't ever underestimate the terrible consequences of Adam and Eve's rebellion against God. Like a deadly virus, their sin infected everything—not only the human race, but all creation. It produced a crop of bitter fruit that is still with us. Look briefly at *six consequences* of their rebellion.

First, death entered the world. We were not meant to die; we were meant to live forever. But now death has invaded the whole creation. The Bible says, "The wages of sin is death" (Romans 6:23). It also declares, "Man is destined to die once, and after that to face judgment" (Hebrews 9:27). It has wisely been said that war doesn't increase the rate of death; it only accelerates it, because the rate is always the same: 100 percent. Medical science may extend our life span by a few years, but death will still overtake us eventually.

Second, we became separated from God. When Adam and Eve were created, God was their friend—and they were His. But the first thing they did after they sinned was to hide from God (Genesis 3:8). Shame and guilt and fear filled their souls, and their fellowship with Him was broken. Now a vast gulf opened up between them and their Creator. The Bible says, "Your iniquities have separated you from your God; your sins have hidden his face from you, so that he will not hear" (Isaiah 59:2).

Third, we became alienated from each other. Originally Adam and Eve walked in perfect harmony, not only with God but with each other. But now this harmony was destroyed. Not only did they hide from God, but they blamed each other for what had happened: "The woman you put here with me—she gave me some fruit from the tree" (Genesis 3:12). Since then human history has been an endless, dismal chronicle of turmoil and conflict.

Fourth, we became subject to God's judgment. God is pure and holy, and sin is an offense to Him. We have broken His law, and before the bar of His perfect justice, there can be only one verdict: *guilty.* Our conscience condemns us, our sins condemn us, and ultimately God's justice will condemn us. The Bible says, "God is a righteous judge" (Psalm 7:11). It also says, "But who can endure the day of his coming? Who can stand when he appears?" (Malachi 3:2).

Fifth, we became slaves of sin. At one time Adam and Eve freely loved God and obeyed Him with all their hearts and souls and minds and strength. But when they turned against God, all that was lost. Sin wrapped its powerful tentacles around their souls, and they became its slaves. God's image within them was defaced, and they no longer had the ability to love and obey God perfectly. Instead, they became spiritually crippled—and so have we. Jesus said, "I tell you the truth, everyone who sins is a slave to sin" (John 8:34).

Sixth, the whole creation was corrupted. We can barely imagine what that original world must have been like: peaceful, beautiful, deathless, perfect. But all that ended as sin's rot spread. God told Adam, "Cursed is the ground because of you. . . . It will produce thorns and thistles for you" (Genesis 3:17–18). Only when God makes all things new at the end of time will "the creation . . . be liberated from its bondage to decay" (Romans 8:21).

Never lose sight of the seriousness of sin. Its corruption has affected everything: our bodies, our minds, our emotions, our wills, our souls, our institutions, our world—everything.

The Depth of Our Sin

Unfortunately most of us have a very shallow view of sin. We think of it only as something we know is wrong. That's true, of course, but sin is far more than this.

For example, think of how we sin by our words. Some sins of the tongue are obvious, such as lying or slander or cursing. But others are more subtle, such as gossiping or speaking unkindly to someone. How often have you gotten in trouble simply because of something you said? The Bible is right: "The tongue also is a fire, a world of evil among the parts of the body. It corrupts the whole person, sets the whole course of his life on fire, and is itself set on fire by hell" (James 3:6).

Or take what goes on in your mind. In God's eyes an evil thought is just as sinful as an evil deed. When we allow our minds to be filled with lust, hate, anger, bitterness, jealousy, greed, envy, selfishness, or even doubt, then we are guilty of sin.

Most of the Ten Commandments deal with outward actions (do not kill, do not commit immorality, do not steal, and so forth). But the final commandment deals with our inner thoughts and motives: "You shall not covet" (Exodus 20:17). Jesus said our thoughts are just as important as our deeds: "You have heard that it was said to those of old, 'You shall not murder.' . . . But I say to you that whoever is angry with his brother without a cause shall be in danger of the judgment" (Matthew 5:21–22 NKJV).

We may hide our thoughts from others, but we can't hide them from God. The Bible says, "The lamp of the LORD searches the spirit of a man; it searches out his inmost being" (Proverbs 20:27).

But we not only sin by what we do or think. We also sin by what we *fail* to do. We should be compassionate to those who are lonely or discouraged or needy, but instead we ignore them. Failing to do right is just as much a sin as doing wrong.

Sin and Sins

We also need to remember that there is a difference between *sin* and *sins*. When we use the word "sin," we usually think of our mis-deeds—actions or habits we know are wrong. But those are specific *sins*, and they are the result of *sin*, the deeper spiritual disease that infects our souls.

Sin is the cause; *sins* are the effect. *Sin* is the tree; *sins* are the fruit. *Sin* is the disease; *sins* are the symptoms. Something is radi-cally wrong with us—and that "something" is *sin*. Through self-discipline we might get rid of some of our *sins*, but our basic problem of *sin* remains untouched and untouchable, lurking just beneath the surface and ready to strike at any moment.

In 1946 I preached in a little town in northeast England. It was right after the war, and I remember it was ice cold, and we had no heat and very little to eat. I was staying with an older, godly business-man, and every night after the service we would come home and in a kind, loving way he would give me more thoughts from the Scriptures. One night he gave me a little booklet which made it clear that sin is a disease that infects us all, while sins are what we do—the outworking of the disease of sin. It was, I think, the first time I had ever thought about this distinction.

Sin is serious—it is, in fact, the most basic problem of the human race. It is my basic problem and yours as well. Don't ever think sin is only a minor misdeed or an occasional outburst of wrongdoing. Sin is far deeper than that. It is a spiritual disease that leaves us weak and powerless. Its hold over us is so strong that only God can overcome it.

Is There Any Hope?

Remember: This world is not the way God meant it to be, and neither are we. Something devastating has happened—and that "something" is sin.

But is this the end of the story? How depressing, how hopeless life would be if it were . . . but it isn't! Life *can* be different. We don't need to be crippled any longer by the disease of sin—because God has provided the cure.

FIVE

CAN WE START OVER?

You have made known to me the path of life;
you will fill me with joy in your presence,
with eternal pleasures at your right hand.

—PSALM 16:11

M ORE THAN ANYTHING ELSE IN LIFE, WE NEED TO find the right path.

Tragically, many people never do. They assume the path they are on must be the only choice, even if it has been difficult and disappointing. Others wonder if any path can be "right"; to them, one way of living is just as good (or bad) as another. And some people simply don't want to bother thinking about it. Down inside, however, they all sense that something is wrong, and they yearn for something better. Perhaps this describes you.

Is There a Right Path?

Yes, we need to find the right path for our journey through life—but is it possible? Does it even exist?

People look for the answers to those questions in all kinds of ways—education, money, success, social standing—hoping these will prove to be the right path. Others look to entertainment or psychology or various kinds of spirituality or the latest self-help fad. Still others assume that if they can only find the right person to share their life, their problems will be over and they will be on the right path. Dozens of other ways could be mentioned.

Some of these may have a place in our lives, of course, if we approach them in the right way. But by themselves, *they lack the power to take us from the wrong road to the right road.* Try as we might, we find ourselves stuck on the same path we've been traveling all our lives.

Is there a right path? And can we find it? The answer to both these questions is *yes*—because *God has provided a new path for us.* The right path is *His path,* and that is the path we need to seek. But where is it to be found?

Our Greatest Need

To find the right path, we first need to remember why we are on the wrong path. The reason can be put in one word: *sin.* In the last chapter we noted some of sin's consequences, but now we need to add one more: *Sin has put us on the wrong path.*

Jesus warned, "Wide is the gate and broad is the road that leads to destruction, and many enter through it" (Matthew 7:13). To the people of his day, the prophet Jeremiah declared, "Ask where the good way is, and walk in it, and you will find rest for your souls. But you said, 'We will not walk in it'" (Jeremiah 6:16). In their stubbornness they refused God's path and chose the wrong road instead—and eventually it led them to destruction.

If we are ever to get on the right path, we must face this problem and deal with it. This is why our greatest need is not economic or political or educational in nature; it is spiritual. *Our greatest need is to have our sins forgiven and our old sinful nature exchanged for a new one.* Only then will we be on the right path—the path God designed for us.

Only God can change us; we cannot change ourselves. It's important to understand this, because millions of people spend their lives trying to conquer sin's power on their own. Some hope, for example, that they can win God's favor by their good deeds or their loyalty to their church or their religious practices. Won't these get me into heaven, they ask? Won't God see my good deeds and reward me with eternal life?

But these efforts—sincere as they are—overlook the power of sin's grip on us. God is holy and pure, and even one sin—just one—will banish us from His presence. The Bible warns, "Whoever keeps the whole law and yet stumbles at just one point is guilty of breaking all of it" (James 2:10).

Our Only Hope

If we cannot save ourselves by our own efforts, is there any hope? Can our lives be different? Can we know for sure that we will go to heaven when we die? The answer is yes—and *the reason is because of what Jesus Christ did for us.* We *can* have our sins forgiven, and we *can* begin life again by God's grace. Our journey through life *can* be different if we travel a new path—God's path.

Even before time began, God knew all about us and planned this new path for us. He looked across the ages and saw that we would be helpless and lost in sin, unable to find the right road on our own. He saw *you.* From all eternity He planned to provide another way—a way that will take us to heaven someday and that gives us purpose and peace in the meantime. That way is Jesus, who alone could say, "I am the way and the truth and the life. No one comes to the Father except through me" (John 14:6).

Sin has put us firmly on the wrong path. But because of Jesus, we can be firmly on the right path—and that's what we need.

Who Was Jesus?

The Christian faith is centered in Jesus Christ, who lived some two thousand years ago in an obscure corner of the Roman Empire. Historians—whether they are religious or not—almost unanimously agree that no other individual has made such a lasting impact on the world. He is the foundation and focal point of the Christian faith, and He always will be. Whenever Christians have lost sight of His teachings, they have betrayed their Lord and brought dishonor to His name. When they have honored and followed Him, however, their lives have been changed and so has their world.

But who was Jesus, and why after two thousand years is He still the most important person who ever lived? Was He just a great man? Or was He more?

The Bible (the source of our information about Jesus) tells us something that staggers our imagination. It tells us that *Jesus was God in human form*. He was a man, fully and completely. But He was more than that: He was also God. He was not just a godly man; *He was God Himself, wrapped in human flesh*. The Bible puts it this way: "In the beginning was the Word, and the Word was with God, and the Word was God. . . . The Word became flesh and made his dwelling among us" (John 1:1, 14).

This is a staggering claim, but Jesus affirmed it repeatedly during His public ministry. "I and the Father are one," He declared

(John 10:30). "Anyone who has seen me has seen the Father," He told His disciples (John 14:9). On one occasion Jesus' appearance was transformed before the eyes of His closest disciples, and for a brief moment His heavenly glory shone through. Then a voice came from heaven saying, "This is my Son, whom I love; with him I am well pleased" (Matthew 17:5).

This also was the consistent witness of the earliest Christians. The apostle Paul put it this way: "He is the image of the invisible God. . . . For God was pleased to have all his fullness dwell in him" (Colossians 1:15, 19). *Jesus Christ was both fully man and fully God.*

This is what we celebrate each year at Christmas. When the angel Gabriel appeared to the Virgin Mary, he told her that "the Holy Spirit will come upon you, and . . . the holy one to be born will be called the Son of God" (Luke 1:35). Later an angel instructed her husband Joseph "to give him the name Jesus [which means 'the Lord saves'], because he will save his people from their sins." This, the Gospel writer adds, was to be done in order to fulfill the prophecy that "'they will call him Immanuel'—which means, 'God with us'" (Matthew 1:21, 23). Never forget: That baby born in Bethlehem's stable was not *a* son of God (only one among many)—He was *the* Son of God, uniquely sent from the Father to become our Savior from sin. He was both fully human and fully divine.

Why is this important? Because *only a divine Savior can save us from our sins.* A mere man could not save us because, like us, he would be a sinner needing God's forgiveness. But because He was God as well as man, Jesus was without sin—thus He alone could bear our sins.

What Did Jesus Do?

But why did Jesus leave heaven's glory and come down to live amid earth's filth and corruption? *He came for one reason: to save us from our sins.* He came to cleanse the blot of sin and guilt that stains our souls and to reconcile us with our Creator. He came to do for us what we could never do for ourselves: take away our sins and implant His life within us by His Holy Spirit.

Jesus did this, the Bible says, through His death on the cross and His resurrection from the dead. He was innocent of any crime, but the authorities—fearful of losing their position—arrested and crucified Him. But they weren't the ones who really executed Jesus. Who is responsible for His death? *I am . . . you are . . . we all are.* Why? Because He voluntarily went to the cross for one reason: to become the final and complete sacrifice for our sins. If we had never sinned, He never would have needed to die. But we have sinned, and He came to remove our guilt. Jesus' death on the cross is a profound mystery we will never fully understand this side of eternity. Its central truth, however, is clear: *By His death and resurrection Jesus made our salvation possible.*

The Meaning of the Cross

The New Testament uses a number of illustrations or images to explain the cross and help us understand its meaning. Let me mention four.

First, by His death Jesus became our sacrifice for sin. I remember many years ago reading Sir James Frazer's *The Golden Bough*, which at the time was a standard anthropological text (in spite of its anti-Christian bias). He said that according to his research virtually every religion in every part of the world had sacrifices for sin. Within every heart, it seems, is an inner awareness of sin and the need to make atonement for it.

In the Old Testament, God accepted the sacrifice of an animal as an offering for sin. But this is no longer necessary, because through His death on the cross, Christ became the final and complete sacrifice for our sins. The Bible says, "He has appeared once for all at the end of the ages to do away with sin by the sacrifice of himself" (Hebrews 9:26). Because of His death for us, we need not fear sin's penalty any longer.

Second, Jesus was our substitute. God's justice demands that sin must be punished; if it isn't, there is no right and wrong, and God is not just. But instead of us having to bear the condemnation we deserve, Christ took upon Himself our guilt and our punishment. He substituted Himself for us.

This imagery of a substitute is vividly illustrated in the life of Abraham. (You can read it in Genesis 22.) Isaac was Abraham's only son, and if Abraham was to become the father of the nation through which the Messiah would come (as God had promised), then Isaac's life must be preserved. One day, however, God commanded Abraham to sacrifice Isaac—something that must have been almost incomprehensible to him. In spite of this, Abraham was determined to obey God—but just as he raised his knife to sacrifice Isaac, God stopped him. Then, we read, "Abraham looked up and there in a thicket he saw a ram caught by its horns. He went over and took the ram and sacrificed it as a burnt offering instead of his son" (Genesis 22:13). God provided a substitute, and the ram took Isaac's place.

In a far greater way, Christ became our substitute by dying in our place. We deserve to die for our sins, but Jesus—who was without sin—took all our sins upon Himself. When our sin and guilt were placed on Him, He deliberately endured God's judgment and wrath for us. This is the heart of the cross: *God judged our sins by taking upon Himself the judgment we deserved.* It is as if a judge fined you for something you did wrong—and then stepped down from the bench and paid the fine himself. The Bible says, "God made him who had no sin to be sin for us" (2 Corinthians 5:21).

Third, Jesus was our redeemer. In the ancient world soldiers captured in battle often were freed only if someone paid a ransom. In the same way, Jesus paid the ransom to free us from our captivity to sin—and the price He paid was his own blood. The Bible says, "The Son of Man did not come to be served, but to serve, and to give his life as a ransom for many" (Matthew 20:28). By His death He frees us from sin's dominion and brings us into God's family. In John's vision of heaven, those surrounding Christ's throne sang, "You are worthy . . . because you were slain, and with your blood you purchased men for God from every tribe and language and people and nation" (Revelation 5:9).

Fourth, Jesus was our conqueror. Never doubt Satan's power or the strength of sin's hold over us. But *by His death and resurrection, Christ defeated Satan and sin!* Satan had done his worst, and during those dark hours on the cross, it looked as if he had won. But he hadn't! Christ broke the bonds of death by His resurrection, and from that moment on, Satan was a defeated foe. When Jesus hung on the cross, a great unseen cosmic battle raged in the heavens— and in the end, Christ triumphed over all the forces of evil and death and hell. The Bible says, "Having disarmed the powers and authorities, he made a public spectacle of them, triumphing over them by the cross" (Colossians 2:15). The final battle has not yet been fought—but the outcome is certain. Satan has been defeated, and Christ is the victor!

What Will You Do with Jesus?

By His death and resurrection, Jesus became our sacrifice . . . our substitute . . . our redeemer . . . our conqueror. He did for us what we could never do for ourselves—and He did it out of love. Think of it: *He loves you so much that He was willing to give His life for you!*

Now He offers you salvation as a free gift—free because He has already paid for it. He wants to forgive your past and set your feet on a new path—His path. "For God so loved the world that he gave his one and only Son, that whoever believes in him shall not perish but have eternal life" (John 3:16).

What must you do? *First, repent of your sins.* The word "repent" means to turn from your sins. It means to change—to change your mind, your way of living, your attitude—with God's help. To repent means more than just being sorry for your sins or having regrets over the past. It means to honestly face your need of forgiveness, and deliberately turn from your sins.

Second, believe in Christ and what He did for you. The word "believe" in the Bible means much more than believing that certain facts are true. It means *to trust*—to put your complete confidence in Christ and what He has done for you and to cast yourself totally on Him for your salvation. You cannot trust your parents' religion or your church membership or anything else. You must come to Christ for yourself and trust Him alone for your salvation.

The Bible says, "To all who received him, to those who believed in his name, he gave the right to become children of God" (John 1:12). Just as a gift must be received before it truly becomes yours, so we must *receive* Christ into our hearts and lives by faith. A small child has absolute trust in his or her father, and we must have absolute faith and trust in Christ. I once asked a brilliant scientist how he came to believe in Jesus, and he replied, "I came as a little child. I had to come by faith." So must you.

Third, commit yourself to follow Christ. Becoming a Christian takes only a single step; *being* a Christian means walking with Christ the rest of your life. Accepting Christ isn't the end but the beginning—the beginning of a whole new life on God's path. Don't let anything keep you from that commitment.

If you have never given your life to Christ or if you are unsure, I invite you to turn to Him now. By a simple prayer of faith, you can give your life to Him today. Perhaps the following prayer will help you make your commitment:

O God, I know I am a sinner. I am sorry for my sins, and I want to turn from them. I trust Christ alone as my Savior, and I confess Him as my Lord. From this moment on, I want to serve Him and follow Him in the fellowship of His church. In Christ's name I pray. Amen.

If you sincerely prayed that prayer, God heard you—and you are now His child forever.

SIX

A NEW BEGINNING

Then He who sat on the throne said, "Behold, I make all things new."
—REVELATION 21:5 NKJV

IF WE DON'T KNOW WHO WE ARE, WE'LL NEVER KNOW how we ought to live.

I still remember the night I made my personal commitment to Jesus Christ, around the time of my seventeenth birthday. A visiting evangelist was preaching in our town in a large temporary structure built for the purpose. At first I wanted nothing to do with those meetings, but finally a friend persuaded me to go, and I found myself transfixed by the evangelist's message (and his colorful way of presenting it). Although thousands were present, he seemed to be speaking directly to me—even when I hid behind the large hat of the woman in front of me! I realize now that God's Spirit was working in my heart, convicting me of my sins and convincing me of my need for Christ.

One night as he gave the invitation for people to commit their lives to Christ, I knew I had resisted long enough, and I finally went forward (although holding out until the final verse of the last hymn). A kindly man explained how I could invite Christ into my life, and at his suggestion I prayed a simple but sincere prayer of commitment.

When I got home, I went upstairs to my room, sensing something important had happened to me—although I wasn't exactly sure what. I didn't feel any strong emotion or dramatic change, but looking out over the moonlit fields of my father's farm, I thought about the step I had just taken. Then for the first time in my life, I spontaneously got down on my knees and prayed: "Lord, I don't know what happened to me tonight, but You know."

Only gradually would I understand my commitment and what it meant. Decades later I am still learning, for the Christian life is one of constant growth.

Different Ways, the Same Reality

People come to Christ in many different ways; your experience won't necessarily be like mine. Some conversions are sudden and dramatic, a radical change from one way of living to another. As Saul of Tarsus approached the city of Damascus on a mission to arrest followers of Jesus, a brilliant light suddenly blinded him. Later he recounted, "I fell to the ground and heard a voice say to me, 'Saul, Saul! Why do you persecute me?'" (Acts 22:7). From that moment on, Saul began serving the One he had once rejected, and later (as the apostle Paul) God used him to spread the Gospel throughout the Roman Empire.

Others come to Christ more slowly, perhaps not even knowing exactly when they have crossed the line from unbelief to belief. The apostle Peter may have been like this—wavering and uncertain at first and only later coming to a firm and decisive commitment to Jesus. Yet the Bible doesn't tell us when that moment of conversion came; Peter himself may not have known. My wife, Ruth, grew up in a strong Christian home. (Her parents were medical missionaries to China.) She cannot recall a time when she didn't believe Jesus was her Savior, even as a child.

The important thing is not *how* we come to Christ, but that we *do* come, and that we are sure we are *now* trusting Christ for our salvation. Are you *certain* of your commitment to Him? If not, don't let another moment go by without making that decision. Nowhere in the Bible are we promised a second chance after death, nor are we promised even one more day of life. The Bible says, "Now is the time of God's favor, now is the day of salvation" (2 Corinthians 6:2).

Is Anything Different?

Whatever your experience, you may feel as I did after giving my life to Christ: "Lord, I don't know what happened to me." You may not even be sure *anything* has happened. Or perhaps you felt very close to God when you first believed in Christ, but now those feelings have faded, and you wonder if your faith was real. I often get letters from people who say their faith is like a roller coaster—up and down, constantly changing. One reason for these reactions is that once we give our lives to Christ, Satan will do everything he can to tempt us or make us doubt God.

But listen: Certain things *do* happen when we give our lives to Christ, and if we understand what they are, it will give us a solid foundation against every doubt Satan hurls against us. God's promise is true: "If anyone is in Christ, he is a new creation; the old has gone, the new has come!" (2 Corinthians 5:17). If you have given your life to Christ, *you are a new creation*—whether you feel like it or not.

What does this mean? What really happens to us when we believe in Christ? Let me list *seven gifts* God gives you when you commit your life to Christ.

A New Relationship

The first thing that happens when we give our lives to Christ is that God gives us a new relationship.

Once we were separated from God because of our sins—and not just separated, but alienated from Him. The Bible says we were "excluded . . . , without hope and without God in the world" (Ephesians 2:12).

But what did Christ do for us? He took away all our sins—not just part of them, but *all* of them! You are forgiven! The one thing that separated you from God—your sin—has now been removed, and therefore you are reconciled to Him. Instead of being God's enemy, you are now His friend. The Bible says, "Since we have been justified through faith, we have peace with God through our Lord Jesus Christ" (Romans 5:1). Think of it: If you know Christ, you are at peace with God. *You are now His friend, and He is now yours.*

We aren't only His friends, however. We are also *His children*. The Bible uses two vivid images to illustrate this. First, it tells us we have been *born again*. Jesus told Nicodemus he needed to be born again, but Nicodemus (a respected religious leader) didn't understand. "How can a man be born when he is old?" he asked (John 3:4). Jesus explained that He was talking about a *spiritual* rebirth: the renewal of our souls by God's Holy Spirit. We now become

God's sons and daughters, born into a new family—His family. The Bible says, "For you have been born again . . . through the living and enduring word of God" (1 Peter 1:23).

A second image the Bible uses is *adoption*. If we have given our lives to Christ, God has adopted us into His family. At one time we were (so to speak) spiritual orphans. We weren't part of God's family, and we had no right to expect anything from Him. But now God has adopted us into His family. We don't deserve it; it is solely because of His mercy and grace. From all eternity, the Bible says, God planned for us "to be adopted as his sons through Jesus Christ" (Ephesians 1:5).

Yes, the first thing that happened when you committed your life to Christ is that *God gave you a new relationship*. He is now your loving heavenly Father, and you are now His child, spiritually reborn into His family. The Bible says, "Be imitators of God, therefore, as dearly loved children" (Ephesians 5:1).

A New Citizenship

The second thing God gives you when you commit your life to Christ is a new citizenship. You are still a citizen of a particular country—but now you are also a citizen of the kingdom of God.

In Jesus' day one of the most coveted privileges a person could have was Roman citizenship. Roman citizens lived throughout the Roman Empire, but most people weren't Roman citizens and could never become one. A Roman citizen paid fewer taxes, and if he went into the army, he automatically became an officer. A Roman citizen couldn't be flogged or put to death by crucifixion (except in very rare cases, such as treason). If found guilty in a Roman court, he had the right to appeal directly to Caesar (which the apostle Paul, a Roman citizen, did on one occasion [Acts 25:11]).

But Jesus said His followers possessed something far greater than Roman citizenship—and that was citizenship in the kingdom of God. In His first recorded sermon, Jesus declared, "The kingdom of God is near. Repent and believe the good news!" (Mark 1:15). God's kingdom, He made clear, wasn't an earthly political kingdom, but a heavenly spiritual kingdom—the realm over which God rules. The Bible says, "Our citizenship is in heaven" (Philippians 3:20).

As long as we are on this earth, we possess dual citizenship. On one hand we owe allegiance to our nation and are called to be good citizens. But we are also citizens of the kingdom of God, that invisible kingdom of which Christ is the head. Our supreme loyalty is to Him, and if someone demands we do wrong, "we must obey God rather than men!" (Acts 5:29). And someday, the Bible tells us, this world's kingdoms will become "the kingdom of our Lord and of his Christ, and he will reign for ever and ever" (Revelation 11:15).

A New Family

Not only does God give us a new relationship with Himself and make us citizens of His kingdom, but He also gives us a new family— the family of God. You aren't just related to God; you are now related to other believers. Everyone who truly believes in Jesus Christ is now your spiritual brother or sister. We are bound together in God's family, not by an organization but by a spiritual relationship. The Bible calls us "members of God's household" (Ephesians 2:19). One of the most frequent terms for Christians in the Bible is "brothers," underlining our family relationship.

In my travels I have often met men and women who were very different from me. And yet after a few minutes it was almost as if we had known each other all our lives. Why? Because we both knew Christ. Our common spiritual bond cut through the barriers that separated us, and we enjoyed fellowship as members of God's family. The Bible says, "Let us do good to all people, especially to those who belong to the family of believers" (Galatians 6:10).

The Bible calls this spiritual family "the church." When you think of church, you probably think of a particular building or group of people, or perhaps your own denomination. But the church is far greater than this. It includes the *whole family of God*—that vast unseen fellowship of men and women throughout the ages who belong to Christ. Paul wrote of "God's household, which is the church of the living God" (1 Timothy 3:15).

This is one reason why you are never alone if you know Christ. You are part of God's family, with brothers and sisters in Christ who love you and want to help you, if you will let them.

A New Purpose

Some people are very focused, using all their energies to reach their goals. Others drift through life with little purpose or direction, living for the moment and never thinking about where they are headed. Most people probably live somewhere in between. But they all have this in common: They are living only for themselves and their own happiness.

But when we come to Christ, God gives us a new purpose. Now we want to live for Christ and not just ourselves. We begin to see other people differently—not for what they can do for us, but for what we can do for them. The Bible says, "We are God's workmanship, created in Christ Jesus to do good works, which God prepared in advance for us to do" (Ephesians 2:10).

When I came to Christ, I had little inkling of what I might do with my life, but down inside I knew something was different. Before my conversion, for example, I tended to be touchy and irritable. Now I deliberately tried to be considerate and courteous. Some may not have noticed, but my parents did—and so did I. Little by little I was beginning to have a new purpose in life: a desire to live for Christ. I was learning that "those who live should no longer live for themselves but for him who died for them and was raised again" (2 Corinthians 5:15).

A New Power

One of the Bible's most comforting truths is that when we come to Christ, God Himself comes to live within us by His Holy Spirit. We are not alone; God is with us!

In fact, even before we believed, His Spirit was already working in us, convicting us of sin and drawing us to God. After we believed, His Spirit didn't stop working; He came to live permanently within us! The Bible says, "If anyone does not have the Spirit of Christ, he does not belong to Christ" (Romans 8:9).

If you know Christ, you don't need to beg for the Holy Spirit to come into your life; He is already there—whether you "feel" His presence or not. Don't confuse the Holy Spirit with an emotional feeling or a particular type of spiritual experience. Instead, accept by faith what God promised: *When you come to Christ, the Holy Spirit comes to live within you.* The Bible says, "Do you not know that your body is a temple of the Holy Spirit, who is in you, whom you have received from God?" (1 Corinthians 6:19).

But *why* has God given us the Holy Spirit? As we will see later, the Spirit has been given for many reasons—but one is to help us live the way we should. *God has given us a new purpose—but without a new power we'll never be able to achieve it.* We are too weak!

But the Bible says, "The Spirit helps us in our weakness" (Romans 8:26). Jesus promised, "You will receive power when the Holy Spirit comes on you" (Acts 1:8). We aren't meant to live the Christian life in our own strength. God has provided His Spirit to help us.

A New Destiny

The word "conversion" means "change"—and the most radical change of all when we come to Christ is that God gives us a new destiny. Once we were headed for hell; now we are headed for heaven. Once we were bound for eternal separation from God; now we will live with Him forever. Once we had no hope of eternal life; now we do. The Bible says, "The wages of sin is death, but the gift of God is eternal life in Christ Jesus our Lord" (Romans 6:23).

Note carefully what this verse says: Eternal life is a *gift*. Many misunderstand this (even some Christians); they still think they must earn their salvation by their own good works. But (as we have seen) we can never be good enough to earn our way into heaven, because God's standard is perfection. God doesn't grade on the curve! Our only hope is Christ, who purchased our salvation at the cost of His own blood and now offers it to us as a free gift. The Bible says, "In his great mercy he has given us new birth into a living hope through the resurrection of Jesus Christ from the dead, and into an inheritance that can never perish, spoil or fade—kept in heaven for you" (1 Peter 1:3–4). What a gift!

In the midst of life's problems and heartaches, never forget: This life is only temporary. One day all our burdens will be cast aside, and we will be with Christ forever. Before us is *a new destiny* when we belong to Him.

A New Journey

Remember: When we come to Christ, *God gives us a whole new life: a new relationship, a new citizenship, a new family, a new purpose, a new power, a new destiny.* Don't ever take lightly what Christ did for you on the cross—and don't ever take lightly what God has given you if you have turned to Christ in repentance and faith. Why not pause right now and thank Him for these gifts to you?

But this isn't the end of His bounty, for God also gives us one final gift: a new journey—a whole new path to follow until the day He takes us to heaven.

In other words, your decision for Christ isn't an end but a beginning—the beginning of a whole new life. We aren't only called to *become* Christians; we are also called to *be* Christians. Don't ever think that faith in Christ is just a type of "spiritual life insurance," something we obtain and then put away until we need it to get into heaven. The Christian life is *a new journey*—one that will take us the rest of our lives.

And the best part is this: We never walk it alone for Christ walks with us.

SEVEN

CAN WE BE SURE?

I know whom I have believed, and am convinced that he is able to guard what I have entrusted to him for that day.

—2 TIMOTHY 1:12

IS UNCERTAINTY THE ONLY CERTAINTY IN LIFE? The daily headlines don't give us much hope. War, famine, terrorism, racial and ethnic conflict, economic disruption, violence—the list is almost endless. Neither do our everyday experiences give us much hope: family and marital breakdowns, sickness, addiction, accidents—again, the list is almost endless. Uncertainty and insecurity seem to be the watchwords of our generation. Any certainty in this uncertain world, many have concluded, is little more than wishful thinking.

Spiritual Uncertainty

Must uncertainty also be true of our spiritual lives? Or can we know—*really know*—that God cares for us and we are securely in His hands forever?

For much of his life, my father doubted this. As a young man he had given his life to Christ after a period of intense spiritual struggle and soul-searching. But gradually his feeling of God's closeness faded, and he began to doubt his salvation. He even wondered if he had committed the unpardonable sin (perhaps because at one point he had felt God might be calling him to preach, and he had turned his back on it). Although he believed he was a Christian, he felt he had slipped away from Christ and might even have lost his salvation.

My father was a man of great integrity and Christian character, and he never doubted the Gospel message. He and my mother attended church regularly (and took us as well), and he participated in the family devotions my mother led each day. But he lacked spiritual confidence, and only later, after many years, did he come into a full assurance of his salvation—an assurance that never left him.

He was not unique. In fact, I often receive letters from men and women who have sincerely committed their lives to Christ but aren't sure if God has really forgiven them. If someone asked them if they knew for certain they would go to heaven when they died, they would have to say no. Like my father, some even wonder if they have committed the unpardonable sin or lost their salvation. The uncertainty of daily life has invaded their spiritual lives, causing them to doubt their salvation.

You can be sure of one thing: *If Satan can't keep you away from Christ, he will at least try to make you doubt your salvation.* The devil's overriding goal is to block God's work—and if he can convince you God doesn't really love you, or that you can't fully trust Him, then he has blocked God's work in your life and achieved his goal. Few things cripple a Christian quicker than a lack of assurance about his or her salvation.

Sin and Doubt

Why do sincere Christians still doubt their eternal destiny? Why do we lack assurance of our salvation?

One reason many Christians aren't sure of their salvation is because they still sin, and they fear God may reject them because of it. "God must be very disappointed in me," one man wrote me. "I don't see how I can still be a Christian when I keep losing my temper." Another said, "I thought I was a Christian, but how can I be one and still do some of the things I do? I guess I'm not a Christian after all." A teenager wrote, "I gave my life to Jesus at a Christian camp this last summer, and I thought He forgave me. But now I'm not sure, because I still sin."

Sin is serious, and later we'll say more about the Christian and sin. At this point, however, notice what these letter writers have in common: They all believe God must be like a vigilant policeman, just waiting to pounce on them if they do something wrong and punish them by taking away their salvation. *But this isn't what the Bible teaches.* Even when we sin, the Bible says, "The LORD is gracious and compassionate, slow to anger and rich in love" (Psalm 145:8).

Suppose someone gave you a computer for your birthday. "This is my gift to you," they said, and you thanked them for being so generous. But suppose they added, "However, I have one requirement. Although I know you've never had a computer before, if you make a mistake on it—even one—then I'm going to take it back. You can't keep this computer unless you're perfect!" What would you think?

Yet many people assume God is like that: giving us the gift of salvation—but then taking it back if we aren't perfect! But it isn't true.

Emotions That Deceive

Other Christians lack assurance about their salvation because they depend solely on their emotions. Perhaps they had deep feelings of joy and peace when they first came to Christ, but over time those emotions faded, and now they think they must not be saved after all. But they don't realize that their emotions are deceiving them. Our emotions go up and down, and if our faith is based only on our feelings, it won't be stable.

Emotions can also deceive us in other ways. Recently I heard about a man whose father was an alcoholic. As a boy he never knew what his father would be like from one day to the next. Sometimes he was kind and gentle, but other times he was very abusive and cruel. When this man later became a Christian, he had a very hard time believing that God wasn't like his father—kind one day, angry the next. It took years (and the help of a wise Christian counselor) for him to understand why he felt this way about God. His emotions had deceived him, and he was only gradually able to overcome them.

Emotions can also deceive us when life becomes hard or turns against us and we get discouraged or depressed. "God must be angry at me," we say. "He doesn't love me after all. Maybe He's even rejected me." We'll see later why God allows hard times to come into our lives, but we must never let our circumstances blot out the sun of God's truth. Our suffering may be great—but Christ's suffering for us was far greater, and He is the final proof of God's love.

Assurance Versus Pride

A final reason why some Christians lack an assurance of their salvation might be called misguided humility. "I don't think we can know we are going to heaven," one man wrote me. "Only a proud person would say he's good enough to get into heaven, and pride is a sin. We won't know until we die, in my opinion."

He was right on one point: Pride *is* a sin, and a proud Christian is a contradiction. God doesn't save us because of who we are or how good we are, nor can we ever claim we are better than others—because we aren't. God has saved us solely by His mercy and grace, and we can't take any credit for our salvation—none at all. The Bible says, "For it is by grace you have been saved, through faith—and this not from yourselves, it is the gift of God—not by works, so that no one can boast" (Ephesians 2:8–9). God's grace—His goodness and love toward us in spite of our sin—is the wellspring of our salvation.

If our confidence was in ourselves, we could rightly be accused of pride. But our confidence must be in Christ and Christ alone. In reality, someone who believes "I won't know if I'm saved until I die" probably is hoping he or she is good enough to get into heaven. Their faith is misplaced, because it is in themselves, not in Christ.

Our Firm Foundation

Can we really *know* God cares for us and that someday He will take us to heaven? Can we *know* He cares for us and will be with us to the end, no matter what happens?

Yes, we *can* know, and in the rest of this chapter, I want to show you why this is true, based on God's Word. Just as a careful builder first lays a solid foundation before constructing a building, so God's

Word gives us a solid foundation for building our spiritual lives. The Bible says, "For no one can lay any foundation other than the one already laid, which is Jesus Christ" (1 Corinthians 3:11).

Why is this important? Because if we aren't sure whether or not God loves us, our journey through life will be hesitant, uncertain, insecure. But if we have confidence in God's love, then our journey will be joyful, assured, and filled with hope. A true Christian isn't prideful or arrogant; his confidence is not in himself but in God, and he humbly trusts Him every day. With the psalmist he says, "My salvation and my honor depend on God; he is my mighty rock, my refuge" (Psalm 62:7).

With this in mind let's examine *three reasons* why we can have assurance, both for this life and the life to come. These are like massive, unmovable stones—solid rocks God has placed under us as our sure foundation.

The Rock of God's Promises

From time to time children write me with their questions about God. One favorite question is this: Is there anything God can't do? I always answer "yes." The one thing God can't do, I explain, is anything wrong. For example, I add, God can never tell a lie; and because of that, we can trust whatever He promises us in His Word, the Bible.

From one end of the Bible to the other, God assures us that He will never go back on His promises. The Bible says, "As for God, his way is perfect; the word of the LORD is flawless" (Psalm 18:30). The Bible also assures us, "I the LORD do not change" (Malachi 3:6).

What does God promise us when we come to Christ? *He promises that we are now His children forever!* The Bible says that nothing "in all creation, will be able to separate us from the love of God that is in Christ Jesus our Lord" (Romans 8:39). Jesus said, "I give them eternal life, and they shall never perish; no one can snatch them out of my hand" (John 10:28). The Bible declares, "God has given us eternal life, and this life is in his Son. He who has the Son has life; he who does not have the Son of God does not have life" (1 John 5:11–12). Could any promise be clearer?

But God's promises didn't begin with Jesus. Immediately after Adam and Eve sinned, God hinted that someday He would send a Savior into the world (Genesis 3:15). As the centuries passed, God revealed more and more of His plan. Repeatedly in the Old Testament He promised that the Messiah (which means "the anointed one") would come to redeem His people, even foretelling the place of His birth and the manner of His death. When He came, God promised, He would die as the final sacrifice for sin and would be victorious over death. Centuries before Jesus' birth, the prophet Isaiah wrote, "He was pierced for our transgressions, he was crushed for our iniquities; the punishment that brought us peace was upon him, and by his wounds we are healed. . . . After the suffering of his soul, he will see the light of life" (Isaiah 53:5, 11). These divine promises, the Bible says, have now been fulfilled in Jesus Christ.

Are you unsure of your salvation? Make certain of your commitment to Christ. Then learn God's promises . . . memorize them . . . thank Him for them . . . and most of all, trust them. Remember: God cannot lie, and you can trust His promises. As the Bible says, "He has given us his very great and precious promises" (2 Peter 1:4).

The Rock of Christ's Finished Work

When Jesus cried, "It is finished" during those last minutes on the cross, He wasn't speaking only of His earthly life (John 19:30).

He was saying that His purpose in coming into the world had now been achieved.

Why did He come? He came for one reason: to give His life for our salvation. Once He did that, His work of redemption was complete. Jesus said, "The Son of Man came to seek and to save what was lost" (Luke 19:10). Salvation has now been accomplished! His purpose in coming has been fulfilled!

You and I can't add *anything* to what Christ did for us because He has done it all. If Christ's death was not enough . . . if we needed to add our own good works to His in order to be saved . . . then we could never know *for sure* that we will go to heaven when we die, because we could never be sure if we had done enough. But the ransom has been fully paid, and Christ's work is finished. The Bible says, "He has appeared once for all at the end of the ages to do away with sin by the sacrifice of himself" (Hebrews 9:26). The Bible also says, "The blood of Jesus, his Son, purifies us from *all* sin" (1 John 1:7, emphasis added).

How do we know Jesus' death on the cross wasn't simply the tragic end of a good man's life? How do we know His death really won our salvation?

We know it for one reason: because Jesus Christ rose from the dead. Death was no stranger to the rough, hardened Roman soldiers who took Jesus' body down from the cross, and they knew beyond doubt that He was dead. Those who collected His body knew it also, wrapping it (according to burial customs) in long strips of cloth and placing it in a cavelike tomb with a huge stone across the entrance. To ensure the body wasn't stolen, the Roman governor, Pontius Pilate, sent soldiers who "made the tomb secure by putting a seal on the stone and posting the guard" (Matthew 27:66).

But on the third day the tomb was empty! When two women

who had followed Him approached the tomb, they discovered the stone had been rolled away, and an angel greeted them with the most amazing words in human history: "He is not here; he has risen, just as he said" (Matthew 28:6). As they left to tell others, Jesus Himself greeted them—the first of many appearances before His ascension into heaven forty days later. Two decades later Paul wrote that on one occasion the risen Jesus "appeared to more than five hundred of the brothers at the same time, most of whom are still living" (1 Corinthians 15:6). The evidence is overwhelming: Jesus Christ came back to life by the power of God.

No event in human history is more startling or more significant. It proves beyond doubt that Jesus was indeed who He claimed to be: the unique Son of God, sent from heaven to save us from our sins. It also confirms that He has conquered for all time the forces of sin and death and hell and Satan. It reminds us as well that Christ is alive, and even now He sits at the right hand of God praying for us.

While preaching in the old Soviet Union some years ago, I asked a Russian Orthodox theologian who accompanied us if he had any suggestions. After a moment he replied, "Preach more about the resurrection." He was right; no event is more central to our faith. Jesus Christ is alive—and that makes all the difference!

Never forget: You can be sure of your salvation *because nothing more remains to be done.* Christ's sacrifice is complete—and the proof is His resurrection from the dead.

The Rock of the Spirit's Witness

As we have seen, some people depend solely on their inner feelings for an assurance of their salvation. If they feel God is close to them, they decide they must be saved, but if those feelings fade, they conclude He has abandoned them. *But this isn't true.* Our emotions aren't a dependable gauge of our true standing with God. Emotions come and go, and a faith that is built solely on our feelings will never be secure.

At the same time, God *has* given us an inner witness to assure us of our salvation: *the witness of the Holy Spirit.* This witness within us isn't just an emotional feeling (although emotions may play a part). Instead, the Spirit's witness is *a settled, inner conviction that the Gospel is true and we now belong to Christ.* The Bible says, "The Spirit himself testifies with our spirit that we are God's children" (Romans 8:16). The Bible also says the Holy Spirit is God's "seal of ownership on us, . . . a deposit, guaranteeing what is to come" (2 Corinthians 1:22).

This is somewhat like being a member of a family. Sometimes you may feel very close to your family; sometimes you may not. But down inside you always know you are part of that family, whether you feel close to them or not. You know you belong to each other; you have a settled, inner conviction that isn't just an emotional feeling. In fact, it isn't based on your feelings at all. It is based on a *fact*, the fact that you were born into that family. In the same way, the Holy Spirit gives us an inner, settled conviction that we have been born into a family—the family of God, who is our heavenly Father.

The Holy Spirit, however, also bears witness to our conversion in another way: by the change in our lives. When Christ lives within us by His Spirit, our lives will be different. No, we won't be perfect, nor will we change instantly overnight. But if *nothing* has changed—in our attitude, our behavior, our priorities—it may indicate we haven't really given our lives to Christ after all. The Bible warns, "No one who lives in him [Christ] keeps on sinning" (1 John 3:6).

The Firm Foundation

Don't let anything—or anyone—ever rob you of your confidence in Christ. Remember: Your salvation depends on what He has done for you, not on what you do for Him. It isn't your hold on God that saves you; it's His hold on you. Your salvation is a free gift, made possible only because God planned it . . . Christ paid for it . . . and the Holy Spirit assures you of it.

Pause right now to thank God for this great gift and the firm foundation you have as a result—a foundation in Christ that can never be shaken.

EIGHT

HEADING IN THE RIGHT DIRECTION

And he died for all, that those who live should no longer live for themselves but for him who died for them and was raised again.

—2 CORINTHIANS 5:15

A BABY ISN'T MEANT TO STAY A BABY FOREVER, AND neither is a new Christian.

It's no accident that the Bible calls us "newborn babies" when we first come to Christ, for that is what we are: spiritual babies (1 Peter 2:2). God has worked in us by His Spirit to change our hearts and adopt us into His family—but like a newborn baby, we are still weak and vulnerable, and we need all the help we can get to grow beyond infancy and become spiritually mature.

But what is spiritual maturity?

Birth and Growth

The birth of each one of our five children was a special event for us, but for me that of our last child, Ned, was especially memorable. The reason was because the doctor allowed me to be with Ruth in the delivery room, and for the first time I had the privilege of actually seeing one of our children being born. As a boy I had often witnessed the birth of animals on my father's farm, but this was different! This tiny newborn (protesting with all the strength his small but powerful lungs could muster) was a human being—and more than that, he was my son! Those who have called the birth of a baby a "miracle" aren't far from the truth. Ned's birth was a unique and moving experience I will never forget.

As Ruth held him for the first time, I found myself silently praying for this child God had entrusted to us. I prayed we would be good and loving parents, and that as the years passed, God would help us point him to Christ. I prayed also that God would protect and safeguard him, and that he would grow up to be a man of God. Ruth and I would repeat that prayer almost daily as Ned grew—as we would for all our children.

As I reflect on it, I realize that behind my prayers for Ned (and behind the prayers of every parent for their children) lurked a hidden fear. It was the fear that something might intervene to stop his growth. A sudden illness, a genetic defect, a devastating accident—a hundred things might go wrong that would hinder his growth or even bring it to an end. Our hearts had always been deeply saddened whenever we had seen this happen, both in our extended family and with close friends.

The point is this: A baby is cute and lovable, *but we don't want a baby to stay a baby forever*. Nor do we want a child or a teenager to remain that way forever. When they do, we know something has gone wrong because they were meant to grow and become mature. A baby is meant to grow into a child, a child into an adolescent, an adolescent into an adult.

Spiritual Birth and Growth

Tragic as it is when a child fails to develop physically or mentally, even more tragic is a Christian who fails to develop spiritually. The reason is simple: *We weren't meant to remain spiritual babies*. Instead, God's goal for us is *spiritual maturity*. The Bible says, "Therefore let us . . . go on to maturity" (Hebrews 6:1). The Bible also urges, "Like newborn babies, crave pure spiritual milk, so that by it you may grow up in your salvation" (1 Peter 2:2). The goal of a child's life is maturity—and the goal of a Christian's life is spiritual maturity.

What is maturity? On a human level we know it isn't just a matter of age. We have all met people who were adults in terms of years yet acted like spoiled little children: self-centered, irresponsible, inconsiderate, impulsive, unwise in the decisions they made. Such a person, we say, is immature, no matter how old they are in years. A mature person, on the other hand, isn't just physically mature; he or she also has grown up emotionally and socially. They have learned to be considerate and responsible and to realize that their actions have consequences, both for themselves and for others.

In a similar way, spiritual maturity isn't just a question of how long we have been a Christian. Sadly, far too many Christians never grow and develop in their faith. If asked, they may be able to give a testimony of what God has done for them—but often it's something that happened many years ago! Spiritually they are in limbo, and if someone examined their spiritual lives five years ago and then looked at them again today, they would see little difference. They have been born again, but they are still babies in Christ.

They are like the Christians to whom Paul wrote in Corinth: "Brothers, I could not address you as spiritual but as worldly—mere infants in Christ" (1 Corinthians 3:1).

Barriers to Spiritual Growth

Why don't we grow in our faith? Sometimes it's because of a particular sin we have tolerated and allowed to block God's work, refusing to admit it or give it up. Or sometimes we don't grow spiritually because we give in to the pressure of those around us who care little for Christ or may even be hostile to Him—family, friends, fellow students, neighbors, coworkers.

In my experience, however, *most Christians fail to grow in their faith either because they don't realize they ought to grow or because they don't know how to grow.* They know Christ died for them and that they will go to heaven someday, but they don't know what ought to be happening to them in the meantime. They remain spiritually weak and immature, never experiencing the fullness of life that Jesus promised His followers. Does this describe you?

You can be sure that Satan delights in an immature Christian. An immature Christian is an ineffective Christian, making little impact for Christ on the lives of others. An immature Christian also is an inconsistent Christian, living for Christ one day and forgetting Him the next. An immature Christian provides plenty of ammunition for those who say they don't believe in Christ because they think the church is full of hypocrites.

Don't let anything—or anyone—stand in the way of your growth in Christ. Just as the relationship between a husband and wife should grow stronger as the years go by, so should your relationship with Christ. Don't take Him for granted, and don't let your love for Him grow cold. Instead, the Bible says, "Grow in the grace and knowledge of our

Lord and Savior Jesus Christ" (2 Peter 3:18). Begin now, by asking God to remove whatever barriers are keeping Him from working in your life. Then make it your goal to become—with God's help—the mature Christian He wants you to be. Ruth and I sometimes watch a video of an old film in which the hero falls in love with a young woman. He tells her, "I can hardly wait for you to grow up!" Is that what God is saying to you?

The Goal

What, however, is spiritual maturity? To put it another way, what exactly does God want to do in our lives as we journey along His path?

The Bible gives us the answer: *God's will is for us to become more and more like Christ.* It is that simple—and also that complex.

Perhaps you've had the experience of having someone come up to you and say, "You look just like your mother!" or "You look just like your brother!" They saw a family resemblance between you and your parents or some other member of your family. Grandparents often spend hours trying to decide whom a newborn baby resembles in the family (usually with little success!). You may even have seen married couples who looked more and more like each other as the years went by.

In a far deeper way, *God's will is that we would bear a family resemblance to His Son.* In other words, God's plan is for us to become more and more like Jesus—not physically, of course, but in the way we think and act and treat other people. From all eternity, the Bible says, God's plan was for us "to be conformed to the likeness of his Son" (Romans 8:29). We are part of His family—and because of that we should bear His likeness!

Do you want to know what God's will is for you? *It is for you to become more and more like Christ.* This is spiritual maturity, and if you make this your goal, it will change your life.

The Key

At this point you may be tempted to say, "Well, that's fine for some people, but it's not for me. I have enough trouble just keeping up with everything I need to do each day. I can't go off in a corner and spend all my time praying or something like that. I'm just an ordinary Christian, not a supersaint!"

But it's a mistake to think God's will is for only a few "super-spiritual" people, or that we must withdraw from our daily responsibilities if we want to become more like Christ. Listen: God's will is for you to become more and more like Christ *right where you are.* Jesus didn't isolate Himself from daily life; He became involved in people's lives wherever He went. At times He withdrew to rest and spend time alone with His heavenly Father—and so should we. But Jesus also knew what it was to live under pressure, yet He never wavered from God's plan for His life. Neither should we. In His last recorded prayer for His followers, He said, "My prayer is not that you take them out of the world" (John 17:15).

How do we become more like Christ? How does it happen? *It happens as we submit every area of our lives to His authority.* We will discuss this in more detail later, but nothing must be excluded from His influence, and nothing must be withheld from His control. Many years ago I heard someone use a little phrase I have never forgotten: "If Christ is to be Lord *at* all, then He must be Lord *of* all." Jesus said, "If anyone would come after me, he must deny himself and take up his cross daily and follow me" (Luke 9:23). John the Baptist declared, "He must become greater; I must become less" (John 3:30). Is this your goal?

Nothing Left Out

When I gave my life to Christ as a teenager, I knew I needed God's forgiveness, and I also knew that my life ought to change. Only gradually, however, did I come to realize that God didn't want just part of me; He wanted *all* of me. Only gradually did I realize that He wanted me to submit *every area of my life* to His authority. I believed Christ was my Lord, but only later did I begin to understand the implications of this for my life. I am still learning.

This, I suspect, is true for most of us. We begin our new lives in Christ joyfully, thankful that God has forgiven us and wanting to leave our old, sinful ways behind. But as time passes, we begin to wonder if we've left them behind after all. Try as we might, old habits remain and little seems to have changed.

What is the problem? It may have several dimensions, but at its heart, we have failed to submit to the daily authority of Jesus. We have ignored His Lordship. Perhaps we have been trying to change our lives in our own strength instead of seeking His help—but whatever the reason, we have not turned every part of our lives over to Him. And when we fail to do that, we block the life-changing work of the Holy Spirit.

Don't take lightly what it means to submit *every area* of your life to Christ's authority. Take your body, for example. God gave it to you—but do you allow its desires to control you? Or what about your mind? Every day you are besieged with ideas and images that dishonor God—but do you allow them to saturate your thinking and influence your behavior? Or think about your motives. Do selfish goals and priorities set the agenda for your daily life? What about your tongue? Would you be ashamed to have Christ overhear your conversations? Would He be pleased with your language? The list could go on and on: our relationships, our finances, our attitude toward those of another race, our concern for those in need, our emotions—everything.

Never forget: *God's will is for us to become more like Christ—and this only happens as we submit every area of our lives to His authority.*

The Battle of the Will

This is why our first spiritual battle once we come to Christ is usually with our *will* (and it will probably continue as long as we live, for our wills can be very stubborn). We want to control our lives, and the idea of handing control over to someone else (even God) goes against the grain. We don't like anyone telling us what to do, and even when what we're doing is foolish, we still dig in our heels and stubbornly resist. This is true in our daily lives, and it's even more true in our spiritual lives.

But there can be no shortcut to spiritual growth. We can't have it both ways. Either we submit ourselves to Christ's authority, or we don't. And if we reject His authority, we will never become like Him. Satan will be the winner—and we will be the losers. We will never experience the joy of knowing God's plan for our lives, nor will we have the joy of having God use us to advance His kingdom.

Do others see something of Christ in your life? Do they see a "family resemblance" to Him by the way you live? If not, *don't let another day go by without committing yourself to God's great plan for you: to make you more and more like Jesus.* Be honest about whatever it is that keeps you from that commitment—and then repent of it, and commit yourself to live under His authority. You will never regret it.

A New Life

Don't make the mistake, however, of thinking that the Christian life is all negative—that is, that it mainly involves denying ourselves and giving up everything we enjoy. Some Christians are like this, I'm afraid; they are known mainly for what they *don't* do, and others don't find much about them to attract them to Christ.

But Jesus wasn't like that. People weren't attracted to Him because of what He *didn't* do; they were attracted to Him because of what He *did* do. They saw in Him a quality of life they had never seen before, and they wanted to experience it for themselves. When they looked at Christ, they saw joy and peace and kindness—and most of all, they saw God's love.

God wants to give us that same quality of life—the life of Jesus. Jesus said to His disciples, "I have told you this so that my joy may be in you and that your joy may be complete" (John 15:11). If your image of the Christian life is negative and cheerless and dull, I have news for you: You are wrong! Listen: *God never removes something from our lives without replacing it with something far better.*

It might not seem so at the time, but later you will understand—and you will marvel at God's wisdom and goodness. If God takes away a bad habit that has enslaved you, He will replace it with a better way of living. If He takes away your gossip or cursing or back-biting, He will replace them with words of love and encourage-ment and praise. If He removes your self-centered motives, He will replace them with the excitement and joy of doing His will.

God's goal isn't just to remove the bad things in our lives; He wants to replace them with good things. *His plan is to remake us from within, by His Holy Spirit.* The Bible says, "Do not conform any longer to the pattern of this world, but be transformed by the renewing of your mind. Then you will be able to test and approve what God's will is—his good, pleasing and perfect will" (Romans 12:2).

That's what God's will is like: *good, pleasing, and perfect.* Why settle for anything less?

SECTION TWO

STRENGTH FOR THE JOURNEY

NINE

PREPARING FOR THE
LONG HAUL

Let us throw off everything that hinders and the sin that so easily
entangles, and let us run with perseverance the race marked out for us.
—HEBREWS 12:1

THE JOURNEY GOD HAS GIVEN US ISN'T A SPRINT BUT
a marathon.

In the 1930s my father was one of the first in our area to have a
radio in his car. Occasionally we would hear programs on it relayed
from Europe—distorted and with a hollow echo, but nevertheless
thrilling to hear. Sometimes we heard the hypnotic voice of a man
named Adolf Hitler, and although I couldn't understand his language, he frightened me in some ways (although I was too young
to fully realize how great a threat he was to world peace).

I will never forget the 1936 Berlin Olympics—probably the first
Olympics to attract any attention on my part. Hitler had planned

for them to be a showcase of Nazi-inspired athletic superiority—but against all odds, an African-American by the name of Jesse Owens stole the show. Americans reacted with excitement and pride as Owens captured an unprecedented four gold medals in track-and-field events, including the 100 meters, the 200 meters, the long jump, and the 4 x 100 relay. Hitler was furious, we read later, but we couldn't have been more thrilled. Jesse Owens was a sprinter, one of the greatest sprinters who ever lived.

Sprint or Marathon?

A sprint is very different from a marathon. A sprint covers only a short distance and lasts just a few seconds, while a marathon covers miles and may last for hours.

But the difference isn't only one of distance or time; it is also in the amount of stamina they require from each runner. The runner in a sprint race—a 100-yard dash, for example, or a 200-meter race—pours all of his energy into those few seconds of intense activity, crossing the finish line drained and exhausted. If he had to run another 100 yards or 200 meters, he might collapse, or at least he would slow down dramatically.

The marathon runner, on the other hand, carefully paces himself, not using up all his energy in the early part of the race but measuring it out, maintaining a steady rate of speed as long as possible. Also running in the 1936 Olympics was another American by the name of Louis Zamperini, whose accomplishments in the 5,000-meter marathon even won Hitler's respect. Years later Louis committed his life to Christ at our 1949 Los Angeles meetings, and he told me once how a marathon runner trains for the long haul, and all his energy is directed toward that goal.

This comparison with the Christian's journey through life isn't exact, of course. We never know, for example, how long our personal journey will last; God may take you home to heaven tomorrow. The marathon runner also trains extensively (often for years) before he enters his first race. We, on the other hand, are already in the midst of the race, learning as we go along and continually drawing strength from the resources God gives us. And, unlike the runner, we do not know in advance exactly what course the path may take—although we have no doubt about the final goal.

The Long Haul

Nevertheless, like the marathon runner, we are in it for the long haul. Our journey—our race—lasts as long as God gives us life, and we aren't meant to wander off the track, or quit and join the spectators, or decide we'll just slow down and take it easy while others pass us by. Our example is Jesus, "who for the joy set before him endured the cross, scorning its shame, and sat down at the right hand of the throne of God" (Hebrews 12:2). He faithfully ran the race God had prepared for Him, even at the cost of His own blood.

Nor are we meant to collapse from exhaustion in the middle of the race, our strength gone and our reserves drained. That will happen if we run it unwisely or depend only on our own resources. We may get by with it for a time, but eventually it will catch up with us. In ourselves we are too weak, and our spiritual resources are too scanty. God didn't intend for us to travel our journey in our own strength anyway, but only with the strength He supplies. This was what Paul meant when he declared, "I can do all things through Christ who strengthens me" (Philippians 4:13 NKJV).

I am convinced the main reason so many Christians become spiritually discouraged and defeated is because they have never discovered this truth. They assume it must be up to them to live the

Christian life, and they never make use of the rich resources God has already provided to strengthen us for the journey. Like guests who have been invited to a banquet but never sit down to the meal, they have never learned to draw their strength from God's resources. But God doesn't want us to be this way. He doesn't want us to fail! In fact, He is far more concerned about your spiritual welfare than you will ever be.

Preparing for the Race

When Jesse Owens won in Berlin, I'm sure many teenagers day-dreamed about someday becoming a second Jesse Owens or Louis Zamperini—yet only a handful would ever make it to the next Olympics (not held until 1948 because of the war). Why? The reason, you might suggest, was because they didn't have the required natural ability. But some probably did have enough talent, and yet none of them would equal Jesse Owens's record.

Why? The reason is because ability alone isn't enough for someone who aspires to be a successful athlete, whether as a runner, a soccer player, a baseball player, a swimmer, a professional golfer, a bicycle racer, or anything else. Coupled with ability must be two other factors: *commitment and discipline*.

Commitment for an athlete means having a strong desire, a driving tenacity, even an overriding compulsion to become the best he possibly can at his sport. He has one goal: to win. Commitment isn't just a hope or a wish or even a deep yearning for him. It goes far beyond that. It means everything else gets put in second place or even set aside as he strives with all his strength to become the best. We sometimes hear that a particular athlete is "totally focused"; the other day I heard a sports broadcaster say this about an outstanding golfer who is known for hitting several buckets of balls even before breakfast. That is his commitment: a total, absolute focus on what they want to achieve.

Commitment for an athlete is essential, but commitment by itself is not enough. Commitment must be coupled with *discipline* if an athlete is ever to achieve her goal. A person may have a driving desire to be the best tennis player she can possibly be, but if she isn't willing to spend time learning the basics of the game, she will never reach her goal. An aspiring tennis player must be disciplined: strengthening her muscles, developing her serve, working on her footwork, learning to put spin on the ball, and so forth. She also must learn the rules of the game, and take care of her body with proper nutrition and exercise.

A lazy athlete will never become a successful athlete, no matter how gifted she is. Even an athlete with less natural ability may become a winner if her commitment and her discipline are stronger than that of her more gifted competitors.

Years after the Berlin Olympics Jesse Owens was asked what it had been like to be a finalist in the 100-meter race. He replied, "It was a lifetime of training for just ten seconds." His victory in that brief race capped years of commitment and discipline, and without them it never would have happened.

The Call to Discipleship

It is no accident that the words *discipline* and *disciple* resemble each other in the English language, for they come from the same Latin root. The most common word in the Gospels for a Christian is "disciple," and discipleship cannot be separated from both commitment and discipline. *To be a disciple is to be committed*—committed to Jesus Christ as our Savior and Lord and committed to following Him every day. *To be a disciple is also to be disciplined*—disciplined in our bodies, disciplined in our minds, disciplined in our souls. Does this describe you?

The New Testament actually uses a number of words to describe the Christian, each of which helps us understand what it means to follow Jesus. As we've already seen, the Bible says the Christian is *a runner* in the "marathon" of the Christian's journey. Paul wrote, "Do you not know that in a race all the runners run, but only one gets the prize? Run in such a way as to get the prize. Everyone who competes in the games goes into strict training." Then he added this personal note: "Therefore I do not run like a man running aimlessly. . . . No, I beat [or discipline] my body and make it my slave" (1 Corinthians 9:24–27). As a "runner" in God's "race," Paul was both *committed* to the goal and *disciplined* to do whatever it took to reach it.

Or again, the Bible compares the Christian to *a soldier*. A soldier is under the command of his superior officer and must be trained and equipped to meet the enemy. He also must be willing to go into battle and even sacrifice his life if necessary. The Bible says, "Be strong in the Lord and in his mighty power. Put on the full armor of God" (Ephesians 6:10–11). Paul urged Timothy, "Endure hardship with us like a good soldier of Christ Jesus. No one serving as a soldier gets involved in civilian affairs—he wants to please his commanding officer" (2 Timothy 2:3–4).

Another word the Bible uses to describe Christians is *brothers* (a general term meaning both brothers and sisters in a family). Brothers aren't just individuals; they are also related to each other. Family ties were very important to first-century Jews and Gentiles, and even when siblings had conflicts (as sometimes happens in families), they usually came together to deal with a family problem or reach a common goal. In a far deeper way, Christians aren't just individuals; they are part of a larger family—the family of God. James (the half brother of Jesus) called his fellow Christians "my dear brothers" (James 1:16). Paul had never met the Christians in the town of Colossae, but he still addressed them as "faithful brothers in Christ" (Colossians 1:2).

However, the most comprehensive word in the Bible for Christians is *disciples.* The twelve men who traveled with Jesus and were closest to Him were called "the disciples," but many others who followed Jesus were called disciples also, including a number of women (Luke 8:2–3). In fact, anyone who wanted to follow Jesus' teaching was called a disciple. When Jesus gave His Sermon on the Mount, for example, we read that "a large crowd of his disciples was there" (Luke 6:17). The Bible also records that several years after Jesus' ministry, "The disciples were called Christians first at Antioch" (Acts 11:26). To be a Christian is to be a *disciple.*

A Learner

Everyone in Jesus' day knew what the word "disciple" meant. The Roman world was filled with philosophers and teachers who gathered students or followers around them, and those followers were called "disciples." John the Baptist had a band of disciples around him, and so did the Pharisees (a group of religious leaders). But Jesus expanded its meaning by saying that everyone who truly believes in Him is called to be a disciple. "Jesus said, 'If you hold to my teaching, you are really my disciples'" (John 8:31).

What is a disciple? *First, a disciple is a learner or a student.* The twelve whom Jesus called to be His closest companions were with Him day and night. They had a personal relationship with Him— walking with Him, eating with Him, sharing in His conversation, observing the way He lived, listening to Him preach to the crowds. But they weren't following Jesus just to enjoy His presence. As Jesus' disciples they had a purpose: to *learn* from Him—absorbing His teaching, learning from His example, even profiting from His rebukes. And this was true for all His disciples, not just the Twelve. To be a disciple is to be a *learner.*

What keeps us from being this kind of disciple? One factor, frankly, may be laziness or at least a lack of discipline. I'm afraid I was at best only an indifferent student when I was growing up. If I was going to follow in my father's footsteps and become a farmer, I thought, why should I bother with subjects like algebra or literature? My problem was a lack of discipline, and only after I turned my life over to Christ did this begin to change.

Or we may not realize how much we need to know and be guided by God's truth. The psalmist was right: "The unfolding of your words gives light; it gives understanding to the simple" (Psalm 119:130). Our journey through life is filled with all kinds of pitfalls and temptations, and unless we allow our minds and hearts to be shaped by Christ's truth, we risk falling into all kinds of errors and dangers. Jesus said, "If you hold to my teaching, you are really my disciples. Then you will know the truth, and the truth will set you free" (John 8:31–32).

A Follower

Second, not only is a disciple a learner, but a disciple is also a follower. Those first disciples of Jesus literally followed Him from place to place, but of course it means far more than that. *To follow Jesus is to follow His teachings.* Jesus said, "You are my friends if you do what I command" (John 15:14). He also said, "By this all men will know that you are my disciples, if you love one another" (John 13:35).

To put it another way, a disciple *seeks to put Jesus' words into action.* I met a man once who was a brilliant scientist, but he admitted sheepishly that at home he couldn't fix a leaky faucet! He had a great deal of knowledge in his head about the way the world works, but he didn't always know how to put it into action. James wrote, "What good is it, my brothers, if a man claims to have faith but has no deeds? . . . As the body without the spirit is dead, so faith without deeds is dead" (James 2:14, 26). A disciple is a *follower* of Jesus.

A Servant

A final dimension of discipleship is this: To be a disciple is to be a servant—a servant of our Master, Jesus Christ.

James and John must have had strong personalities; the Bible calls them "Sons of Thunder" (Mark 3:17). One day as Jesus neared the end of His ministry, they said to Him, "We want you to do for us whatever we ask." They added, "Let one of us sit at your right and the other at your left in your glory" (Mark 10:35, 37). They wanted to act like kings, ruling over everyone else!

But Jesus rebuked them and told them they didn't understand what it meant to be His disciples: "Instead, whoever wants to become great among you must be your servant" (Mark 10:43). (The irony is that Jesus had already told His disciples only days before, "If anyone wants to be first, he must be the very last, and the servant of all" [Mark 9:35]. How often do we fail to hear what God is trying to tell us?) To be a disciple is to be a *servant*.

The Race Before Us

The Christian's journey through life isn't a sprint but a marathon. Are you prepared for it? How can you be prepared? *It begins with a commitment to be His disciple—to be Christ's learner, Christ's follower, and Christ's servant.* Are you that kind of disciple? Is this your commitment, and are you disciplined in carrying it out? Only then will you be prepared for the journey.

Discipleship is the commitment of a lifetime. Let it begin in your life today.

TEN

THE UNENDING BATTLE

Dear friends, do not be surprised at the painful trial you are suffering, as though something strange were happening to you.

— I PETER 4:12

THE CHRISTIAN LIFE ISN'T A PLAYGROUND BUT A battlefield.

In early 1959 preparations were almost complete for the most extensive evangelistic outreach we had ever attempted, a continent-wide mission across Australia. The invitations in each city had come from broad-based committees representing almost every denomination, and for over a year our staff had been working with them to prepare the meetings. Tens of thousands of volunteers had been recruited, and home prayer meetings had been organized in every city—five thousand in Sydney alone. Arrangements had also been made to relay the meetings by telephone line to hundreds of towns and settlements throughout Australia's vast outback. Ruth couldn't join me due to Ned's birth the year before, and neither of us looked forward to an extended separation. Nevertheless, we believed God had opened the door to evangelism in Australia, and I was looking forward to it with great anticipation.

Just days before I was scheduled to depart, I noticed that something seemed to be wrong with my vision. When I looked at the ground, it appeared ridged or wavy, and shortly afterward I experienced a sharp pain in my left eye and lost peripheral vision. The doctor's diagnosis was not encouraging: I had a rare but serious problem that could lead to blindness if left untreated—and the only treatment was total rest. The Australian meetings had to be delayed, and my own schedule once the meetings started would have to be greatly curtailed.

Why did it happen? Did God cause the delay—or was the devil trying to stop us? Or was I somehow at fault?

I still don't know the answer. I do know that God used those unexpected weeks of quiet to prepare me in ways I wouldn't have experienced otherwise. The disruption in our plans also caused people to pray more intensely, and in spite of the changes, God worked in remarkable ways once the meetings began. But I still don't know why God let it happen.

It wasn't the first time I experienced a serious roadblock in our work, nor would it be the last. In fact, I don't think I have ever undertaken a major evangelistic outreach without encountering some kind of problem, either in my own life or in the mission itself. Like my Australian experience, I seldom know exactly why it happens—but it does. You have probably faced similar difficulties in your own life, for none of us is exempt from problems and troubles.

A Paradox?

Occasionally I meet people who sincerely believe that if they follow Christ, their lives should be free of problems. After all, they say, didn't Jesus promise us peace? Won't God take away our troubles and give us health and prosperity, if we only have enough faith?

The Bible, however, doesn't promise this. Yes, it promises peace, but it also promises tribulation and conflict. On the surface, I know, this sounds like a paradox, and in a way it is. After all, how can we be at peace and also at war at the same time?

The key is to understand what Jesus meant when He said, "Peace I leave with you; my peace I give you" (John 14:27). His promise is true: We *do* have peace when we follow Christ—an inner peace that comes from a deep and abiding trust in His promises. One dimension of this is our *peace with God*. When warring nations sign a peace treaty, the fighting between them stops—and this is what has happened between us and God. At one time we were at war with God, but now "we have peace with God through our Lord Jesus Christ" (Romans 5:1). In addition, when we walk with Christ, we have *peace in our hearts.* The wars that once raged in our hearts have ended. So have our conflicts with other people, and we come to have *peace with others*. When we know Christ, we truly have peace—peace with God, peace in our hearts, and peace with others.

This peace is real—just as real as God Himself. It is an *inner* peace—a peace in our souls and minds and emotions—that keeps us calm even in the midst of life's worst storms. But notice: This doesn't mean we'll always be free from trials and conflicts. Yes, Christ gives us *inner peace*—but He hasn't promised to always give us *outer peace* or freedom from problems and difficulties. In fact, our problems may become greater when we know Christ, because our commitment to

Him may put us at odds with an unbelieving world. Jesus declared, "In this world you will have trouble" (John 16:33). He also warned, "'No servant is greater than his master.' If they persecuted me, they will persecute you also" (John 15:20).

The Cosmic Conflict

Why is our journey through life beset with so many problems and heartaches, even for Christians? What is behind all the trials and tribulations that plague us? We will explore this in more detail later when we look at the Christian and temptation, but first we need to examine one truth that is often overlooked.

In 1985 I visited Romania, which at that time was still under Communist rule. Romania, however, has a strong Christian heritage dating back over a thousand years, and shortly after our arrival a church leader took me for a tour of some of their medieval cathedrals. Unlike the cathedrals of Western Europe with their elaborate stained glass windows, these were decorated inside and outside with magnificent frescoes depicting stories and themes from the Bible. (Very few people had Bibles or could read in medieval Europe, and artwork like this was used to teach them the Bible.)

One fresco especially made an impression on me. It covered an entire wall and showed people struggling upward on a ladder, climbing a staircase toward heaven. Surrounding them were numerous angels, encouraging and helping them on their journey—but below were numerous demons, pulling at their heels and trying to drag them off the ladder and into the fires below.

This scene, although fanciful, vividly reminded me that *you and I are part of a vast spiritual conflict we can only barely perceive, but which affects everything that happens on this planet.* It is the continual conflict between good and evil . . . right and wrong . . . life and death . . .

heaven and hell. But most of all, it is the age-old conflict between God and Satan. More than any fanciful Hollywood drama, this is the true "war of the worlds." The Bible says, "For our struggle is not against flesh and blood, but against the rulers, against the authorities, against the powers of this dark world and against the spiritual forces of evil in the heavenly realms" (Ephesians 6:12).

The Bible only gives us faint glimpses of this conflict, and we must be careful not to speculate or go beyond what it tells us. Nor must we become preoccupied with it. Nevertheless, the Bible suggests that our earthly struggles are but a reflection of a much greater cosmic struggle—a struggle that won't end until the final battle is fought and Satan is cast "into the eternal fire prepared for the devil and his angels" (Matthew 25:41).

Why do I mention this? The reason is because *you and I are part of this struggle*. The battle isn't only cosmic; it is also personal. Satan is real, and he will do everything he can to pull us away from God. If we have truly given our lives to Christ, our salvation is secure, for it depends on Christ's work on the cross and not on us. But Satan can still discourage us and make us weak and ineffective—and it happens all the time.

Three Errors

We need to take this spiritual conflict seriously, for we are all part of it. If we don't, we may fall into one of several errors—and God's plan to make us more like Christ will suffer.

The first error some people make is this: Evil isn't real. They believe evil is only an illusion, or simply an absence of good. Others say evil is merely another name for psychological or social maladjustment. When confronted with evil in its most brutal forms, however, they have no answer, because they cannot admit its reality or its terrible impact on humanity. If we deny evil's stark reality, we will never be prepared to fight it. A good friend told me once that he had eventually faced the fact that his own father wasn't only malicious and mean, but thoroughly evil. My friend was very thankful Christ had delivered him from the grip of his background.

A second error says almost the opposite: Evil is real, and we'll never be able to overcome it. Some believe God and Satan are equals, locked in an endless struggle without victory on either side. Why fight evil? they say; it won't do any good. They fail to see that *while Satan is powerful, God is all-powerful.* They also fail to see that through His death and resurrection, Jesus "disarmed the [demonic] powers and authorities, . . . triumphing over them by the cross" (Colossians 2:15). As we saw in chapter 4, Satan is real—but he is also a defeated foe! He is still at work—but the final outcome is not in doubt. Don't give in to despair when life turns against you. You are on the winning side if you know Christ!

A third error may be the most dangerous; even Christians can fall into it, often without realizing it. It goes like this: Evil is real, but I must fight it on my own. Instead of depending on God to help us, we rely on ourselves. Instead of realizing our utter helplessness in the face of sin and admitting our need for the Holy Spirit's help, we assume we must try to gain victory in our own strength. We fail to realize that God has already given us all the resources we need for victory.

Don't underestimate the dangers we face along this journey God has set before us. The devil works in many ways—sometimes openly, more often indirectly. But *his goal is always the same: to turn us away from God.* If he can distract us, or take us down a side road, or discourage us, or get us to yield to temptation—then he has succeeded.

But don't underestimate God's willingness to help! He loves us and wants to help us. The prophet Zephaniah's words are just as true today as when he first penned them: "The LORD your God is with you, he is mighty to save. He will take great delight in you, he will quiet you with his love, he will rejoice over you with singing" (Zephaniah 3:17).

Strength for the Conflict

"What is wrong with me?" someone wrote me recently. "I gave my life to Jesus two years ago, but I just can't seem to do what's right." Perhaps you have felt this way.

How do we find strength for the conflict? How do we stay on course? I have often thought about this, reflecting not only on my own spiritual struggles but those I have seen in the lives of other Christians. How do we gain victory each day in the midst of this spiritual conflict?

The answer, I'm convinced, can be stated very simply: *The key to spiritual victory is to stay close to God.* The Bible puts it this way: "Submit yourselves, then, to God. Resist the devil, and he will flee from you. Come near to God and he will come near to you" (James 4:7–8). *Submit . . . resist . . . come near*—this is what we must do if we are to gain spiritual victory.

We have already seen what it means to submit to God. It means to turn every area of our lives over to Christ. It means to renounce control over our lives and hand ourselves over instead to His authority. Have you submitted every part of your life to Christ's Lordship? That must be your first step.

Then we are told to *resist the devil*. How do we do this? The word translated "resist" was used to describe a soldier's response when attacked and means to actively oppose or take a firm stand against an enemy. Just as a soldier resists an enemy who attacks him, so we are commanded to resist the devil's attacks. When we resist him, the Bible says, he will flee in defeat.

Finally, we are told to *come near to God*. Remember: *The closer you are to God, the farther you are from the devil.* That doesn't mean he'll give up tempting you, but it does mean his chance of success is greatly lessened. The psalmist said, "He is my loving God and my fortress . . . in whom I take refuge" (Psalm 144:2).

Time Alone With God

The question remains, however: How do we come near to God?

First, remember two important truths. One, if you know Christ, you have a personal relationship with God. God isn't a remote, forbidding figure who doesn't want anything to do with you. He is your loving heavenly Father, and even now His Son is praying for you. Therefore, the Bible says, "let us draw near to God with a sincere heart in full assurance of faith" (Hebrews 10:22). You can come near to God because He wants you to!

The second truth is this: You also have a personal relationship with your brothers and sisters in Christ. One of the ways we draw near to God is through our fellowship with other Christians—praying together, worshipping together, studying God's Word together, sharing our burdens, and encouraging each other.

With these two truths in mind, how shall we come near to God? *The key is to spend time with Him.* If I could give only one piece of advice to a new Christian, it would be this: *Develop the discipline of spending time alone with God every day.* Whether you call it your quiet time or daily devotions or some other term, there is no substitute for a daily time alone with God.

How can you develop this practice? *First, set aside a time.* Yes, it may seem impossible to find even ten extra minutes in your busy day. But the real question is this: *How important to you is your relationship with God?* You find time for meals and other things you think important. Every day has exactly 1,440 minutes; can't you find even ten of them to be with your heavenly Father? Don't wait until you have some spare time; you'll probably never have any! Instead, set aside a regular time each day, a time when you are fresh and won't be interrupted (even if it's only a few minutes at first). Don't wait until you're too sleepy or too preoccupied. Doesn't God deserve the best minutes of our day?

Second, have a pattern. My daily quiet time always includes at least three things: *Bible reading, prayer, and reflection (or meditation).* From time to time I may vary the order or spend more time on one than another, but all three are important to me. When we read the Bible, God speaks to us—and we need to hear His voice. One morning I was visiting a conference center near our home and saw an old preacher reading his Bible. I spoke to him, but he didn't reply. Later, I asked if I had offended him somehow, and he said, "If I had been in prayer, talking to God, I would have spoken to you. But when I am reading the Bible, He is speaking to me." He had a good point: When God speaks to us, He should have our full attention.

Prayer and reflection are likewise important. When we pray, we speak to God—and we need to share our deepest joys and burdens with Him. When we reflect, we meditate on God's Word, and we ask God to help us apply it to our lives. Some people keep a journal to record what God is teaching them. Many also keep a prayer list, so they remember who needs their prayers (and also can record God's answers).

Finally, practice God's presence all day long. The psalmist said, "Oh, how I love your law! I meditate on it all day long" (Psalm 119:97). The Bible tells us to "pray continually" (1 Thessalonians 5:17). When I talk with someone, I often find myself praying silently for them. Frequently during the day a Bible verse I read that morning will come into my mind. If something unexpected comes up, I can commit it immediately to God and seek His wisdom. The Bible says, "The LORD is near to all who call on him" (Psalm 145:18). Learn to practice God's presence every waking hour.

Peace in the Midst of the Storm

Never forget: We are part of a vast unseen spiritual conflict that will only end when Christ returns. But we are *not* helpless pawns at the mercy of forces beyond our control. Instead, we have a choice every day—the choice to come near to God or to drift away from Him.

Don't give Satan a foothold, but discipline yourself to stay close to God. He alone is your security.

ELEVEN

OUR UNFAILING GUIDE

Your word is a lamp to my feet and a light for my path.

—Psalm 119:105

Faith grows when it is planted in the fertile soil of God's Word.

Not only are we saved by faith but we also live by faith, because we need God's grace and help at every turn. As the Bible says, "We walk by faith, not by sight" (2 Corinthians 5:7 NKJV).

But how can our faith grow stronger?

Can Our Faith Grow?

"My faith is so weak," a man wrote me recently. "I want to have a strong faith but how can I?" His plea could be echoed by countless

Christians. Is strong faith something reserved for only a few special people, they ask? Does faith mean shutting out our doubts and pretending they don't exist? Can faith really grow and become stronger?

The answer to this last question is *Yes*—because God *wants* our faith to grow stronger. Furthermore, He has given us the resources to achieve this. They are like tools in the hands of a skilled woodworker, giving him the ability to shape even the roughest piece of wood into something useful and beautiful.

The Bible—God's Tool

The first tool God has given us to strengthen our faith is *the Bible*. The Bible is essential to our spiritual growth—so essential that lasting spiritual maturity is impossible without it. *If our faith isn't rooted in the Bible, it will wither like a plant pulled out of the soil.* Only a strong faith—a faith based on God's Word—will protect us from temptation and doubt. Otherwise we will find ourselves "tossed back and forth by the waves, and blown here and there by every wind of teaching and by the cunning and craftiness of men in their deceitful scheming" (Ephesians 4:14).

Do you want your faith to grow? Then let the Bible begin to saturate your mind and soul. One of my most enduring memories of my mother is her sitting quietly in her favorite chair, reading her well-worn Bible every day. This was her practice right up to the end of her life and was the reason she had such an unwavering faith. The Bible says, "Faith comes from hearing the message, and the message is heard through the word of Christ" (Romans 10:17). Faith doesn't just happen; it grows when it is planted in the fertile soil of God's Word.

Don't take your Bible for granted! For centuries ordinary believers had no access to the Bible; Bibles had to be painstakingly copied by hand and were very expensive. The only access most people had to the Bible was by hearing it read in church. The invention of the printing press changed all that, however, and today the Bible is readily available in multiple translations and hundreds of languages around the world—even on the Internet. In spite of this, I'm afraid most Bibles remain unopened and unread. Don't let this be true of yours!

The Power of God's Word

Why is the Bible so crucial to our spiritual development? For one reason: *There is power in the Word of God—the power to change our lives.* "'Is not my word like fire,' declares the LORD, 'and like a hammer that breaks a rock in pieces?'" (Jeremiah 23:29).

God spoke—and the heavens were formed. God spoke—and the Red Sea parted so the Israelites could escape from slavery. God spoke—and Jesus Christ rose from the dead. God spoke—and Saul, the hate-filled persecutor, was converted and became Paul the apostle. Yes, there is power in the Word of God. When I quote the words of the Bible in my preaching, I know that the Holy Spirit will take those words and supernaturally use them to bring conviction and new life to others. I know too that when I prayerfully study the Bible on my own, God will use it to change me. He can do the same for you.

What Is the Bible?

What makes the Bible so different from other books? At first glance it looks like any other book (although you may be intimidated by its size). You also might wonder if it's of any use to us today, since it mostly tells about events that happened thousands of years ago. And yet people in every generation have found its message indispensable, and its influence on individuals and society over the centuries has been enormous. Why? What is the Bible?

For one thing, the Bible is *a collection of books*, written by dozens of authors over many hundreds of years. Some are very brief—less than a page—while others are much longer. But in spite of their diversity, when you examine them, you discover *they all have a common theme: God's relationship with the human race.*

This is one reason why the books of the Bible are just as relevant today as when they were written. The Bible deals with *timeless questions*: Who are we? Where did we come from? Why are we here? Where are we going? How should we live?

Can you think of any questions more important than these? How can we ignore them?

The Word of God

But the Bible is important for a much greater reason: *The Bible is the Word of God.* Yes, various human authors wrote it—but *behind them was another Author: the Spirit of God.* Even when they weren't fully aware of it, God was guiding them so that what they wrote wasn't just their own words, but God's Word. The apostle Peter wrote, "No prophecy of Scripture came about by the prophet's own interpretation. For prophecy never had its origin in the will of man, but men spoke from God as they were carried along by the Holy Spirit" (2 Peter 1:20–21). God wanted to speak to us in words we could understand—and the Bible contains those words.

The Bible isn't just a collection of men's ideas about God, nor is it a guidebook for living that people developed over the centuries. It is *the Word of God*—and that makes all the difference. This means the Bible is *our authority* in everything it touches. This means the Bible is *our guide* to show us how to live. Most of all, this means the Bible is *our instructor*, teaching us about God and His plan of salvation in Christ. The Old Testament points toward Christ's coming; the New Testament tells of His arrival. From Genesis to Revelation we see God's great plan unfold—His plan to win a lost humanity back to Himself. The central theme of the Bible is *salvation*, and the central personality of the Bible is *Christ*.

The Bible is God's gift to us. It came *from* God, and it points us *to* God. The Bible says of itself, "All Scripture is given by inspiration of God, and is profitable for doctrine, for reproof, for correction, for instruction in righteousness, that the man of God may be complete, thoroughly equipped for every good work" (2 Timothy 3:16–17 NKJV).

Can We Trust It?

Since the Bible is God's Word, we shouldn't be surprised if Satan tries to convince us otherwise. The very first question in the Bible came from Satan's lips, casting doubt on what God had told Adam and Eve: "Did God really say . . . ?" (Genesis 3:1). Then he became bolder, flatly denying what God had said: "You will not surely die" (Genesis 3:4). Ever since that dark day in the Garden of Eden, one of Satan's most persistent strategies has been to make us doubt the truthfulness and authority of God's Word.

In the summer of 1949, my team and I were preparing for the most intensive evangelistic mission we had ever attempted, a citywide outreach in Los Angeles, California. Although the press had ignored it, several hundred churches had come together to prepare and pray for the planned three-week-long event. We believed God had led us there, and many were praying He would use the meetings to bring many to Christ.

Just weeks before the mission was to start, however, I experienced a major crisis of faith—the most intense of my life. Some months before, a fellow evangelist whom I respected greatly had begun to express doubts about the Bible, urging me to "face facts" and change my belief that the Bible was the inspired Word of God. "Billy," he said, "you're fifty years out-of-date. People no longer accept the Bible as being inspired the way you do. Your faith is too simple." I knew from my own reading that some modern theologians shared his views.

For months doubts about the Bible swirled through my mind, finally coming to a boil during a conference at which I was speaking in the mountains east of Los Angeles. One night, alone in my cabin at the conference, I studied carefully what the Bible said about its divine origin. I recalled that the prophets clearly believed they were speaking God's Word; they used the phrase "Thus says the Lord" (or similar words) hundreds of times. I also knew that archaeological discoveries had repeatedly confirmed the Bible's historical accuracy.

Especially significant to me, however, was Jesus' own view of Scripture. He not only quoted it frequently, but also accepted it as the Word of God. While praying for His disciples, He said, "Sanctify them by the truth; your word is truth" (John 17:17). He also told them, "I tell you the truth, until heaven and earth disappear, not the smallest letter, not the least stroke of a pen, will by any means disappear from the Law" (Matthew 5:18). Shouldn't I have the same view of Scripture as my Lord?

Finally I went for a walk in the moonlit forest. I knelt down with my Bible on a tree stump in front of me and began praying. I don't recall my exact words, but my prayer went something like this: "O Lord, there are many things in this book I don't understand. There are many problems in it for which I have no solution. . . . But,

Father, by faith I am going to accept this as Thy Word. From this moment on I am going to trust the Bible as the Word of God."

When I got up from my knees, I sensed God's presence in a way I hadn't felt for months. Not all my questions were answered, but I knew a major spiritual battle had been fought—and won. I never doubted the Bible's divine inspiration again, and immediately my preaching took on a new confidence. This was, I believe, one reason why our Los Angeles meetings had to be extended from three weeks to eight.

Don't let anyone shake your confidence in the Bible as God's Word. If you have questions about it, don't use them as an excuse to turn your back on God. Instead, face your doubts and seek answers; you aren't the first person to ask them. (Your local Christian bookstore can help you.) In addition, read the Bible for yourself with an open heart and mind. Ask God to show you if it truly is His Word—and He will.

Your life will never be the same once you trust the Bible as God's Word. God will begin to use it to change your life.

An Impossible Task?

"I know I ought to read the Bible," someone wrote me recently, "but it's too big. I guess it's only for preachers and scholars." Perhaps you have felt this way.

The Bible *is* big—so big that even the greatest scholar will never exhaust its riches. But the Bible isn't just for preachers and scholars! God *wants* to speak to you through His Word, and no matter who you are, the Bible can come alive to you. You may never understand *everything* in the Bible, but you can understand *something.* Samuel was still a boy, but God answered his simple prayer: "Speak, LORD, for your servant is listening" (1 Samuel 3:9). Make that your prayer as well.

Why does the Bible remain a closed book to many? One reason is because *we don't realize how much we need it*. If I suggested you stop eating for a few months, you'd ignore me—and rightly so. We need food in order to survive, and without food we'll grow weak and eventually die. My son Franklin, who heads a major Christian humanitarian organization called Samaritan's Purse, has told me how heartbreaking it is to hold a child dying of starvation who is too weak even to cry.

Yet many Christians are spiritually starved and weak because they ignore the spiritual "food" God has provided in the Bible. *The Bible is not an option; it is a necessity*. You cannot grow spiritually strong without it. Job said, "I have treasured the words of his mouth more than my daily bread" (Job 23:12). Is the Bible this important to you?

Discovering the Bible for Ourselves

How can you discover the Bible's message? How can the Bible become part of your life?

First, learn the Bible from others. God has given some people a special gift to understand the Bible and teach it to others. The Bible says that "in the church God has appointed . . . teachers" (1 Corinthians 12:28). Listen carefully when your pastor preaches from the Bible. In addition, seek out a Bible class in your church or community where the Bible is faithfully taught. Also, check your local Christian radio station (if you live in a country that permits religious broadcasting); some of today's most gifted Bible teachers are on radio. Investigate spending part of your vacation at a conference center devoted to Bible teaching. Many people find daily devotional books based on the Bible helpful; although they may only examine a verse or two each day, God can use them to encourage you.

One of the most significant spiritual movements in recent decades has been the explosion in small group Bible studies. All over the world Christians are coming together to read the Bible and share their insights. The Bible says, "Let the word of Christ dwell in you richly as you teach and admonish one another" (Colossians 3:16). Jesus promised, "Where two or three are gathered together in My name, I am there in the midst of them" (Matthew 18:20 NKJV).

Second, learn the Bible on your own. If you have never read the Bible, or you started reading it once but got bogged down, let me encourage you to discover the Bible for yourself.

How can you do this? *First, come to the Bible joyfully.* Bible reading shouldn't be a burden but a joy! I vividly remember the day I received Ruth's letter saying she had decided to accept my proposal for marriage. I probably read and reread it dozens of times that day! God wants to talk with us through His Word—in fact, it is His "love letter" to us. Why shouldn't we come to it joyfully?

Then come to the Bible prayerfully and expectantly. Ask God to speak to you through its pages—and then expect Him to do so. This doesn't mean every time we open the Bible we'll find something new; God may be underlining truths we already know. But let the psalmist's prayer become yours: "Open my eyes that I may see wonderful things in your law" (Psalm 119:18).

In addition, come to the Bible systematically. Some people open their Bibles almost at random or simply reread passages they already know. While God can certainly speak to us through any passage, we also need to remember that the Bible wasn't written that way. Get in the habit of reading the Bible the way it was written: one book at a time. I often suggest people begin by reading through one of the Gospels (such as John), perhaps only a few paragraphs at a time. Later you can read Acts (which tells of the early Christians) or some of the New Testament letters. Psalms in the Old Testament (the "hymnbook" of the Bible) has blessed generations of believers, while Proverbs gives practical guidance for daily living. Psalms teaches us how to relate to God, and Proverbs teaches us how to relate to others.

Also, come to the Bible thoughtfully. In other words, be sure you understand what you are reading. Several years ago a woman told me that her grandmother reads a chapter of the Bible every day. Then she added, "But whenever I ask her what she's just read, she can't tell me. Reading the Bible is just a habit that doesn't seem to make any impression on her."

Focus on what the passage is really saying. What is happening in it? What is its central point or primary teaching? What does it say about God, or about Jesus, or about someone's response to God?

Finally, come to the Bible obediently. James wrote, "Do not merely listen to the word, and so deceive yourselves. Do what it says" (James 1:22). Is God pointing out a truth you should believe, or something you should do? Is He revealing a sin for which you need to repent? Remember: *God never leads us to do anything that is contrary to His Word.* But the opposite is also true: *God always leads us to do everything that is in agreement with His Word.*

God gave the Bible to us because He wants us to know Him and love Him and serve Him. Most of all, *He gave it to us so we can become more like Christ.* Make the Bible part of your life—beginning today.

TWELVE

KEEPING IN CONTACT

This is the confidence we have in approaching God: that if we ask anything according to his will, he hears us.

—I JOHN 5:14

PRAYER IS NOT AN OPTION BUT A NECESSITY.
I don't think I have ever met a busier man than my father-in-law, Dr. L. Nelson Bell. As a missionary surgeon in China for twenty-five years, he operated on thousands of patients annually. During one brief period of civil unrest, he treated over six hundred gunshot wounds. When the Bells were forced to return to America by the outbreak of World War II, he not only resumed a busy medical practice but (among other things) became editor of two influential Christian magazines and an active leader in his denomination. After Ruth and I were married, he became one of

my closest friends and advisers, someone whose wise counsel I always respected. I never met anyone who was more disciplined or more determined to make every minute count.

Yet my most lasting memory of Dr. Bell is his commitment to prayer. Most mornings he would be up by four thirty or five o'clock, alone in his study reading his well-worn Bible and spending extended time in prayer. If anyone had an excuse to bypass this, it was Dr. Bell—but he saw his time alone with God as the most important event of the day. He never drew attention to it (much less bragged about it), but occasionally he would quote the psalmist's words: "O God, thou art my God; early will I seek thee: my soul thirsteth for thee" (Psalm 63:1 KJV).

Prayer for Dr. Bell wasn't a hurried sentence or two at the end of the day or a hasty afterthought when facing a crisis. Prayer for him was a constant, moment-by-moment practice that penetrated his whole life. Prayer for him was also a joyful experience, an opportunity to come daily into God's presence.

The Privilege of Prayer

Unfortunately, however, for many people prayer isn't a joy but a burden. When they fail to pray, they feel guilty; when they do pray, they worry that they might not be doing it correctly. Or their prayers are wooden and lifeless, perhaps only repeating words learned in childhood but never engaging their minds or hearts.

But this is the opposite of what prayer should be. Prayer shouldn't be a *burden* but a *privilege*—a privilege God has graciously given us because He *wants* our fellowship. Remember: Jesus Christ died to destroy the barrier of sin that separates us from God, and when we give our lives to Him, we have a personal relationship with God. In fact, we have access to God in prayer only because of what Christ did for us on the cross.

But central to any relationship is *communication*. It's true on a human level; what kind of relationship do two people have who never talk with each other? In a far greater way, our relationship with God involves communication—not just an occasional brief chat, but a deep sharing of ourselves and our concerns with God. Because Christ has opened heaven's door for us, the Bible says, we should "approach the throne of grace with confidence, so that we may receive mercy and find grace to help us in our time of need" (Hebrews 4:16).

What Is Prayer?

Our relationship with God involves communication, and that, quite simply, is what prayer is: *talking with God*. In the Bible God speaks to us; in prayer we speak to God. Both are essential—and both are gifts God has given us so we can know Him. Prayer is a gift from God's hand just as much as the Bible, and He has given us the privilege of prayer because He loves us and wants our fellowship. Jesus said, "The true worshipers will worship the Father in spirit and truth, for they are the kind of worshipers the Father seeks" (John 4:23). Think of it: God *seeks* our fellowship!

Strength Through Prayer

Why do we *need* to pray? The reason is because the Christian life is a journey, and we need God's strength and guidance along the way. One of the major ways He supplies these is through prayer. God doesn't leave us to our own resources! Instead, He "has given us *everything we need* for life and godliness through our knowledge of him who called us by his own glory and goodness" (2 Peter 1:3, emphasis added). Prayer is part of the *"everything we need"* God has given us.

Every man or woman whose life has ever counted for God has been a person of prayer. A prayerless Christian is a powerless Christian. A prayerless Christian is also a contradiction, because we should yearn for fellowship with the One who redeemed us. Throughout both the Bible and the history of the church, those who made the greatest impact for God were those who prayed the most.

Most of all, Jesus demonstrated the importance of prayer by His own example. His whole ministry was saturated with prayer. On one occasion, "very early in the morning, while it was still dark, Jesus got up, left the house and went off to a solitary place, where he prayed" (Mark 1:35). On another occasion, "Jesus was praying in a certain place. When he finished, one of his disciples said to him, 'Lord, teach us to pray'" (Luke 11:1). He responded by giving them what came to be His most-quoted words, the Lord's Prayer. As His death approached, He withdrew to the Garden of Gethsemane, a secluded place outside the walls of Jerusalem, to pray, "And being in anguish, he prayed more earnestly, and his sweat was like drops of blood falling to the ground" (Luke 22:44). His last words from the cross were a prayer: "Father, into your hands I commit my spirit" (Luke 23:46). If prayer was this important to the Son of God during His journey on earth, shouldn't it be important to us?

Bringing God Our Needs

"I don't see any reason to pray," a young man wrote me recently. "After all, God already knows what I want, so why should I bother telling Him?"

He was right up to a point. God is sovereign, and He knows all about us: "Your Father knows what you need before you ask him"

(Matthew 6:8). Yet God still commands us to pray for ourselves and for others, and He often responds only as we pray. This is a mystery we will never fully understand this side of eternity.

One of God's most comforting promises is that we can bring *every* need and burden to Him: "Cast your cares on the LORD and he will sustain you; he will never let the righteous fall" (Psalm 55:22). The Bible also says, "The prayer of a righteous man is powerful and effective" (James 5:16). One of my strongest memories of our trips to Africa and India was the prayer meetings we attended—sometimes with thousands gathered in the early morning. I have seldom heard such fervent prayer, and the reason their prayer was so fervent was because they deeply believed prayer is "powerful and effective." God's Word is filled with promises about prayer, and He repeatedly tells us to bring our burdens to Him.

In fact, God *urges* us to bring our concerns to Him—not just petitions about our own needs, but also intercessions for others. The Bible says, "Do not be anxious about anything, but in everything, by prayer and petition, with thanksgiving, present your requests to God. And the peace of God, which transcends all understanding, will guard your hearts and your minds in Christ Jesus" (Philippians 4:6–7). Paul often asked others to pray for him: "Brothers, pray for us" (1 Thessalonians 5:25). Just as an earthly father wants his children to come to him with their requests, so our heavenly Father wants us to come to Him.

Praise and Thanksgiving

As that young man wrote, "God already knows what I want"—but if all we do is ask God for things *we* want, our prayers quickly become selfish. Although the thought might shock us, we begin to think of God as little more than a glorified Santa Claus to whom we turn only when we want something. But God is far greater than this. Remember: *God isn't our servant; we are His servants.*

True prayer begins with seeing God as He really is—and that is why *praise* should be a regular part of our prayers. When we praise God, our focus is on Him, not on ourselves. Many of the psalms are actually prayers of praise, and it is no accident that the word "praise" occurs in the book of Psalms over two hundred times. The Lord's Prayer begins with praise: "Our Father which art in heaven, Hallowed be thy name" (Matthew 6:9 KJV). Paul began one of his letters, "Praise be to the God and Father of our Lord Jesus Christ, who has blessed us in the heavenly realms with every spiritual blessing in Christ" (Ephesians 1:3).

A second dimension of prayer which helps us focus on God is *thanksgiving*, which is closely related to praise. The Bible says, "Enter his gates with thanksgiving and his courts with praise; give thanks to him and praise his name" (Psalm 100:4).

Why should we give thanks? One reason is because everything we have comes from God: "Every good and perfect gift is from above, coming down from the Father" (James 1:17). We can't take credit for anything—even our successes. God gave us our abilities; He arranged our circumstances; He blessed our efforts. Therefore, the Bible says, "Give thanks to the LORD, for he is good; his love endures forever" (Psalm 106:1). We also are to "give thanks in all circumstances, for this is God's will for you in Christ Jesus" (1 Thessalonians 5:18). How long has it been since you paused to thank God for all He has done for you?

Confessing Our Sins

Bringing our needs to God . . . offering praise and thanksgiving . . . these are important elements of prayer. But something else is equally important: *confessing our sins.*

If you have never opened your heart and life to Jesus Christ, the very first prayer you need to make is one of *confession*. Tell God you know you are a sinner and you want to turn from your sins. Then by faith ask Christ to take away your sins and come into your life as your Lord and Savior—and He will. The Bible says, "Everyone who believes in him receives forgiveness of sins through his name" (Acts 10:43). This is God's promise to you, and to all who turn to Him in repentance and faith. Why delay any longer giving your life to Christ?

Even when we know Christ, however, we still sin, and we still need to come to Him for cleansing and restoration. When you know you have sinned, don't let anything—shame, guilt, pride, fear, or anything else—keep you from confessing it to God and seeking His forgiveness. One of the Bible's greatest promises is found in 1 John 1:9: "If we confess our sins, he is faithful and just and will forgive us our sins and purify us from all unrighteousness." Seek God's forgiveness, and then make the psalmist's prayer yours: "Create in me a pure heart, O God, and renew a steadfast spirit within me" (Psalm 51:10).

Overcoming the Barriers

We may be convinced of the importance of prayer and yet still not pray. Why? What are the hindrances to prayer? There may be many reasons why we don't pray: lack of discipline, unconfessed sin, failure to see our need of God's help, unconcern for others, doubt that God will answer our prayers, even a lack of assurance that we can come directly to God. Whatever the reason, ask God to give you a greater hunger for Himself and a deeper desire for His fellowship. Then be honest about whatever is keeping you from prayer, and ask God to help you deal with it.

For many, however, the main barrier to a more effective prayer life is simply a feeling that they don't know how to pray. "I know I need to pray," someone wrote recently, "but I'm not sure how. I'm afraid I might upset God."

But God delights in even our most childlike efforts. At one time you didn't know how to talk—but that didn't keep you from learning your first words and later forming a simple sentence. Few things bring greater joy to a mother or father than hearing their baby's first words—and the same is true of God. You are a child of God if you know Christ, and He *welcomes* your prayers. He is much more concerned about our hearts than our eloquence. The Bible says, "A broken and contrite heart, O God, you will not despise" (Psalm 51:17). Remember: Prayer is simply talking with God.

Learning to Pray

How can you make prayer a part of your daily life? Let me suggest six guidelines that have helped me.

First, have the right attitude. A friend of mine likes to define prayer as "a declaration of dependence"—and he has a point. We will only pray when we realize how dependent we are on God and we trust Him to hear our prayers and answer them according to His will. Recently I saw a documentary on television about the bombing of London during the Second World War. One man in the program said that when the bombs began to fall, he began praying for the first time in his life. I'm sure the same is true for countless people who never think about God, but suddenly find themselves in a crisis that is beyond them and cry out for help. They are realizing—even if dimly—that they are dependent on God after all.

Prideful, self-sufficient people will never pray, because they don't believe they need God's help. The Bible reminds us that "God opposes the proud but gives grace to the humble" (1 Peter 5:5).

Second, seek God's will in your prayers. God wants us to bring our every concern to Him in prayer and to be persistent in our praying. But we don't see the whole picture, and sometimes we ask for things that are unwise or even wrong. Once Jesus rebuked His disciples because "You don't know what you are asking" (Mark 10:38). James wrote, "When you ask, you do not receive, because you ask with wrong motives" (James 4:3). Ask above all for God's will to be done: "Thy will be done in earth, as it is in heaven" (Matthew 6:10 KJV).

How do we know God's will? In chapter 24 we'll examine this more closely, but for the present remember that God *wants* us to know His will and He reveals it to us both through the Bible and through the guidance of His Spirit. Seek God's will when you pray, and He will help you know it.

Third, bring everything to God in prayer. God loves us, and He is concerned about every detail of our lives, both big and small. I have known young people who prayed about minor things—but then didn't pray about their choice of college or their career or their future spouse. On the other hand I've also known people who prayed only when they faced a crisis. The Bible says, "In everything . . . present your requests to God" (Philippians 4:6).

Fourth, learn to pray at all times, and in all situations. Nothing can replace a daily time spent alone with God in prayer. But we also can be in an attitude of prayer throughout the day—sitting in a car or at our desks, working in the kitchen, even talking with someone on the phone. The Bible says, "Pray continually" (1 Thessalonians 5:17). When Daniel's life was in danger because he refused to stop worshipping God, "he went home to his upstairs room. . . . Three times a day he got down on his knees and prayed, . . . *just as he had done before*" (Daniel 6:10, emphasis added).

Fifth, trust God for the outcome. One of the most frequent questions people ask me concerns unanswered prayer. "God must be deaf," someone bluntly wrote me. "My prayers never get above the ceiling," another wrote. But God knows what is best for us, and we need to learn to trust Him for the outcome. Sometimes God answers "Yes" when we ask Him for something. But sometimes His answer is "Not yet" or even "No." And sometimes His answer is simply "Trust Me, even if you don't understand."

Ruth's father, Dr. Bell, always kept a list of people for whom he was praying. After his death Ruth found one of his prayer lists. ("Mostly illegible," she commented. "You know how doctors write!") On it was a specific concern about one of our children. Not until five years after his death was that prayer answered—a vivid reminder of God's faithfulness in answering prayer according to His timetable, not ours.

Finally, learn to listen. Prayer is speaking to God—but sometimes He uses our times of prayerful silence to speak to us in return. He may simply give us an inner assurance of His presence, or He may guide us in a certain direction. The Bible says, "Be still before the LORD and wait patiently for him" (Psalm 37:7).

Begin today making prayer central in your life. Pray because of Jesus' example. Pray because God has commanded it. Pray because Christ died to give us access to the Father. Pray because God is worthy of your praise and thanksgiving. Pray because you need His forgiveness and cleansing and His guidance and protection. Pray because others need your prayers.

Pray most of all because God *wants* your fellowship and you *need* His fellowship on this journey He has set before you.

THIRTEEN

TRAVELING TOGETHER

For where two or three are gathered together in My name, I am there in the midst of them.

—MATTHEW 18:20 NKJV

WE NOT ONLY BELONG TO GOD, WE ALSO BELONG to each other.

We aren't traveling alone on this journey God has given; others are traveling it with us. But unlike a race or a marathon, we aren't competing with each other or trying to get ahead of them and win. We are traveling together on this journey, sharing its joys and bearing each other's burdens and heartaches. If someone stumbles, we help them get to their feet; if someone veers off course, we urge them back. On this journey we are all brothers and sisters in the same family—the family of God.

This family is what the New Testament calls *the church*. In its fullest sense "the church" isn't just a particular building or congregation but the spiritual fellowship of all who belong to Jesus Christ. If we belong to Christ, we also belong to each other; if we have committed our lives to Him, we are also committed to each other. The reason is simple: *We need each other*. The word we translate "church" occurs more than one hundred times in the New Testament, indicating its importance.

Across The World

In 1959 a friend invited my colleague Grady Wilson and me to join him on a trip to Moscow. I was going strictly as a tourist; Soviet authorities would not permit me to preach. I nervously approached the woman at the immigration booth after we landed and handed her my passport. She inspected it carefully, then, looking around to be sure no one was watching, gave me a bright smile and silently pointed upward—the Christian "One Way" sign. In the midst of the Soviet Union's fierce atheism, here was a fellow believer in Christ.

Several days later I stood with a crowd just outside the Kremlin wall watching people lay wreaths as part of their annual Victory Day celebration. A man quietly slipped up beside me, his chest covered with medals from his military service. Without saying a word he used the tip of his cane to draw a cross in the dirt at our feet. Here again was a fellow believer.

On that same visit I was standing in the drizzle outside our hotel when a bus stopped to let passengers off. A woman on the bus looked directly at me, perhaps recognizing me as a foreigner because of my clothes. Then she deliberately traced a cross on her fogged window. I nodded and smiled to acknowledge her gesture. Although we never spoke, I sensed a common bond with her because of Christ.

Did those three people I saw in Moscow have any contact with other believers, or were they isolated and alone, as so many were during those dark days? I have no way of knowing, of course. But I know they yearned for contact with other Christians; otherwise they would not have signaled their faith to me.

During that trip I attended three services at the Moscow Baptist Church, the only non-Orthodox congregation permitted by the Soviet authorities in that city of over seven million. We sat in the back, hearing (through whispered translation) two sermons from the Bible at each two-hour-long service. (More than twenty-five years later I would finally have the privilege of preaching in this church.) Hundreds not only filled the pews and jammed the aisles in the sweltering heat but also clustered outside, listening intently at the windows. One look at their faces told me volumes about the depth of their faith in Christ and their eagerness to hear the Word of God. In spite of the hardships and risks they faced, church to them wasn't a burden but a joy.

Not Alone

One of my greatest privileges over the years has been the opportunity to meet Christians in many different parts of the world. We might have been of different races or denominations or cultures—but almost instantly we realized we had something in common that overcame every human barrier: We belonged to Christ. God, I came to realize, has His people almost everywhere—even in the most unlikely places—and we are spiritually united because of our faith in Christ.

We come to God as individuals; we must each make our own personal commitment to Christ. We cannot depend on our parents' faith, or what others did on our behalf when we were young, or on our church membership (important as these may be). We must each decide personally whether or not we will trust Christ and follow Him as our Lord and Savior.

But *we aren't only individual believers*. In God's eyes we are also part of a group: the body of Christ, "which is the church" (Colossians 1:24). A solitary Christian is almost a contradiction, because we each are part of a larger whole. Just as there is something wrong when a brother or sister becomes alienated from the rest of their family, so there is something wrong when Christians refuse to have anything to do with their fellow Christians. We are on this journey together, and God wants us to live the Christian life together.

What Is the Church?

I wonder what picture comes into your mind when you hear the word "church." A building? A denomination? A particular congregation? A social club?

Some of these definitions may have a place, but in the Bible the word "church" has two basic meanings. *First, it means a local group of Christians,* or all the Christians in a particular city or area. We read, for example, about "the church at Jerusalem" (Acts 8:1) or "the church at Antioch" (Acts 13:1) or "the church of God in Corinth" (1 Corinthians 1:2). Nowhere in the New Testament does "church" refer to a church building, since there were none in the first century (Christians mostly met in homes.)

Second, the word "church" in the Bible refers to the company of all believers, who are spiritually united by their relationship with Christ. The church isn't just a local congregation; it includes all believers everywhere—even those who have died and are now in heaven. As my mother approached death, she was not only looking forward to being with Christ, but also to being reunited with friends and family who had already entered heaven. If you belong to Christ, you are part of this great invisible fellowship of believers across the ages. The Bible tells us that "Christ is the head of the church, his body, of which he is the Savior" (Ephesians 5:23).

The Gift of Each Other

The Bible is God's gift to you, but your fellow Christians are His gift to you also. *God has given us to one another.* One of the main tools God uses to shape us and make us more like Christ is our fellowship with other Christians. In fact, *unless we have active contact with other believers our spiritual lives will be stunted.* The Bible says, "As iron sharpens iron, so one man sharpens another" (Proverbs 27:17). Our fellowship with other believers is a gift from God.

Some people have problems with the church, or at least with the idea of being part of a local congregation. One man wrote me recently, "I go to church sometimes, but to be honest I feel closer to God when I take a hike in the woods or watch a beautiful sunset." Another was more blunt: "I feel God's presence on the golf course more than in a stuffy old church!" One woman's letter especially saddened me: "I'd never gone to church before, and when I got up enough courage to go last week, no one even spoke to me. Why should I bother with church?"

Why Bother?

Her question is one many people ask, even those with a strong commitment to Christ. Why should we come together as part of a local congregation? I find at least four reasons in the Bible.

First, we should come together to worship God. God is worthy of our praise, and we honor Him when we worship together. In the

Old Testament God's people were commanded to "enter his gates with thanksgiving and his courts with praise; give thanks to him and praise his name" (Psalm 100:4). The Bible tells us to come together to "sing psalms, hymns and spiritual songs with gratitude in your hearts to God" (Colossians 3:16).

If you have visited various churches, you know they differ in the way they worship. Some are very informal in their services, others are very formal, and most are somewhere in between. Some churches stress the place of the sacraments (such as the Lord's Supper) more than others.

Is only one style of worship right and all others wrong? Of course not. One style may be more comfortable for you than another; the important thing is that it should turn your heart toward God in worship and praise. (Don't, however, look down on those who prefer other styles of worship. God is more concerned about the attitude of our hearts than the way we express it.) Worship isn't supposed to be entertainment; we don't come together to enjoy ourselves but to worship God. Jesus said, "The true worshipers will worship the Father in spirit and truth, for they are the kind of worshipers the Father seeks" (John 4:23). Think of that: God *seeks* those who will truly worship Him.

Second, we should come together to hear God's Word. God speaks to us when we study the Bible on our own, but He also uses others to teach and challenge us from the Bible. In fact, God has given some people a special gift for preaching or teaching the Bible, and one reason we should come together is to learn from them. The Bible says that God "gave some . . . to be pastors and teachers" (Ephesians 4:11). Paul wrote, "Let the word of Christ dwell in you richly as you teach and admonish one another with all wisdom" (Colossians 3:16).

From time to time people write me saying, "I don't get anything out of church." I often discover they go at most only once a week and have never explored other opportunities their church may offer to learn God's Word—in classes, small group Bible studies, special events, retreats, and so forth. I sometimes suggest they also take notes on their pastor's sermon. Not only will it help them remember the main points—it also may encourage their pastor to prepare more carefully!

Third, we should come together to encourage one another. I have never met a person who didn't have problems of some kind. I also have never met a Christian who didn't face temptations or pressures, or sometimes even wondered if it was worth it being a Christian. This is why we *need* each other's encouragement and wisdom. The Bible says, "Let us not give up meeting together, as some are in the habit of doing, but let us encourage one another—and all the more as you see the Day [of Christ's return] approaching" (Hebrews 10:25).

Sometimes we encourage someone without even being aware of it. I can't begin to count the times I have heard a preacher or Bible teacher and said to myself afterward, "That message was exactly what I needed!" Even the example you set by attending church may encourage someone who is searching for God, although you may never know it.

We also encourage one another on a personal level. Some of my greatest encouragement over the years has come from godly friends who were willing to pray and share their wisdom with me. Whenever we are with other believers—whether in a church service with hundreds of people or just sharing a cup of coffee with a Christian friend—God can lift us up and increase our faith through their encouragement and counsel. Husbands and wives should encourage each other also by praying and reading the Bible together.

The writer of Hebrews said, "Encourage one another daily . . . so that none of you may be hardened by sin's deceitfulness" (Hebrews 3:13). Paul told the Thessalonian Christians to "encourage one another and build each other up" (1 Thessalonians 5:11). Paul's companion on his first missionary journey was a man named Barnabas, "which means Son of Encouragement" (Acts 4:36). Barnabas was known for his ability to encourage others. May this be true of us as well.

Fourth, we should come together so we can reach out to others with Christ's love. Some years ago I read about a farm family in one of our Midwestern states whose little boy wandered away from home and got lost. All around were large fields of lush wheat, almost ready to be harvested. Hundreds of friends and neighbors frantically searched everywhere, but without success. Someone could pass within a few feet of the boy, they knew, but not see him because of the thick, tall wheat.

Finally, after two days had passed, the father in desperation suggested the searchers join hands and sweep across the fields together. Some two thousand did, and after walking only a quarter of a mile, they came upon the boy's lifeless body. The father, his heart broken, said that if they had only joined hands sooner, his son might have been saved.

All around us are people who are lost and separated from their heavenly Father, and we have a responsibility to tell them about Him. They need someone who will love them and point them to Christ. But how much more could we do if we joined hands with other Christians? Very few of us can support a missionary by ourselves, or start a homeless shelter, or send a planeload of food to a famine-stricken country, or start a united prayer movement in our community. But together we can! The Bible says pastors and teachers are called "to prepare God's people for works of service" (Ephesians 4:12).

Finding a Church

Christian fellowship isn't limited to a church congregation; some of your deepest fellowship may be with just one or two others.

Jesus had only twelve disciples (and one of them wasn't even a true disciple)—but He poured His life into them, and they made an impact on the world. Perhaps God is calling you to befriend one or two younger Christians and help them grow in their faith. Paul told his young coworker Timothy, "The things you have heard me say . . . entrust to reliable men who will also be qualified to teach others" (2 Timothy 2:2).

But fellowship on a personal level isn't a substitute for congregational fellowship. If you are in a church where Christ is preached and the Bible is taught, thank God for it, and take advantage of every opportunity it offers to nourish you spiritually. If you don't have a church home (or you aren't growing spiritually in your present church), ask God to lead you to the church He has for you. If you are a new believer or you don't come from a church background, don't be embarrassed if you don't understand everything at first. People who love Christ won't look down on you if you sit at the wrong time or can't find the right page in the hymnal; they care for you and want to help you.

How do you find the "right" church for you? Seek the counsel of other Christians in your area; find out all you can about various churches; visit as many as you can and find one that makes you feel welcome. In addition, think through your particular needs. For example, if you have children, you will want to find a church with an active, Christ-centered youth program. While the weekly services are very important, find out what other programs the church offers to meet your specific needs: Bible studies, recovery programs, groups for people your age, etc. Note also any opportunities for service through the choir, social service ministries, evangelism, etc. If you have never been baptized, make this part of your public commitment as you join a church.

Most of all, pray for God's guidance, because He knows the

right church for you. No church is perfect, but don't let that discourage you. Someone has said that if you ever find one that is, it will stop being perfect the minute you join!

Don't take this journey God has given you alone. God is with you, and so are His people. You need them—and they need you.

FOURTEEN

OUR CONSTANT HELPER

But you will receive power when the Holy Spirit comes on you.

—ACTS 1:8

W HAT MAKES A CHRISTIAN DIFFERENT FROM ANYONE else in the world?

This question could, of course, be answered in several ways. One Christian might say he is different from his non-Christian friends because he belongs to a church. Another might reply that she is different because she knows she has been forgiven of her sins and is going to heaven. Someone else might say Christians are different because of what they believe: The Bible is the Word of God, Jesus was the divine Son of God who died for our sins, and so forth. Still others might suggest that what makes Christians different is the way they live (although a cynic might respond that he doesn't see anything different about the Christians he knows).

The Spirit Within

Each of these may contain an element of truth, but they aren't the whole picture. In fact, they overlook the most important truth—one we need to understand as we travel along the journey God has given us. It is this: *What makes Christians different from everyone else is that God Himself lives within them by His Holy Spirit.* When we come to Christ and give our lives to Him, God actually takes up residence within us. We may not always feel different or be aware of His presence, but Jesus' promise to His disciples has *already* been fulfilled: "I will ask the Father, and he will give you another Counselor to be with you forever—the Spirit of truth" (John 14:16–17).

The night I came forward at the end of an evangelistic meeting to commit my life to Christ I didn't feel any strong emotion. The woman standing next to me was weeping, and I even wondered if there was something wrong with me because I didn't feel as she did.

But down inside I knew something *was* different, and later I realized it was because the Holy Spirit had come to live permanently within me. The Bible says, "If anyone does not have the Spirit of Christ, he does not belong to Christ" (Romans 8:9). *If you have given your life to Jesus Christ, God now lives within you by His Spirit.* You don't need to beg for Him to come into your life if you are a Christian; He already has! You need only acknowledge His presence and then submit in faith to His power.

Our Need for God's Power

As humans we have two great spiritual needs. The first is *forgiveness*, which God made possible by sending His Son into the world to die for our sins. Our second need, however, is for *goodness*, which God also made possible by sending the Holy Spirit to dwell within us.

If we are to live the way God meant us to live . . . if we are to become more like Christ . . . if we are to travel our journey wisely . . . then we need *both* God's forgiveness and goodness. We need the work of the Son *for* us, and we need the work of the Holy Spirit *in* us. *To the great gift of forgiveness God adds the great gift of the Holy Spirit.* As a friend of mine once said, "I need Jesus Christ for my eternal life, and the Holy Spirit of God for my internal life."

Can the Holy Spirit really change us? Many years ago a clergyman in a poor part of London became burdened for the dockworkers in his parish. Their work was hard, thankless, and poorly paid, and he decided that if he was ever to reach them with the Gospel of Christ he must become one of them. Day after day he dressed like them and stood in line waiting for a job, never telling who he really was. Finally one winter's day he was hired to help unload a freighter, moving goods in a wheelbarrow from boat to dock along a narrow plank. On one trip he felt the plank rock violently, and he lost his footing and fell into the cold river. Laughter rang out, and he realized one of the men had deliberately jiggled the plank to make him fall.

His first impulse was to react in anger (for he had often struggled with his temper)—but almost instantly he sensed the power of the Holy Spirit overcoming his anger and giving him peace. He grinned and joined in their laughter, and to his surprise the culprit dropped his load and helped him out of the muck. His tormentor-turned-rescuer, taken aback by his calm reaction, began talking with him. Later the man shamefacedly revealed that he had once been a highly respected physician, but alcohol had robbed him of both his profession and his family. The clergyman led him to Christ, and in time the man was reunited with his family and restored to his position. But here is the point: It would never have happened if the Spirit of God hadn't conquered the clergyman's temper and replaced it with the gentleness and love of Christ. The Holy Spirit made the difference.

Transformed from Within

Many Christians fail to understand this. They know they should be better persons, and they struggle with all their might to change their behavior. But most of their attempts at self-improvement fail, and they end up frustrated and discouraged. They can echo the words of the apostle Paul: "I have the desire to do what is good, but I cannot carry it out. For what I do is not the good I want to do; no, the evil I do not want to do—this I keep on doing" (Romans 7:18–19).

What is the problem? The problem is that we are relying on our own strength *instead of the strength of the Holy Spirit*. We not only need to know how God wants us to live; we also need the power to achieve it. And God has given us that power by giving us His Holy Spirit. He gives us the Bible to teach us and other Christians to encourage us—but *He also gives us His Spirit to change us*. Not only do we have other Christians *around* us, but we have the Holy Spirit *within* us. He is our constant, unchanging companion on the journey.

Who Is the Holy Spirit?

People have all kinds of ideas about the Holy Spirit—some based on the Bible, and some not. Some compare the Holy Spirit to an impersonal spiritual force, somewhat like electricity or gravity. Others think of the Spirit only in terms of emotion or feeling; if they think they feel God's presence within them, they label that feeling "the Holy Spirit." Still others think only of the gifts the Spirit may grant them. These, however, miss the real point.

The Bible tells us *three important truths* about the Holy Spirit.

First, He is a person. We shouldn't refer to the Spirit as "it"; instead we should always refer to the Spirit as "He"—because the Holy Spirit is *a person.* He has all the attributes or characteristics of a person: He speaks to us, He commands us, He intercedes for us, He hears us, He guides us, and so forth. We also can lie to Him or insult Him; we can even blaspheme Him or grieve Him. None of these would be possible if He were simply an impersonal force—but they *are* possible, because He is a person. "The Spirit *himself* [*not "itself"*] testifies with our spirit that we are God's children" (Romans 8:16, emphasis added).

Second, He is a power. The Holy Spirit is the unseen channel or instrument of God's power in the world, the One through whom God works to accomplish His will. Before the worlds were created, "the Spirit of God was hovering over the waters" (Genesis 1:2). Job declared, "The Spirit of God has made me" (Job 33:4). We read of Samson that "the Spirit of the LORD came upon him in power" so he was able to free himself from his captors (Judges 15:14). When God chose Bezalel to oversee the construction of the sanctuary or tabernacle where people would come to worship, He said, "I have filled him with the Spirit of God, with skill, ability and knowledge in all kinds of crafts" (Exodus 31:3).

Greater still is the Spirit's power to use God's Word to convict us of sin and give us new birth. Night after night as I have preached the Gospel in different parts of the world and asked people to respond by giving their lives to Christ, I have felt a deep burden for them afterward. Sometimes I feel so helpless and inadequate, and wonder if I have done enough to make the Gospel clear. But I also know that only the Holy Spirit can open their eyes to the truth, and if we return years later to the same area we'll often meet people who started their spiritual journey at that moment. The Bible says, "My word . . . will not return to me empty, but will accomplish what I desire and achieve the purpose for which I sent it" (Isaiah

55:11). Jesus said, "Flesh gives birth to flesh, but the Spirit gives birth to spirit" (John 3:6). The Bible also states that "you have been born again, not of perishable seed, but of imperishable, through the living and enduring word of God" (1 Peter 1:23). And once we have been born again, the Holy Spirit has the power to keep us in God's family and change our lives. He is God's "seal of ownership on us, . . . guaranteeing what is to come" (2 Corinthians 1:22).

Third, He is God. Just as Jesus is fully divine, so too the Holy Spirit is fully divine. The Bible says He is eternal—just as God is eternal. The Bible also says He is present everywhere and is all-knowing and all-powerful—again, attributes that belong exclusively to God. (Satan isn't this way, incidentally; he is powerful, for example—but not all-powerful.)

Furthermore the Bible explicitly declares the Holy Spirit to be God: "The Lord is the Spirit" (2 Corinthians 3:17). On occasion the Bible calls Him "the Spirit of Christ" or "the Spirit of God"—again indicating His divine nature. *The Holy Spirit is God Himself.* Just as God is a Person, so is the Holy Spirit; just as God is all-powerful, so is the Holy Spirit. *What is true of God is also true of the Holy Spirit, because He is God.*

The Mystery of the Trinity

At this point you may be asking how it's possible for the Holy Spirit to be God and also be separate from God. In the same way, how can Jesus be fully God yet somehow be separate from God, His heavenly Father?

One of the Bible's most profound truths—and one of the hardest for us to understand—is what theologians call *the Trinity.* The Bible clearly teaches that God comes to us in three distinct ways: as Father, Son, and Holy Spirit. At the end of one of his letters, Paul wrote, "May the grace of the Lord Jesus Christ, and the love of

God, and the fellowship of the Holy Spirit be with you all" (2 Corinthians 13:14). All three—Father, Son, and Holy Spirit— are distinct, yet they are also united as one. We do not worship three Gods (as Christians have sometimes been accused of doing); we worship one God, who reveals Himself to us in three persons.

How can we visualize this? When St. Patrick first brought Christianity to Ireland, it is said that he used a clover leaf to explain the Trinity to new converts: three separate leaves, combined in only one plant. Others have used the sun to illustrate the Trinity: The sun is an object in space, but it also produces both light and heat—yet it is still one. Water can be a solid or a liquid or a gas, but it is all water. Sometimes when I go into a church, I notice what are called "trefoil" windows, windows in the form of three interlocking circles. Each circle is separate, yet together they form a single design, symbolizing the Trinity.

The young son of a friend of mine was asking his father how God the Father could be God, and Jesus the Son could also be God. Wouldn't this make Jesus His own father, he asked? (Children have a way of asking complicated theological questions!) They were sitting in the family car at the time, and with a sudden inspiration my friend replied something like this: "Son, under this car's hood is one battery, yet I can use it to turn on the lights, blow the horn, or start the car. How that happens is a mystery to me—but it happens!"

These illustrations may help us understand the truth of the Trinity, but none of them fully explains it. Ultimately it is a mystery we will never fully understand this side of heaven. I am often reminded of Paul's words: "Now we see but a poor reflection as in a mirror; then we shall see face to face. Now I know in part; then I shall know fully" (1 Corinthians 13:12). But this doesn't take away from its truth. We worship God as Father, Son, and Holy Spirit, for that is who He is: the Holy Trinity.

Why Has He Come?

As we have seen, the Holy Spirit worked at the dawn of creation, and His work continued throughout the Old Testament. At the beginning of the New Testament, He also appeared; the angel told the Virgin Mary that "the Holy Spirit will come upon you, and the power of the Most High will overshadow you. So the holy one to be born will be called the Son of God" (Luke 1:35).

It wasn't until Pentecost, however, following Jesus' ascension into heaven, that the Holy Spirit came in a special way upon the disciples (Acts 2). Up to that time Jesus had been physically present with them, but He promised that once He departed, the Holy Spirit would take His place. (This is why the Bible says that during Jesus' earthly ministry, "the Spirit had not been given, since Jesus had not yet been glorified" [John 7:39]). The Spirit's presence would be just as real as Christ's presence had been to them.

It's instructive to note some of the terms Jesus used to describe the Holy Spirit's work. The Spirit, He said, *will convict us of our sins*: "When he comes, he will convict the world of guilt in regard to sin and righteousness and judgment" (John 16:8). Before we can even come to Christ, the Holy Spirit must first convict us of our sins and open our eyes to the truth of the Gospel.

He also *will be our teacher and guide*: "But when he, the Spirit of truth, comes, he will guide you into all truth" (John 16:13). This is why the Bible is so important, because the same Spirit who guided its writing now wants to help us understand it—and apart from Him we can't fully grasp its meaning. He also guides us each day as we seek God's will for our lives.

In addition, Jesus said, the Spirit *will help us tell others about Christ*: "You will receive power when the Holy Spirit comes on you; and you will be my witnesses . . . to the ends of the earth" (Acts 1:8).

The Spirit goes ahead of us when we witness—preparing the way, giving us the words, and granting us courage.

One of the most memorable men I have ever met came to the United States as a refugee from Soviet Georgia. He had earned three doctoral degrees and held a position at a prestigious university, but in spite of that he felt depressed and unhappy. One day he stopped at a shoeshine stand and asked the man polishing his shoes why he was always so happy. Humbly but boldly the man replied that it was because he knew Jesus loved him, and it was because of Jesus that he was happy. The professor scornfully dismissed his words but found he could not escape them. As a result of this man's simple witness, he began searching for God—a search that led to his commitment to Jesus Christ. Later he left his prestigious post to teach at the Christian college Ruth and I attended, and his life influenced me greatly. And it all began because the Holy Spirit gave an uneducated man the courage to witness to someone with a brilliant mind but an empty heart—a heart the Spirit had already prepared. The Spirit truly helps us witness.

More Like Christ

The Bible gives many other reasons why the Holy Spirit has been given to us; we shall explore some of these in more detail later. However, let me summarize them this way: *The Holy Spirit has been given to help us become more like Christ.* We can't become like Christ on our own; we need God's help. And He has given us His help by sending us His Holy Spirit.

Are you trying to live the Christian life on your own, or are you turning to Him each day for the help you need? Pause right now to thank God that He has come to live within you by His Holy Spirit. Because of Him you are never alone.

FIFTEEN

STRENGTH FOR EACH DAY

But grow in the grace and knowledge of our Lord and Savior Jesus Christ.

—2 PETER 3:18

Becoming a Christian is the work of a moment; being a Christian is the work of a lifetime.

Many years ago (so the story goes) engineers made plans to construct a suspension bridge over a deep river gorge. The biggest problem was how to get the heavy steel cables from one side of the gorge to the other. Helicopters hadn't been invented, and the turbulent, rock-strewn river below made it too dangerous to transfer the cables by boat.

The solution? One day the engineers flew a kite over the gorge. As it hovered over the opposite shore, they deliberately grounded it, which meant the two sides of the river were now linked by a thin kite string. They then tied a slightly heavier string to one end of the kite string and carefully hauled it across to the other side. Once it was in place they tied a still stronger cord to the end of that string and pulled it across. They repeated this process several more times, graduating to a thin rope, then on to stronger ropes—until eventually they were able to pull the heavy steel cables across the gorge and construct the bridge.

What if they had stopped with the kite string? Or what if they had decided to take a month off to celebrate the kite's successful flight? Not only would the bridge never have been built, but that thin kite string probably would have been destroyed by the elements.

Growing Toward Maturity

Spiritual growth is somewhat like the construction of that bridge. At first our faith may be small and fragile, in danger of being swept away by the storms and temptations that buffet us. But that isn't God's will! Just as the link between the two sides of that river gradually grew stronger and stronger, so God's will is for our faith to grow stronger and stronger. God's will isn't simply our conversion, but our *spiritual maturity*.

It is tragic when a new Christian never grows in his or her faith but remains a spiritual "baby." Like the kite string, they have taken the first vital step—but then stopped. Jesus warned us against welcoming the Word of God but then allowing it to wither or be choked out by the cares of this world, like seeds planted among rocks or thorns (Luke 8:1–15). Instead, He said, we should be "those with a noble and good heart, who hear the word, retain it, and by persevering produce a crop" (Luke 8:15).

Crops don't grow overnight. They take time to mature, with lots of hard work on the part of the farmer. The day I was born, my mother spent several hours that morning picking beans on our farm and preparing them for canning. She knew it needed to be done and felt she couldn't afford to relax. What would our world be like if farmers ignored their fields or neglected to harvest their crops? Yet we let this happen to our souls, leaving us spiritually weak and ineffective. What is the answer?

Focusing on the Goal

Words like "discipleship" and "spiritual maturity" have an impressive ring to them, but what exactly do they mean?

They all focus on an important truth we saw earlier: *God's goal is for us to become more like Christ.* Paul declared to one group of new Christians, "My dear children, . . . I am again in the pains of childbirth until Christ is formed in you" (Galatians 4:19). To another he wrote, "We . . . are being transformed into his likeness with ever-increasing glory, which comes from the Lord, who is the Spirit" (2 Corinthians 3:18). Just as children often bear the likeness of their parents, so we, as members of Christ's family, are to bear His likeness.

We will never achieve this completely, not as long as we are on this earth. Only in heaven will this fully happen, for then "we shall be like him, for we shall see him as he is" (1 John 3:2). But until that day our mandate is clear: We are to "become blameless and pure, children of God without fault in a crooked and depraved generation" (Philippians 2:15). Is this happening in your life?

The Likeness of Christ

When I was a young Christian, I met a man who was a well-known Christian leader in certain circles. As I observed him, I couldn't help but be impressed by his zeal for the truth and his staunch defense of the faith. But in time I realized something was missing: a love for others (especially those who disagreed with him). Was this how Jesus would have acted, I asked myself? In God's providence this man's negative example forced me to face my own need to be filled with more of Christ's love.

What does it mean to be like Christ? As we saw earlier, it means *Christ becomes Lord of every area of our lives.* Let me give three examples (although I could list others).

First, it means Christ becomes Lord of our character. A man told me once that he refused to deal with a certain businessman in his community. The reason, he said, was because the man claimed to be a Christian but was always cutting corners, never delivering quite what he promised, and taking advantage of every loophole he could find. Sadly, his character didn't reflect Christ.

Second, it also means Christ becomes Lord of our actions. A college student wrote me recently to say he had no use for Christianity. He then added, "One reason I'm not a Christian is because I've never met anyone who acts like one." What an indictment! I wrote back urging him to look not only at Christians but at Christ (for only He is perfect, and only He can save us), but his impression of Christians still saddened me. If our lives don't reflect Christ, why should we expect anyone to believe what we preach? Paul told Timothy to "flee from all this [evil], and pursue righteousness, godliness, faith, love, endurance and gentleness" (1 Timothy 6:11).

Third, becoming more like Christ means He becomes Lord of our attitudes. Our inner attitudes determine our outward actions—but sadly, they may not reflect Christ. Why are some Christians so negative and critical? Why are some so sour or grumpy or arrogant or impatient? Why are some so anxious and filled with worry, or lazy and undisciplined, or undependable and irresponsible? Why are some so domineering or harsh toward others? God calls us to be like Christ in our attitudes.

The Humility of Christ

One of the most memorable experiences of my life was the opportunity to visit a remote, mountainous corner of India called Nagaland. Nagaland has one of the largest concentrations of Christians in India, and the occasion was the one-hundredth anniversary of the coming of missionaries to that area. Tens of thousands came to the celebration—some walking for days over rough jungle trails. One hundred thousand people, we were told, would be gathering each morning for a Bible study, in addition to the evening evangelistic meetings.

When we arrived at Government House, where we were to stay, a man unloaded our baggage from the car, then took our shoes to wipe the mud off them. I protested, saying we could do that, but he insisted. Only later did I discover that he would be leading the Bible study for those one hundred thousand people the next morning! Here was a man who truly exemplified the attitude of Christ by his humility and his willingness to serve others. I have never forgotten his example.

The Bible says, "The fruit of the Spirit is love, joy, peace, patience, kindness, goodness, faithfulness, gentleness and self-control" (Galatians 5:22–23). There are nine characteristics in that list, and every one of them should mark our lives if we belong to Christ—because they marked His life. Do you want to know what it means to be like Christ? Begin by asking God to help you understand those nine characteristics and then, by the power of the Holy Spirit, to make them part of your life.

This doesn't mean, however, that God wants to erase our personalities—although He does want to take the sharp edges off them! We are all different, because God made us that way. Saul of Tarsus had what we today might call a "type A" personality—hard driving, determined, energetic, absolutely focused on his goal of destroying the Christian faith. But God intervened and replaced Saul's hatred of Christ with love. His basic personality didn't change, but God redirected his energies and used him instead (as the apostle Paul) to advance the Gospel. Paul's young companion Timothy, on the other hand, had a different personality—shy, sensitive, perhaps even a bit introverted. But God helped Timothy overcome his shyness so he could reach out to others, and God also used his sensitive nature to make him an effective and caring pastor.

The Path to Transformation

What does it take for us to become more like Christ? As we have seen, we can't do it in our own strength; *only the power of the Holy Spirit can change us*.

This is why the Bible commands, "Do not get drunk on wine. . . . Instead, be filled with the Spirit" (Ephesians 5:18). When a person is drunk, we say they are "under the influence" of alcohol (often with tragic results, as almost every newscast confirms). In other words, alcohol is controlling them. In like manner, to be "filled with the Spirit" simply means to be under the influence or control of the Holy Spirit. But how does that happen? How do we release the Holy Spirit's power to change us?

First, it requires repentance. This means asking God to show us areas of our lives where sin still rules and we haven't allowed Christ to be Lord—and then deliberately turning from those sins.

The water for our home in the mountains of North Carolina comes from a spring above the house. When we moved there, the old-timers in the area told us this particular spring would always flow, even in the worst drought—and they were right. One year, however, we had an abnormally cold winter, and one day we found ourselves without water. Ice had formed in the pipe running from the spring, and we had to dig through the frozen ground and use a blowtorch to melt it. Only then did the flow resume.

I have often compared that spring to the Holy Spirit. No matter the circumstances, the Holy Spirit's flow is always available to us— just like that spring. But sin is like the ice that blocked our pipe. We allow the spiritual coldness of a hostile world to freeze our souls and cut off the Spirit's life-giving water.

The only way to clear the blockage and restore the flow is through repentance. If your spiritual life is dry and barren, begin by praying the psalmist's prayer: "Search me, O God, and know my heart. . . . See if there is any offensive way in me" (Psalm 139:23–24). Ask God to show you any area of your life where sin still rules, and then repent of it.

Daily Submission

Second, becoming more like Christ requires submission. Every day a battle rages in our hearts between our wills and God's will. God now lives within us by His Holy Spirit, but our old nature is still alive, striving to gain the upper hand and control us. Instead of reflecting Christ in our lives, we reflect the unbelieving world.

This is why Jesus told His disciples, "If anyone would come after me, he must deny himself and take up his cross daily and follow me" (Luke 9:23). His words must have shocked them; in the first century a cross was a symbol of shame and death, and the only person who took up a cross was someone who was about to die (as Jesus would do later). But that was what Jesus meant. Our old nature—our selfishness, our evil desires, our old attitudes and patterns of living—must die. The Bible says, "Put to death, therefore, whatever belongs to your earthly nature" (Colossians 3:5). Paul knew what this meant by personal experience: "I have been crucified with Christ and I no longer live, but Christ lives in me" (Galatians 2:20).

To submit to Christ means *to commit every area of our lives to His authority*, asking Him to change us according to His will. It means we turn from everything wrong and ask God to replace it all with that which is good and pure. The Bible compares this to a change of clothing—casting aside our old, filthy rags and putting on new, clean garments: "You were taught, with regard to your former way of life, to put off your old self, which is being corrupted by its deceitful desires; . . . and to put on the new self, created to be like God in true righteousness and holiness" (Ephesians 4:22, 24).

Where has Christ been left out of your life? In your character? Your attitudes? Your actions? Or in some other part, such as your time or money or a relationship? Be honest with yourself—and with God. Remember: You cannot deceive God. The psalmist prayed, "Cleanse me from secret faults" (Psalm 19:12 NKJV). Let that be your prayer.

Then submit every area of your life to Christ's authority. The Bible says, "Submit yourselves, then, to God. Resist the devil, and he will flee from you. Come near to God and he will come near to you" (James 4:7–8).

Trust and Obey

Finally, the key to releasing the transforming power of the Holy Spirit involves not only repentance and submission, but also obedience and trust.

When a soldier submits to the authority of his commanding officer, he obeys what that officer tells him to do. If a patient submits to a doctor's treatment, he or she does what the doctor says to do. If a football player submits to the direction of his coach, he does what the coach instructs him to do. And *when we submit ourselves to the King of kings and the Lord of lords, we obey what He tells us to do, because we know His way is right.*

As we have seen, God shows us His will first of all through His Word, the Bible. How many problems would we avoid if we knew God's Word and obeyed it? The Bible doesn't give us a rule for every conceivable situation, but it does cover far more than most of us realize. It also gives us *principles* by which we are to guide our lives. God's Word isn't to be debated or dissected; it is to be *done*. The psalmist said, "I have kept my feet from every evil path so that I might obey your word" (Psalm 119:101).

God also leads us by His Spirit, especially when we face difficult decisions—and when He does, we must obey, regardless of the cost. I have experienced this repeatedly in my own life. Sometimes obedience came easily—but sometimes it was a struggle even to know what was right. I can recall numerous times when we were weighing whether or not God wanted us to expand our ministry in certain ways, such as through films or television, or we were trying to decide which invitations to accept for an evangelistic outreach. Logic alone wasn't enough. Only as we prayed, studied the Scriptures, and sought the godly advice of others would the answer eventually come, confirmed by the inner voice of the Holy Spirit saying, "This is the way; walk in it" (Isaiah 30:21).

A New Start Every Day

Repentance . . . submission . . . obedience . . . these are the steps we must take for God to fill us with His Spirit so we become more like Christ. And we must take these steps *daily*, because we need

God's help daily. Being filled with the Holy Spirit isn't a once-for-all event, but *a continuous reality every day of our lives*. Is it for you?

Personally I find it helpful to begin each day by silently committing it to God (even before I get up), thanking Him that I belong to Him and that He knows what the day holds for me. Then I ask Him to use me that day for His glory, and to cleanse me from every sin that might hinder this.

Then I step out in faith, believing His Spirit will fill me as I obey His Word and trust in Him. I won't always be aware of His presence, but at the end of the day, I know I'll be able to look back and thank Him for being with me and guiding me. He had promised to be with me that day—and He was.

This can be your experience also, as you yield your life daily to Christ's Lordship. Give each day to Him, so that at its end you can look back and thank Him for being with you, as He promised.

SECTION THREE

———

CHALLENGES ALONG THE WAY

SIXTEEN

PRONE TO WANDER

Watch and pray so that you will not fall into temptation. The spirit is willing, but the body is weak.

—MATTHEW 26:41

I F GOD IS FOR US, WHY DO WE HAVE SO MANY PROBLEMS? Christians aren't exempt from them; we too experience illness, temptation, disappointment, grief, and a hundred other problems we could list. Our journey through life is filled with all kinds of hazards and bumps in the road, and will be until we enter heaven. They may change as we get older, but they never completely go away.

In Danger of Collapse

A few miles from our home is a small lake, fed by a clear mountain stream tumbling down the valley from the surrounding mountains.

Our children often played there when they were young and even went swimming in its cold waters. (The mantel over our living room fireplace is actually made from a plank of wood that was once the lake's diving board.) The lake was formed many years ago by constructing a sturdy concrete dam across the stream.

Because the mountains near us form a natural barrier for weather fronts, we often get a fair amount of rainfall. A few years ago, however, we had several days of exceptionally heavy rain, turning the normally placid stream into a raging, debris-choked torrent. People standing on its swollen banks could even hear large stones rumbling beneath the stream's surface, swept along by the water's force.

Soon fears grew that the dam might collapse. Water began seeping through weak spots in the embankment and spurting through tiny cracks in the concrete. The police ordered those living below the dam to evacuate, fearing a sudden collapse. Thankfully the rains subsided and the dam held (although later it had to undergo extensive and costly repairs).

That incident reminds me of the ways problems and temptations assail us. Just as the dam was battered by the surging waters, so we are often battered by life's problems and temptations, even to the point of moral and spiritual collapse. We live in a hostile world that constantly seeks to pull us away from God, and sometimes its pressures are enormous. In other words, *one reason we are vulnerable to life's stresses and temptations is because of what happens around us.*

And just as those raging waters sought out weak places in the dam, so problems and temptations seek out the weak places in our lives. A dam may be 99 percent solid—but if 1 percent is weak, eventually the whole structure may be destroyed. The same is true of our lives. Problems and temptations always exploit our weaknesses—always. In other words, *we are also vulnerable to life's stresses and temptations because of our own inner weaknesses.* And like that weakened dam, they often prove very costly to repair.

Confronting Our Problems

Why do we have so many problems, even as Christians? One reason (as we've seen) is because we are part of a vast spiritual conflict—one that won't end until Satan's final defeat at the end of time. In addition, our old sinful nature is still alive, competing with the new nature God has given us. The Holy Spirit now lives within us, but this doesn't free us from life's problems or guarantee that we'll never sin. In fact, one reason the Holy Spirit has been given to us is because God knows how weak we are. The Bible says, "The Spirit helps us in our weakness" (Romans 8:26).

The real issue, however, isn't *why* we have problems and temptations but *how we will respond* to them. In the next few chapters, we'll be seeing what the Bible has to say about these. The Bible is intensely practical, and one of the reasons God gave it to us is so we'll be better prepared to deal with life's problems and temptations. Unfortunately, all too often we respond to these in ways that don't reflect Christ, yet we may not even realize it. When we do that, Satan is the winner and the cause of Christ suffers.

In this chapter we will examine the subject of *temptation*. We all face temptations of one kind or another, for temptation is universal. But where does it come from, and why do we find it so hard to resist? How should we face temptation, and what should we do when we fail? And how can we keep from failing in the future?

What Is Temptation?

Have you ever tried to define temptation? Simply speaking, temptation is *being urged or enticed to do something wrong*.

Temptation isn't the same thing as sin, and it isn't a sin to be tempted. Temptation is being *enticed* to do wrong; sin is actually *doing it. It isn't a sin to be tempted, but it is a sin to give in to the temptation.* At the beginning of His ministry, "Jesus was led by the Spirit into the desert to be tempted by the devil" (Matthew 4:1). But Jesus didn't give in to Satan's temptations (although they were very intense and alluring). The Bible says Jesus was "tempted in every way, just as we are—yet was without sin" (Hebrews 4:15). Whenever I am tempted to do something wrong, I gain great strength from those words about Jesus. You and I will never face a temptation He doesn't understand, for He was tempted "in every way, just as we are." He knows what we are going through when we are tempted, because He has already been there. But He also points the way to victory, because He faced temptation's challenge—and overcame it. So can we.

The World, the Flesh, and the Devil

Where does temptation come from? Ultimately, all evil (and therefore all temptation) comes from our adversary, Satan. The Bible says, "Your enemy the devil prowls around like a roaring lion looking for someone to devour" (1 Peter 5:8). Just as a lion stalks a herd of animals looking for the weak and vulnerable, so the devil stalks us, trying to find where we are weak.

But the devil is very clever, and he seldom attacks us directly and openly. He doesn't carry a sign saying, "Look! I'm the devil, and I've come to destroy you!" Many years ago I was speaking at a university in Adelaide, Australia, and a group of students came running into the crowd with signs saying, "I'm the devil! I'm the devil!" But that's not the way the devil operates; he's much more cunning than that. Instead, he may disguise himself; the Bible says that sometimes the devil even "masquerades as an angel of light" (2 Corinthians 11:14). He often hides in the background, only working behind the scenes.

How does he tempt us? The Bible says he seeks to tempt us in two ways. *First, he uses pressures from outside*—from the world around us. Remember the dam? If we hadn't had a prolonged rain, it never would have been in danger. But the rain-swollen stream attacked it from the outside—and the same happens to us.

The Bible calls this pressure *"the world."* This doesn't mean the physical world but the unbelieving world's system of values—its ways of thinking and acting. It refers to the standards and behavior of a world that is separated from God, a world in rebellion against its Creator.

Never forget: We live in an upside-down world, in which people hate what they should love and love what they should hate. This is why the Bible warns, "Do not love the world or the things in the world. If you love the world, the love of the Father is not in you." It then lists the marks of a worldly attitude: "These are the ways of the world: wanting to please our sinful selves, wanting the sinful things we see, and being too proud of what we have. None of these come from the Father, but all of them come from the world" (1 John 2:15–16 NCV).

Worldliness is an inner attitude that puts self at the center of life instead of God. Its outlook is limited to the present, and its values come from our pride and selfish desires. Paul rebuked the Christians in Corinth because, although they believed in Christ, they were spiritually immature and still acting like unbelievers: "For since there is jealousy and quarreling among you, are you not worldly?" (1 Corinthians 3:3).

Temptations from Within

The second way Satan tempts us is from within ourselves—from what the Bible calls *"the flesh."* "Flesh" doesn't refer here just to our physical bodies, but to the desires and appetites that attempt to rule us. "Flesh" means far more than sexual lust (although it includes that). It means *a determination to satisfy our own desires and appetites* instead of seeking to please God. The Bible says, "Those who live according to the flesh set their minds on the things of the flesh" (Romans 8:5 ESV). James wrote, "Each one is tempted when, by his own evil desire, he is dragged away and enticed" (James 1:14).

God gave us our bodies, and we are to take care of them and use them for His glory. But all too often we allow our bodies to rule us, instead of us ruling them. For some this may take the form of slavery to alcohol or drugs or lust, or to some other habit or passion. For others it may take the form of something that isn't necessarily wrong in itself, but we allow it to become the focus of our lives, and it becomes our idol.

This is why the Bible urges us "to offer your bodies as living sacrifices, holy and pleasing to God—this is your spiritual act of worship" (Romans 12:1). The Bible also says, "Clothe yourselves with the Lord Jesus Christ, and do not think about how to gratify the desires of the sinful nature" (Romans 13:14). Have you committed your body to Christ?

The Way of Escape

The real question, however, is this: *How should we deal with temptation?* How can we resist it? Recently a young man wrote me, "I wish I weren't so weak. I make all sorts of resolutions, but then I get with my friends and end up doing whatever they do. I just don't seem to be able to resist." Perhaps you can identify with him. Just as the heavy rains revealed the weaknesses in that dam near our home, so temptation reveals the weaknesses in our lives.

Let me suggest *four steps* to deal with temptation—and conquer it.

First, recognize it. People have told me repeatedly, "I can't believe I did that. I didn't even realize what I was doing until it was too late." Satan had deceived them into thinking something wasn't really a sin, or that it wouldn't hurt them.

Some claim there is no such thing as right and wrong, and therefore we shouldn't worry about temptation. But God says otherwise. Don't forget: Temptation means *being tempted to do wrong in the eyes of God.* Label sin for what it is: *sin.*

This is why we need to know what the Bible teaches about right and wrong. Every day we are battered by messages—from the media, advertising, entertainment, celebrities, even our friends—with one underlying theme: "Live for yourself." The world hammers away at us, trying to shape us into its mold and make us believe that sin isn't really sin. After all, isn't everyone doing it? But God says, "Do not conform any longer to the pattern of this world, but be transformed by the renewing of your mind" (Romans 12:2).

Ask God to help you recognize temptation when it comes. Alarm bells should go off in your soul! Don't look only for obvious temptations. Look also for the subtle ones—temptations of the tongue or emotions or thoughts or motives. The psalmist prayed, "Search me, O God, and know my heart" (Psalm 139:23).

Admittedly, we sometimes face "gray areas," things that aren't necessarily forbidden by the Bible but still may not belong in our lives. When you are unsure whether or not something is wrong, ask yourself these questions: Does this glorify God? Can I offer a prayer of thanksgiving for it? Does it draw me closer to Christ, or does it make me preoccupied with this world? Will it harm my health or hurt me in some other way? Will it cause someone else to stumble spiritually or morally (especially a less mature Christian)? I have never forgotten what a wise Christian said to me many years ago: "When in doubt—don't!"

Flee from Temptation

Second, when temptation comes, reject it. Martin Luther said you can't keep birds from flying over your head, but you can keep them from building nests in your hair! You and I can't avoid temptation—but we can keep it from overpowering us.

Don't savor temptations; don't dwell on them or toy with them or replay them over and over in your mind. The more you think about a particular temptation, the more enticing it becomes. Did you ever play with magnets when you were young? If you did, you probably noticed that the closer they got to each other, the harder it was to keep them apart. Temptation is like that. The closer we let it come to us, the stronger its attraction. In fact, if you don't look out, it will become almost impossible to pull away.

Don't let that happen! *Handle temptation the same way you would a deadly snake or a vial of lethal poison—for that is what it is.* The only way to deal with temptation is to reject it—immediately and forcefully. Paul told Timothy to *"flee* the evil desires of youth" (2 Timothy 2:22). The Corinthians were commanded to *"flee* from idolatry" (1 Corinthians 10:14). The Bible says, "*Flee* from sexual immorality" (1 Corinthians 6:18, emphases added). No, we can't flee from temptation in our own strength—but God will give us the strength we need, if we'll only seek it. A friend of mine says, "When the devil knocks, I just send Jesus to the door!"

Halfway measures won't do. Temptation requires definite, decisive action. It may mean turning off the computer or television . . . or parting company with someone . . . or sharing your struggle with a mature Christian who can encourage you and hold you accountable. Occasionally I receive letters from people who changed jobs because a person or situation at work was tempting them to do wrong.

One of the most important passages in the Bible about temptation is found in 1 Corinthians 10:13; I urge you to memorize it. It says, "No temptation has seized you except what is common to man. And God is faithful; he will not let you be tempted beyond what you can bear. But when you are tempted, he will also provide a way out so that you can stand up under it." Yes, God gives us "a way out"! Ask Him to show it to you—*and then take it.*

Learn from Temptation

Third, learn from your encounters with temptation. In other words, reflect on the temptations you've faced so you'll be better prepared to fight them in the future. Are you especially vulnerable around certain people, doing what they do because you want them to like you? Are you especially tempted when you get in certain situations or go to particular places? What weakness in your life is Satan trying to exploit? Is he appealing, for example, to your pride? A friend of mine who is a seminary professor once listed the Christian leaders he knew who had fallen into sexual sin. Almost without exception, he said, the real cause was their pride. God sometimes allows us to be tempted so we will realize our weaknesses and seek His help to overcome them. Don't just fight temptation—learn from it.

Learn to avoid situations where you will be vulnerable. One woman wrote me about her struggles with overeating. The only way to conquer it, she found, was to avoid certain sections of the supermarket. Once the foods she needed to avoid were in her refrigerator it was too late.

When We Fail

Fourth, repent when you fail, and immediately seek God's forgiveness and restoration. Sin breaks our *fellowship* with God—but it doesn't end our *relationship*. We are still His children, even when we disobey. We feel guilty and ashamed, and sometimes we simply want to hide. But God still loves us, and He wants to forgive us and welcome us back! When you fail, repent and claim God's promise of forgiveness and restoration.

One woman told me how she yielded to temptation and ended up destroying her family. She then added, "The thing that upsets me the most is that I know God will never forgive me." This is what Satan wants us to believe—but it isn't true! The Bible promises, "If we confess our sins, he is faithful and just and will forgive us our sins and purify us from all unrighteousness" (1 John 1:9). This is God's promise to you. Believe it!

The only sin God cannot forgive is the sin of refusing His forgiveness. When you sin, don't excuse it or ignore it or blame it on someone else. Admit it . . . repent of it . . . and then rejoice that God has fully forgiven you.

SEVENTEEN

CONFRONTING THE ENEMIES WITHIN

Create in me a clean heart, O God,
and renew a right spirit within me.

—Psalm 51:10 ESV

ONE OF SHAKESPEARE'S CHARACTERS HAD IT RIGHT:
The fault lies within ourselves.

Recently I heard about a woman who seemed to be a perfect example of Christian character: active in her church, respected in her community, above reproach in her personal life, always available to lend a helping hand to others.

But one day her doctor gave her the bad news: She had only months to live. Almost instantly she became a totally different person. She quit her job, dropped her old friends, and turned her back on her church. She announced that she had been good long enough and intended to spend her last days catching up on all the fun she had missed. Bars and nightclubs became her regular haunts, and she began running around with a new set of acquaintances who had no use for morality or virtue. Until the day she died, she scorned everything she had practiced the rest of her life. Her only appearance in church during those last months was on the day of her funeral, in her coffin.

Why Did It Happen?

How could someone who was apparently so upstanding and honorable suddenly throw it all overboard? How could someone who had openly identified herself as a Christian abruptly turn her back on decency and morality—and even common sense?

Only God knew her heart and mind, of course, and only He knows why she acted the way she did during those last months. Only God knows also if her professed faith in Christ was genuine, or if it was false and meant only to impress others. We must never set ourselves up as anyone's final judge.

But one thing is clear: *Her faith had not changed her on the inside.* Until those final months her outward behavior was beyond reproach; she avoided what was wrong and did what was right. Down inside, however—in the deepest recesses of her heart where no one could see—she secretly envied those who lived only to please themselves, and her envy finally overwhelmed her.

In other words, to her the Christian life was only a matter of outward behavior. She apparently never understood one of the Bible's most important truths: *God not only wants to change our actions; He also wants to change our hearts.* In other words, *God wants to change us both on the outside and the inside.* The apostle Paul put it this way: "Do not offer the parts of your body to sin, as instruments of wickedness, but rather . . . offer the parts of your body to him

[God] as instruments of righteousness" (Romans 6:13). He also wrote, "Be transformed by the renewing of your mind" (Romans 12:2). *Both* our bodies *and* our minds need to be committed to Christ, for only then can He begin changing us into the people He wants us to be.

What Difference Does It Make?

Why is God so concerned with what goes on inside of us? After all, what difference does it make, as long as we act the way we're supposed to?

The reason is simple: *This is God's will.* As we have seen, God's will is for us to become more and more like Christ. When we allow sinful thoughts and emotions to govern us, however, we fall far short of His plan. Christ was pure *both* within and without—and that must be our goal as well. The Bible says, "It is God's will that you should be sanctified [i.e., pure]" (1 Thessalonians 4:3). The Bible also tells us to "purify ourselves from everything that contaminates *body and spirit*" (2 Corinthians 7:1, emphasis added). Some of Jesus' strongest words were directed at those who were moral on the outside, but inside were filled with evil thoughts and desires: "Woe to you, . . . you hypocrites! You are like whitewashed tombs, which look beautiful on the outside but on the inside are full of dead men's bones and everything unclean" (Matthew 23:27).

The Danger Within

Why are our inner lives so important? *One reason is because our thoughts determine our actions.* Sometimes we say, "I acted without thinking," and it may seem true. But on a deeper level, our actions are always a reflection of our inner thoughts. In fact, sometimes it's almost impossible to separate our thoughts from our actions. Jesus put it this way: "For out of the heart come evil thoughts, murder, adultery, sexual immorality, theft, false testimony, slander" (Matthew 15:19). This is why we need to submit our lives to Christ every day, for only He can transform our hearts and minds.

Another reason, however, why God is concerned about what goes on inside of us is because He loves us and He knows how destructive wrong thoughts and emotions can be. They poison our souls and also harm our bodies. Psychologists are discovering that what the Bible taught centuries ago is true: Our minds and bodies are very closely linked. Someone who is constantly angry, for example, is much more likely to end up with a heart attack or stroke or other physical malady. When King David refused to confess his adultery with Bathsheba and suppressed his feelings of guilt, he paid a price both spiritually and physically: "When I kept silent, my bones wasted away. . . . My strength was sapped" (Psalm 32:3–4). Only when he faced his sin and sought God's forgiveness did his health return. The Bible says, "A cheerful heart is good medicine, but a crushed spirit dries up the bones" (Proverbs 17:22).

Sin, like a deadly cancer, has invaded every area of our lives: our bodies, our minds, our emotions, our wills—everything. Don't take sin lightly! But Jesus Christ came to conquer sin. He came not only to forgive us; He also came to free us from sin's power and transform us by His Spirit. The Bible says, "Once you were alienated from God. . . . But now he has reconciled you . . . to present you holy in his sight, without blemish and free from accusation" (Colossians 1:21–22).

Holy . . . without blemish . . . free from accusation—this is God's purpose for you every day. But how does it happen?

The Enemy Within: Pride

Many centuries ago Pope Gregory the Great divided all sin into seven categories: pride, anger, envy, impurity, gluttony, slothfulness, and greed. Over time these came to be called "the seven deadly sins," and while no single Bible passage lists them exactly this way, they each occur frequently in Scripture.

It is no accident that he listed pride first, for self-centered pride is at the root of almost every other sin. Pride caused Satan to rebel against God. Isaiah's description of the king of Babylon's pride is also a picture of Satan: "I will ascend to heaven; I will raise my throne above the stars of God. . . . I will make myself like the Most High" (Isaiah 14:13–14). (Notice, incidentally, how often the words "I" and "my" occur here, for the essence of pride is found in its middle letter: *I*.) Satan appealed to Adam and Eve's pride, claiming that if they followed him, they would "be like God" (Genesis 3:5). What a temptation: to become like God! Ever since that fateful day, the human race has been ensnared by pride—and paid a terrible price as a result. The Bible warns, "Pride goes before destruction, a haughty spirit before a fall" (Proverbs 16:18).

Pride That Destroys

Why is pride so destructive? *For one thing, pride blinds us to our faults.* Pride tells us we are better than we really are, so we feel no need to repent of our sins or mend our ways. The prideful, self-righteous man in one of Jesus' stories prayed, "God, I thank you that I am not like other men." Nearby another man was also praying— but with a far different attitude: "God, have mercy on me, a sinner"

(Luke 18:11, 13). God heard his prayer, but not that of the prideful man who was blind to his own sin.

In addition, pride also cuts us off from others. We can be proud for many reasons: our possessions, physical appearance, abilities, social position, achievements, and so forth. Whatever the reason, however, pride always puts us above others—and cuts us off from them as a result. No one likes an arrogant, prideful person.

Pride also is at the root of prejudice and racism, which have caused unimaginable suffering and violence throughout history. Prejudice and racism are sins in God's eyes and have no place in the heart of any true follower of Jesus Christ. God created all humanity, and in His eyes no race or ethnic group is either superior or inferior to any other. The ground at the foot of the cross is level, for with His blood Christ "purchased men for God from *every* tribe and language and people and nation" (Revelation 5:9, emphasis added). What possible excuse can we give for despising any person for whom Christ died?

Most of all, pride cuts us off from God. King Uzziah was one of the best rulers Judah ever had, but the Bible says that "after Uzziah became powerful, his pride led to his downfall. He was unfaithful to the LORD his God" (2 Chronicles 26:16). God had blessed him, but instead of giving God the credit, he turned away from Him. When pride controls us, we think we don't need God, and we claim glory for ourselves. We forget that God has said, "I will not give My glory to another" (Isaiah 48:11 NKJV).

Even Christians can be driven by subtle forms of pride, looking down on others (including fellow believers) and exalting themselves at the expense of others. They forget that "God opposes the proud but gives grace to the humble" (1 Peter 5:5). They forget too that the Bible says, "What does the LORD require of you? To act justly and to love mercy and to walk humbly with your God" (Micah 6:8).

Does this mean pride is *always* wrong? No, it isn't—if properly understood. It's not wrong to take pride in a job well done, for example, or in the accomplishments of those we love—as long as we acknowledge that God gave us our abilities and He alone deserves the credit. Nor is it wrong to have a proper sense of self-esteem and self-confidence. When we tear ourselves down or think less of ourselves than we should, we are refusing to accept ourselves as God made us. The key is balance—avoiding both selfish, ego-centric pride and unjustified self-loathing. The Bible says, "Do not think of yourself more highly than you ought, but rather think of yourself with sober judgment" (Romans 12:3).

Dealing with Pride

What is the answer to sinful pride? *First, admit it and confess it to God, and humbly seek His forgiveness.* Self-centered pride is a sin, and we must confront it honestly, and humbly seek God's forgiveness and help. The Bible says, "Humble yourselves, therefore, under God's mighty hand" (1 Peter 5:6).

In addition, learn to walk in God's presence every day. Once you understand how great God is, your boasting and pride will begin to fade. Pride flees when we compare ourselves to God instead of other people.

The Enemy Within: Envy and Greed

As I write, news reports tell almost daily about still another case of corporate greed or accounting fraud—sometimes involving billions of dollars. Shocking as they are, however, such scandals aren't new; they only differ in details from stories I read as a boy.

Envy and greed have been with us since Adam and Eve were

expelled from the Garden of Eden—or even before. Satan appealed not only to their pride when he tempted them; he appealed also to their envy and greed by urging them to want more than God had given them. The Bible has many stories of envy and greed. Joseph's brothers were envious of him because of their father's favoritism and in their greed sold him into slavery. King Ahab coveted Naboth's vineyard and allowed Queen Jezebel to plot Naboth's death and seize his land. Judas, driven by greed, betrayed Jesus for thirty pieces of silver. Ananias and Sapphira likewise harbored greed in their hearts, secretly withholding from God's work part of the money they had received from a sale of land.

In every instance, however, envy and greed proved to be destructive. Adam and Eve were expelled from the Garden of Eden; Joseph's brothers lived in fear once their treachery was revealed; King Ahab died in battle and the dogs licked up his blood; Judas committed suicide; Ananias and Sapphira fell dead. The Bible warns, "A heart at peace gives life to the body, but envy rots the bones" (Proverbs 14:30). Envy and greed always—*always*—exact a terrible price. I have never met an envious or greedy person who was at peace.

Envy and greed aren't identical, but they are closely related. When we envy someone, we easily become obsessed with getting what they have. Envy and greed often focus on money, but we can also be greedy for other things, such as beauty, status, possessions, fame, or power. The Bible sees greed as a form of idolatry, because a greedy person worships things instead of God. Greed and envy have their roots in selfishness, driving us into madly pursuing what we don't already have. Envy and greed may seem harmless on the surface, but they easily develop into abuse, violence, and even war. James describes this sequence well: "What causes fights and quarrels among you? Don't they come from your desires that battle within you? You want something but don't get it. You kill and covet, but you cannot have what you want. You quarrel and fight" (James 4:1–2).

Greed and envy not only harm society, they also hurt us personally. Almost every week I receive at least one letter from someone whose family is being torn apart by an addiction to gambling, an activity based squarely on greed. Countless families live on the brink of bankruptcy because of uncontrolled debt—driven by envy and greed (often through the excessive use of credit cards). Marriage counselors say the number one cause of marital strife is money. Our prisons are filled with men and women whose lives have been destroyed by their greed.

Envy and greed aren't restricted to the rich; a poor person can be just as consumed by them as someone with great wealth. Sadly, Christians aren't immune to envy and greed either. The Bible warns, "The love of money is a root of all kinds of evil" (1 Timothy 6:10).

Confronting Envy and Greed

It isn't wrong to want to provide a decent living for our families, of course; God knows our needs, and the Bible encourages us to be diligent and thrifty (as well as generous). Nor is it necessarily wrong to want to be successful; God is honored when we use the gifts He has given us to their fullest. But envy and greed easily creep into our lives and overwhelm our best intentions. Don't let that happen to you!

First, ask God to show you if envy or greed have gripped your heart—and then confess it and repent of it. Don't be deceived: Envy and greed are sins, and they can destroy you. Most of the Ten Commandments deal with our actions—do not steal, do not kill, do not commit adultery, and so forth. But the final commandment deals with our inner motives—and specifically envy and greed:

"You shall not covet . . . anything that belongs to your neighbor" (Exodus 20:17). When Jesus was interpreting the Ten Commandments in the Sermon on the Mount, He dealt with the inner problem, not just the outward action. For example, He said we commit murder in our heart by hating someone or being angry with them, and we commit adultery by having lust in our heart.

Then ask God to help you to learn the secret of true contentment. How does this happen? One way is to make thanksgiving a part of your daily life. Envy and greed starve on a steady diet of thanksgiving! The Bible says, "Give thanks in all circumstances, for this is God's will for you in Christ Jesus" (1 Thessalonians 5:18).

Finally, learn to trust God in everything. The Bible says, "Keep your lives free from the love of money and be content with what you have, because God has said, 'Never will I leave you; never will I forsake you'" (Hebrews 13:5). When we learn to trust God for our needs, Paul's experience will become ours: "I have learned to be content whatever the circumstances" (Philippians 4:11).

What does God see when He looks within your heart and mind? Does He see compassion and contentment—or pride and envy and greed? You may hide your inmost thoughts from others, but you cannot hide them from God. Pause right now and recommit your whole life to Christ—including your inmost thoughts and desires. Then ask God to begin changing you from within by the power of His Spirit.

EIGHTEEN

EMOTIONS THAT DEFEAT US

Above all else, guard your heart,
for it is the wellspring of life.

—PROVERBS 4:23

A CHAIN IS ONLY AS STRONG AS ITS WEAKEST LINK, and so is our character.

My wife, Ruth, was born and raised in China, where her parents were medical missionaries. Almost from the beginning of our marriage, she yearned to take me back to the land of her birth—a land whose people and ancient culture she dearly loved. But the Second World War, followed by Mao's Communism, made it impossible. We continued to hope and pray, however, and eventually—after almost half a century—the door finally opened for us to visit China and speak in some of its newly opened churches.

One of the highlights of that trip was our visit to the Great Wall.

I'll never forget sitting atop it, surrounded by curious school children who had probably never seen an American. They quickly overcame their shyness (due to a Chinese-American friend who was traveling with us) and began singing some rousing children's songs for us. We responded with two or three songs of our own, including "Jesus Loves Me," which they immediately demanded our Chinese-speaking friend teach them!

Parts of the Great Wall date back before Christ, and it still stretches across hundreds of miles of rugged mountainous terrain. It remains one of the most remarkable construction projects in history and is, I'm told, one of the few man-made objects visible from space. It was built for one purpose: to keep out barbarians bent on destroying Chinese civilization.

As we exited through one of the gates in the Great Wall, I couldn't help recalling something I had read years before. At first the Great Wall was a success; its height and well-guarded gates repelled every invasion. But eventually the enemy succeeded. How? The solution was simple: They found a gatekeeper of weak character and bribed him into leaving his gate unlocked.

Gaps in the Wall

Our lives are often like the Great Wall: strong and fortified at some points—but weak and vulnerable at others. And where will Satan attack? Not where he knows we are strong and he stands no chance of victory. Instead, *Satan will always attack us where we are weak*. Like China's invaders, he looks for a weak "gatekeeper"—a weakness in our character, an unconfessed sin, a harmful habit—so he can invade our lives and reap destruction.

In the last chapter we saw one of those "gates" through which the devil may come, that of our inner motives. When we allow pride or envy or greed to control us, Satan will exploit it. But our adversary tries other "gates" also, and in this chapter we'll examine one of them: the "gate" of our emotions.

Emotions—God's Gift?

Emotions in themselves aren't wrong or sinful—not at all. God gave our emotions to us, and we shouldn't despise or deny them. If we didn't experience emotions, we couldn't know God's peace and joy. When Jesus was asked what the greatest commandment was, He replied, "Love the Lord your God with all your heart and with all your soul and with all your mind" (Matthew 22:37). Heart . . . soul . . . mind—*all* are involved in loving God.

God experiences emotion—and so do we, because we were made in His image. How empty our lives would be if we had no emotions! I once visited a friend whose mind had been ravaged by Alzheimer's disease. He had always been an active, alert person— but now he sat staring vacantly into space, not even aware of my presence. He had lost all capacity for emotion. Emotions are a gift from God and a fundamental part of life.

The older I get the more I marvel at the complexity of our minds. The psalmist exclaimed, "I praise you because I am fearfully and wonderfully made" (Psalm 139:14). I used to think this verse referred only to our bodies, but I realize now that it applies to our whole beings, including our minds and emotions. God made you a unique, complex person, and just as your body is uniquely yours, so too is your personality. We truly are "fearfully and wonderfully made"!

Like everything else, however, our emotions have been cor- rupted by sin. Emotions aren't bad in themselves, but they can become twisted or even destructive. They may even become so overwhelming that we require professional help to restore us to health. We still have much to learn about the human mind, but I'm thankful for gifted counselors and psychologists who seek to help those suffering from serious emotional problems.

Most of the time, however, our emotions simply lead us astray—and when they do, they become spiritually dangerous. And you can be certain of this: Satan will try to use them to gain victory over us. In fact, *one of Satan's chief ways of attacking us is through our emotions*. Learn to guard the "gate" of your emotions!

Emotions That Destroy: Anger and Bitterness

Every destructive emotion bears its own harvest, but anger's fruit is the most bitter of all. Uncontrolled anger is a devastating sin, and no one is exempt from its havoc. It shatters friendships and destroys marriages; it causes abuse in families and discord in business; it breeds violence in the community and war between nations. Its recoil, like that of a high-powered rifle, often hurts the one who wields it as well as its target. Anger makes us lash out at others, destroying relationships and revealing our true nature. The history of the human race is largely the history of its anger.

Nor are Christians exempt from anger's grip. After Jesus' arrest Peter angrily denied his Lord: "He began to call down curses on himself and he swore to them, 'I don't know this man you're talking about'" (Mark 14:71). Paul had to urge the Ephesian Christians to "get rid of all bitterness, rage and anger, brawling and slander, along with every form of malice" (Ephesians 4:31). How many churches have been torn apart by someone's anger? How many people have been turned away from Christ because of a Christian's anger?

We get angry when others hurt us, both by what they say and what they do. We get angry too when we don't get our own way or our plans and dreams are frustrated. Anger may arise in an instant, erupting like a volcano and raining destruction on everyone in sight. Often, however, anger simmers just below the surface, sometimes for a lifetime. Like a corrosive acid, this kind of anger eats away at our bodies and souls, yet we may not even be aware of its presence.

Some people are angry at God. Sometimes I get letters from people who have been touched by tragedy—but instead of seeking God's help, they angrily blame Him for what happened. As a result they cut themselves off from the peace and joy He alone can give us, even when we don't understand.

Is anger ever justified? Yes—when it is caused by injustice and sin instead of our selfishness or hurt pride. God is angry when His righteousness is scorned; Jesus forcefully drove out from the temple those who were callously making money from God's people (Matthew 21:12–13). We must be careful, however; sometimes our so-called "righteous indignation" is little more than a cover for lovelessness or self-righteousness.

Anger and bitterness (as well as hatred, jealousy, and resentment, their offspring) aren't identical, but they are closely related. Bitterness is anger gone sour, an attitude of deep discontent that poisons our souls and destroys our peace. My wife has said that a bitter, sour Christian is one of Satan's greatest trophies—and she's right. The Bible says, "See to it . . . that no bitter root grows up to cause trouble and defile many" (Hebrews 12:15). Are anger or bitterness keeping you from becoming the person God wants you to be?

Conquering Anger

Can we overcome our anger, instead of constantly being overcome by it? Yes—with God's help. Peter's anger was channeled into boldness for Christ. Paul's anger against Christians was replaced with a burning passion to spread the Gospel. The Bible commands us "to be made new in the attitude of your minds; and to put on the new self, created to be like God in true righteousness and holiness" (Ephesians 4:23–24). Is this your goal?

How should we deal with anger? The answer is *decisively! The first step in gaining victory over unjustified anger is to want to get rid of it—and the key to that is to see it for what it is: sin in God's eyes.* Jesus warned, "Anyone who is angry with his brother will be subject to judgment" (Matthew 5:22).

This means we must stop making excuses for our anger or bad temper—blaming it on our parents, for example, or claiming we have every right to be angry because of something that happened to us in the past. We also must face honestly the toll anger and bitterness take on our lives. *They are our enemies!* The Bible says, "An angry man stirs up dissension, and a hot-tempered one commits many sins" (Proverbs 29:22). It also says, "Refrain from anger and turn from wrath; . . . it leads only to evil" (Psalm 37:8). Never underestimate anger's destructive power.

The second step—as with every other sin—is to confess it to God, and seek His forgiveness and help. On the cross Christ took upon Himself every sin you ever committed—including your anger. God in His love and mercy not only promises to forgive our anger, but to cleanse it from our lives if we will let Him. No matter its cause, commit your anger to God, and ask Him to replace it with the Holy Spirit's fruit of "love, joy, peace, patience, kindness, goodness, faithfulness, gentleness and self-control" (Galatians 5:22–23). Notice: Anger is the exact opposite of every one of these. Anger flees when the Spirit's fruit fills our hearts.

Then take practical steps to deal with your anger. When are you especially susceptible to anger? Avoid those situations when possible—and when you can't, pray about them in advance and ask God to help you. When you fail, be quick to seek not only God's forgiveness, but also the forgiveness of those you hurt. If you have been harboring anger or bitterness or jealousy in your heart toward someone—a parent, an ex-spouse, a boss—hand it over to Christ, and ask Him to help you let it go.

In addition, discover the transforming power of forgiving others. Jesus said, "Bless those who curse you, pray for those who mistreat you" (Luke 6:28). You can't stay angry if you obey this command. Deliberately act toward others the way you should, even if you don't feel like it; changing our behavior eventually changes our emotions. The Bible says, "Be kind and compassionate to one another, forgiving each other, just as in Christ God forgave you" (Ephesians 4:32).

Emotions That Destroy: Worry and Fear

Is it any wonder that fear and anxiety have become the hallmarks of our age? Recently I received a letter from a woman living in the heart of one of our most crime-riddled cities. "I have five locks on my door," she wrote, "but I'm so fearful I can hardly sleep."

Fear has its place; if we didn't fear danger, our lives would be in constant peril. A small child must be taught to fear the busy street or the unguarded pill bottle. A soldier or policeman knows even a moment's inattention is dangerous. The Bible says, "A prudent man sees danger and takes refuge, but the simple keep going and suffer for it" (Proverbs 22:3). We shouldn't just fear physical danger, however; most of all we should be on guard against moral and spiritual danger. The Bible says, "Be self-controlled and alert. Your enemy the devil prowls around like a roaring lion looking for someone to devour" (1 Peter 5:8).

Fear has its place, but fear also can become overwhelming—

and then it becomes sin. Why? Because *fear causes us to doubt God's promises and disbelieve His love.* Fear can paralyze us and keep us from believing God and stepping out in faith. The devil loves a fearful Christian! God told the ancient Israelites that He would be with them and help them conquer the Promised Land. But fear seized them, and they refused to obey. As a result they were forced to wander in Sinai's wilderness for forty years (Numbers 14). They allowed fear to paralyze them, and an entire generation missed God's blessing. This can happen to us.

Most people yearn for one thing more than anything else: inner peace. Without it they have no lasting happiness or security. I'm also convinced, however, that this is exactly what most people are missing—and the main reason is anxiety and fear.

Conquering Our Fears

Can we conquer our anxieties and fears? Or must we spend our lives consumed by worry?

Let me respond with another question: What is the opposite of fear? For the Christian there can be only one answer: *The opposite of fear is trust—trust in God and His unchanging love.* Once we realize God is in control and He holds us in His loving hands, we can meet life's dangers and uncertainties with confidence. After all, *if we can trust God for our eternal salvation, can't we also trust Him for our lives right now?* The psalmist declared, "The LORD is with me; I will not be afraid" (Psalm 118:6).

Let's be honest, however: It's hard to trust God when danger threatens or everything seems to be collapsing around us. Fear comes much easier to us than faith. But never forget: *Fear can banish faith, but faith can banish fear.* Faith isn't pretending our problems don't exist, nor is it simply blind optimism. Faith points us beyond our problems to the hope we have in Christ. True faith involves *trust*—trust in what Christ has done for us, and trust in God's goodness and mercy.

How should you deal with anxiety and fear? *First, turn them over to Christ.* Don't deny them—and don't cling to them. Confess them to Christ, and then ask Him to lift them from your shoulders. The psalmist wrote, "Cast your cares on the LORD and he will sustain you; he will never let the righteous fall" (Psalm 55:22). Peter echoed this truth: "Cast all your anxiety on him because he cares for you" (1 Peter 5:7).

Second, stand firmly on God's promises. In the Bible God has given us "very great and precious promises" (2 Peter 1:4)—and every one of them reminds us that we can trust our lives into His hands. You can trust God's promises, for He cannot lie! God's promises in the Old Testament are just as applicable and relevant to us today as those in the New Testament, and both Testaments contain God's principles for life. Fear vanishes when it is exposed to the promises of God's Word.

What are those promises? One is that God is with you, no matter how difficult or confusing life becomes. He says, "Never will I leave you; never will I forsake you" (Hebrews 13:5). Jesus declared, "Surely I am with you always, to the very end of the age" (Matthew 28:20). *You are never alone if you know Christ—never.* I have never forgotten the familiar words from Psalm 23 my mother taught me as a child: "Yea, though I walk through the valley of the shadow of death, I will fear no evil: for thou art with me; thy rod and thy staff they comfort me" (v. 4 KJV). Saturate your mind and heart with the promises of God's Word.

God also promises us hope—hope that someday all the evils and injustices of this life will be destroyed. Jesus warned, "In this world you will have trouble." But He immediately added, "But take heart!

I have overcome the world" (John 16:33). Everything that makes you fearful or anxious is only temporary, for when Christ returns they will be destroyed.

Pray Without Ceasing

Finally, pray diligently and in faith. I'm amazed how easy it is to become anxious over something—but then forget to pray about it. Anxiety and fear are like baby tigers: The more you feed them, the stronger they grow.

But God has another way—*the way of prayer*. The Bible's answer to worry couldn't be clearer: "Do not be anxious about *anything*, but in *everything*, by prayer and petition, with thanksgiving, present your requests to God." Then comes God's promise: "And the peace of God, which transcends all understanding, will guard your hearts and your minds in Christ Jesus" (Philippians 4:6–7, emphasis added).

How should you pray? Pray first of all for strength in the face of whatever you fear, for God helps us hold on in the midst of life's storms. Pray also for wisdom to deal with whatever is worrying you; some practical steps may change the situation.

Pray as well that God will act to change your circumstances, according to His will. He doesn't always do what we want Him to— but He knows what's best for us, and He can be trusted. God is sovereign, and no situation is beyond His control. Over her desk my wife has these words: "Fear not the future; God is already there."

Emotions enrich our lives, but sometimes they also can overwhelm us or lead us astray. But we can learn to keep them in balance—with God's help.

NINETEEN

THINGS THAT DESTROY

Whether you eat or drink or whatever you do, do it all for the glory of God.

—1 CORINTHIANS 10:31

THE DEVIL DOESN'T NEED TO INVENT ANY NEW TEMP-
tations; the old ones work as well as they ever have.

We never seem to learn; we fall for exactly the same temptations past generations did and suffer exactly the same consequences. Perhaps the writer of Ecclesiastes had this in mind when he wrote, "What has been done will be done again; there is nothing new under the sun" (Ecclesiastes 1:9).

The Downward Path

Not long ago I watched a man virtually destroy both himself and his family. He was active in his church, successful in his chosen profession, and widely respected in his community. I had only met him casually, but others spoke of his apparent sincerity and faith.

Unknown to them, however, he harbored a secret—a hidden sin that he not only tolerated, but allowed to flourish. His job took him out of town from time to time, and whenever he thought he was safely away from anyone who might know him, he indulged in behavior he knew was wrong—but did anyway. He got by with it for years, no doubt believing he could continue indefinitely. He apparently thought the Bible's warning didn't apply to him: "You may be sure that your sin will find you out" (Numbers 32:23).

But his sin *did* find him out—and when it did, his world collapsed. The details aren't important, but in less than twenty-four hours he not only found his name on the front page of his local newspaper, but everything he had worked for in life vanished. He lost it all: his reputation, his job, his friends, his influence, even the love and respect of his wife and children. More than that, he brought disgrace on the name of Christ. The last I heard he had moved to another part of the country, working in a job far below his abilities while trying to salvage something from the wreckage of his life.

Had he ever stopped to think about the consequences of what he was doing? Did it ever occur to him that he was leaving himself open to humiliation and disgrace? Has he, even now, honestly faced his sin and sought God's forgiveness and help? I have no way of knowing, but I feel a great sadness whenever I think of him, and I pray for him.

The Danger of Self-Deception

Unfortunately, this man's experience isn't unique, for none of us is exempt from the dangers of sin and self-deception. The Bible warns, "If you think you are standing firm, be careful that you don't fall!" (1 Corinthians 10:12). While most situations aren't this dramatic, all too often men and women—even those who sincerely believe in Christ—deceive themselves into thinking they can keep doing things that God has clearly labeled sin but never suffer any consequences. They also forget that their behavior dishonors God and compromises their witness for Christ. They fail as well to see that it blocks God's blessing and keeps Him from fulfilling His purpose in their lives.

In the last few chapters we examined some of the hazards and roadblocks that threaten our spiritual journey. Like the cracks in that dam near our home or the unguarded gate in China's Great Wall, wrong motives and uncontrolled emotions can break through our defenses and overwhelm us.

But there is another crack in the dam—another unguarded gate—through which the devil will try to enter our lives, and that is *our behavior*. We can mask our motives . . . we may conceal our true feelings . . . but we can't hide our actions. People judge us not by what we think or believe, but by what we do—and when our lives don't measure up, we lose their respect and they conclude our faith isn't real.

Rules or Relationship?

This doesn't mean the Christian faith is only a set of rules—a list of dos and don'ts to be obeyed. Sadly, some people see it that way, and their lives are joyless as a result. They are constantly trying to please God, forgetting that *the Christian faith isn't a set of rules but a relationship*—a personal, intimate, daily walk with the living God. When our faith becomes nothing more than a series of rules and regulations, joy flees and our love for Christ grows cold. Yes, rules have their place—but just as a healthy marriage is more than a set of rules, so too is a healthy relationship with Christ.

At the same time, our behavior *does* matter. Why? Because *how we act toward someone is a reflection of our feelings about them.* When you truly love someone, you want to please and honor them by the way you act. In other words, how you treat someone shows whether or not you really care about them. Acting disrespectfully or ignoring their wishes shows you don't really love them, no matter what you say.

In a far greater way, the same is true of our relationship with Christ. *If we truly love Christ, we will want to please and honor Him by the way we live.* Even the thought of hurting Him or bringing disgrace to His name will be abhorrent to us. Jesus' words should be engraved on the heart of every believer: "If you love me, you will obey what I command" (John 14:15).

The Devil's Lures

All sin is serious, and in God's eyes there is no such thing as an unimportant or harmless sin. But some sins *are* more serious to us than others, and the reason is because their consequences are more serious. This is why Satan, our unrelenting adversary, will do everything he can to entice us into committing them. Never forget: Satan's goal is to turn us away from God, and he knows there is no quicker way of doing this than drawing us into open sin.

As a boy on my father's farm, I sometimes had to set traps for the rabbits that ate our crops. My father always knew exactly what kind of bait to use—bait so tempting it would blind them to danger and lure them into the trap. Satan is like that. He wants to lure us into his traps, and he knows exactly what kind of "bait" will appeal to us. He knows what we're like, and *he will attack us exactly where we are weakest.*

With this in mind, let's examine *four qualities or traits of character* that God wants to implant in our lives, and then see how Satan will try to undermine them.

The Christian's Character: Integrity

When Ruth and I took our first trip to China, our host in Beijing was a man whose sincerity and personal warmth immediately made us feel welcome. A distinguished retired diplomat who had been ambassador to the United States, we soon discovered he was known throughout China by a nickname: *Mr. Integrity*. When we asked why, we were told it was because everyone knew his character was above reproach.

How much more should we Christians be known for our integrity! *Integrity* means that our lives match what we say. Integrity means we are trustworthy and dependable, and our character is above reproach. Integrity means that if our private life was suddenly exposed, we'd have no reason to be ashamed or embarrassed. Integrity means our outward life is consistent with our inner convictions. A person of integrity is like Daniel of old, whose enemies diligently searched for his weaknesses, but in the end "could find no corruption in him, because he was trustworthy and neither corrupt nor negligent" (Daniel 6:4). King David prayed, "I know, my God, that you test the heart and are pleased with integrity" (1 Chronicles 29:17).

What do others see when they look at your life? What do those who know you best say about you—your spouse, your children, your friends, your coworkers? Do they see inconsistencies in any area of your life—money, relationships, speech, possessions, or any of a hundred other areas? Satan rejoices when we are inconsistent, because he knows that an inconsistent Christian is an ineffective Christian—or worse. Almost every week I hear from someone who says they don't want anything to do with Christ because "Christians are just a bunch of hypocrites." Sometimes their complaint is very general—but all too often, I'm afraid, they tell of someone they know who claims to be a Christian but whose life doesn't measure up. I always reply by urging them to look instead at Christ, for only He is perfect and worthy of our allegiance. But their criticism still stings, because I know that all too often people turn away from Christ because of some Christian's hypocrisy or inconsistency. When they do, Satan has gained another victory.

Ask God right now to help you become a person of *integrity*—someone whose life is consistent before others and before God. No matter how others behave, make it your goal to live consistently for Christ. Even Jesus' detractors had to admit, "Teacher, we know you are a man of integrity" (Mark 12:14).

The Christian's Character: Honesty

Honesty means exactly what it says: We are honest and trust-worthy in all our dealings. People can trust our word, because we refuse to lie or shade the truth (even if it seems to be to our advantage). They also know we won't use half-truths or deceit to take advantage of them. The Bible says that in the last days God's servants will be honored because "no lie was found in their mouths; they are blameless" (Revelation 14:5). The Old Testament commanded, "Do not lie. Do not deceive one another" (Leviticus 19:11).

Few things will discredit us quicker than a reputation for dis-honesty. Once people conclude we can't be trusted, it's almost impossible to reverse their opinion. This is why Satan will do every-thing he can to persuade us that it doesn't really matter whether or not we tell the truth (or even that "truth" doesn't exist). We shouldn't be surprised; after all, the Bible says of Satan that "there is no truth in him. When he lies, he speaks his native language, for he is a liar and the father of lies" (John 8:44).

Dishonesty isn't limited to the outright lie, however. It also can take the form of gossip—tearing down others through half-truths or unsubstantiated rumors. "A gossip betrays a confidence; so avoid a man who talks too much," the Bible says (Proverbs 20:19). Paul rebuked the immature believers in Corinth because of their "slander, gossip, arrogance and disorder" (2 Corinthians 12:20).

Why is a dishonest tongue detestable to God? One reason is because God's will (as we have seen) is for us to become more like Christ, of whom "no deceit was found in his mouth" (1 Peter 2:22). Dozens of times Jesus declared, "I tell you the truth." Another reason God despises dishonesty is because it springs from sinful motives. How often do we tell a lie simply because we are trying to build ourselves up in the eyes of others? How often do we gossip because we want to appear to be "in the know," or because we're trying to make ourselves appear better than someone else?

But dishonesty can take other forms. When a student cheats on a test or someone pilfers from their office or fakes their time sheet or cheats on their taxes, they are acting dishonestly. When business executives commit accounting fraud or exploit their workers or swindle someone, they are acting dishonestly. The Bible's command is clear: "Be careful to do what is right in the eyes of everybody" (Romans 12:17).

The Christian's Character: Purity

You already know it: We live in a sex-saturated world. No one is exempt; we all are constantly bombarded with advertising and entertainment that is deliberately designed to appeal to our sexual appetites. Repeatedly we are urged to cast aside moral restraints and give free rein to lust, carnality, and even perversion. Our generation has become like that of Jeremiah's day: "They have no shame at all; they do not even know how to blush" (Jeremiah 6:15).

In reality, however, the world of the New Testament wasn't much different from our own. Immorality and perversion were everywhere, sanctioned by some of the pagan religions of the day. To take a stand for morality and sexual purity was to put yourself in the minority, swimming against the stream of your surroundings and risking scorn and even rejection. But God's standards were clear, and they have not changed: When we come to Christ, God calls us to live lives of purity. Paul told the Christians in Corinth, a city noted for its blatant immorality, to "flee from sexual immorality. All other sins a man commits are outside his body, but he who sins sexually sins against his own body" (1 Corinthians 6:18).

We'll look at God's plan for our sexuality more fully in chapter 25. The important thing to remember here, however, is that God gave sex to us, and we can only fulfill His plan for this powerful, wonderful gift by following His commands. Almost nothing can bring us greater pleasure—but almost nothing will bring us greater heartache when it is misused. Almost daily someone writes me telling how an illicit sexual relationship has almost destroyed them. Without exception they thought they could get by with it—but to their sorrow they now know better.

Don't give Satan even a toehold in this vital area of your life! He knows your weakness, and he'll do everything he can to bring you down. *No area of your life is more vulnerable!* Men, avoid the second look, the "innocent" invitation, the "accidental" touch! Women, avoid the suggestive clothing, the playful banter, the flirtatious smile! "It all started so casually," one woman wrote me, "but before we knew it, it was out of control. I'd give anything to be able to change the past."

The time to deal with sexual temptation is *now*, not when it comes crashing down upon you. *Now* is the time to commit your body and mind to God; *now* is the time to take your stand for purity; *now* is the time to plan ahead and know exactly how you'll react to sexual temptation. Remember what we said earlier about dealing with temptation: *Recognize it* for what it is, and then *reject it—immediately and without compromise.*

The Christian's Character: Freedom

When most of us hear the word "freedom," we think of political freedom, or perhaps the freedom to live without restraints. But to the earliest Christians the word "freedom" conjured up a much different image. Historians estimate that in the first century at least half the people in the Roman Empire were slaves, and the word "freedom" for them meant freedom from slavery.

Slavery was a terrible institution; I recall as a boy hearing my African-American friends describe their ancestors' suffering as slaves in the American South. But Jesus said there is an even worse type of slavery, and that is slavery to sin: "I tell you the truth, everyone who sins is a slave to sin." But then He added, "If the Son sets you free, you will be free indeed" (John 8:34, 36).

Think of it: In Christ we are free—free from sin's slavery, free from sin's guilt and fear, free from sin's consequences, even free from sin's power. Freedom from sin is the rightful privilege of every child of God, because Christ has set us free! It isn't the freedom to do anything we want (for if we did, we'd become sin's slaves all over again), but the freedom to serve Christ. The Bible says that someday "the creation itself will be liberated from its bondage to decay and brought into the glorious freedom of the children of God" (Romans 8:21).

But Satan will do everything he can to pull us back into slavery—often, slavery to a particular sin. Some of the most heartbreaking letters I receive are from people who tell how alcohol or drugs have ravaged their lives and destroyed their families. Others become slaves to debt or food or a harmful habit or some type of psychological disorder. What began as an apparently harmless pastime has ended up as a frightening, overpowering addiction or obsession they cannot break on their own.

Does this describe you? Has some particular sin gained such a strong grip on your life that you can no longer resist it? If so, face it honestly, and seek God's help to deliver you. Turn your whole life—including this problem—over to Christ, and ask Him to give you the help you need. The reasons why you have fallen into this problem may be deep and complex (even going back to childhood), and your pastor or doctor may be able to suggest a trained counselor or program in your community to help you understand it and overcome it. God wants you to be free—free from this problem and free to love Christ and serve Him with all your heart.

Don't be sin's slave any longer, but by faith submit your heart and life to Christ and allow His Spirit to control you. And if you already know Christ, don't let Satan gain any advantage over you, but "stand firm, then, and do not let yourselves be burdened again by a yoke of slavery" (Galatians 5:1).

TWENTY

WHEN LIFE TURNS AGAINST US

We are hard pressed on every side, but not crushed; perplexed, but not in despair.

—2 CORINTHIANS 4:8

I T'S THE MOST-ASKED QUESTION IN THE WORLD: WHY? Why is there so much evil? Why do innocent children die from cancer and abuse and starvation? Why is the world wracked by natural disasters and war and disease? Why is there so much disappointment? Why do good people suffer just as much as bad people—and sometimes even more? If God is so loving and kind (we ask), why doesn't He do something? *Why?*

A Nation in Crisis

None of us will ever forget September 11, 2001. Within minutes our world changed forever as two hijacked airliners plowed into the twin towers of America's tallest building, the World Trade Center in New York City, and a third slammed into the Pentagon in Washington, D.C. Thousands were killed in that merciless terrorist attack, including hundreds of heroic fire, police, and emergency personnel. The attack would have been even more devastating had it not been for a courageous band of passengers who took control of a fourth hijacked plane, sacrificing their lives to keep it from reaching its intended target—probably the White House or the United States Capitol. (One of those fearless passengers had recently graduated from the college Ruth and I attended.)

I was invited by the president to speak three days later at a special service of prayer and remembrance in Washington's National Cathedral. I had participated in a similar event a few years earlier memorializing the victims of the bombing of the Federal Building in Oklahoma City—but this service was undoubtedly one of the hardest things I ever had to do. What could I say to bring comfort and hope to a nation in crisis? How could I possibly explain to those who were grieving why God hadn't intervened—when I didn't know the answer myself?

"I have been asked hundreds of times in my life why God allows tragedy and suffering," I told the congregation that day. "I really do not know the answer totally, even to my own satisfaction. I have to accept, by faith, that God is sovereign, and He is a God of love and mercy and compassion in the midst of suffering."

Does that sound like a contradiction? Perhaps it does, at least to our limited minds. Yet both are true: Evil is real—but so is God's power and love. And because He is all-powerful and loving we can cling to Him in trust and faith, even when we don't understand.

The Mystery of Suffering

Evil and suffering are real, whether we see them on our television screens or confront them in the privacy of our own lives. They aren't an illusion, nor are they simply an absence of good. None of us is immune from their grasp; suffering and tragedy touch us all, no matter who we are. The writer of Ecclesiastes asked, "What does a man get for all the toil and anxious striving with which he labors under the sun? All his days his work is pain and grief; even at night his mind does not rest" (Ecclesiastes 2:22–23). We are fallen creatures living in a fallen world that has been twisted and corrupted by sin, and we all share in its brokenness. Most of all, we share in its tragic legacy of disease and death.

But God is also real! He is just as real as our pain and heartache—and even more so, for someday they will vanish, but He will still remain. In the midst of life's tragedies, He wants to assure us of His presence and love—even if we don't understand why He allowed them to happen. He knows what we are going through, for He experienced evil's fiercest assault when His beloved Son suffered the pangs of death and hell. God understands our suffering, for Christ endured far greater suffering than we ever will. The Cross tells us that God understands our pain and confusion—but more than that, it tells us He loves us.

Can we believe this? Can we honestly believe God is loving and kind when there is so much suffering and sorrow in the world? Yes, we can—but not because we have all the answers, for we don't. We know God loves us for one reason: Christ died and rose again *for us*. Even when we don't understand why bad things happen, the cross tells us God loves us and cares for us. The greatest suffering in human history was Christ's suffering on the cross. Only hours before His arrest Jesus prayed, "My Father, if it is possible, may this cup be taken from me" (Matthew 26:39). The "cup" of which He spoke symbolized all the suffering He was about to endure. What was in that "cup"? It contained all the sins of the whole human race, and now He was about to partake of it. Think of what was in that "cup": every murder, every adultery, every theft, every injustice, every evil deed or thought—all the sins of the whole human race had been poured into that "cup." No wonder He asked the Father if there was any other way for our salvation to be won! But there was no other way. The sinless Son of God was about to have all our sins transferred to Him, so God's full judgment could fall on Him instead of us. Jesus' suffering wasn't simply that of a man dying a cruel and painful death—terrible as that was. His greatest suffering was the spiritual agony He endured as He took upon Himself the death and hell you and I deserve.

Yet by allowing His Son to suffer the pangs of death and hell, God demonstrated how much He loves us. If He didn't love us, He never would have allowed His Son to leave heaven's glory and die for us.

How Will We React?

"I don't want anything to do with God," a woman angrily wrote me recently. "Our baby died last month of SIDS [sudden infant death syndrome], and I'm very bitter at God. I'll never get over it." My heart went out to her; almost nothing is as painful as the loss of a child, and I understand her emotions (as does God). But my heart went out to her for another reason: She desperately needed comfort and strength to deal with this tragedy—and yet she was cutting herself off from the only One who could provide them. The psalmist's words are true: "God is our refuge and strength, an ever-present help in trouble" (Psalm 46:1).

Whether we realize it or not, every time life turns against us we stand at a crossroads. When disappointment or tragedy or suffering strike, we have a decision to make: *Will we turn away from God, or will we turn toward Him?* Will we refuse His help, or will we seek it? Will we depend on ourselves for the strength we need, or will we depend on Him? *Which road will we take?* One road leads to doubt, anger, bitterness, fear, hopelessness, and despair. The other leads to hope, comfort, peace, strength, and joy. *Which will it be?*

As we have already seen, our journey through life is never smooth and untroubled. Life isn't always fair, nor is it always the way we wish it were. Disappointment, tragedy, grief, failure, disability, illness, injustice, rejection, suffering, grief—these *will* come our way, sometimes at the most unexpected times or in the most unexpected ways.

When they do, it's natural to ask, "Why, Lord? Why did You let this happen to me?" It's not wrong to ask this; God may even answer our cry (or at least give us a hint), because He has lessons to teach us through this experience.

But the most important question we should ask when life turns against us isn't *"Why?"* but *"What?" "What do You want me to do, Lord? How should I react to this situation? What response do You want me to make?"*

When we fail to ask this, we almost always end up taking the wrong road, reacting in bitterness or anger or jealousy or revenge, or even despair. And when we do, we always pay a terrible price—*always*. Reacting in an unspiritual, ungodly way never solves anything, and almost always makes the situation worse. Not only do we poison our own souls, but we end up poisoning our relationships—with others and with God. The Bible says of such a person, "All his days he eats in darkness, with great frustration, affliction and anger" (Ecclesiastes 5:17). Who wants to be around someone like that? Who honestly wants to *be* someone like that?

Preparing for Adversity

Nevertheless it's not easy to react in the right way when life turns against us. Almost before we realize it, our emotions overwhelm us and we find ourselves swept away in a flood of anger or frustration or despair. Even if we stop to reconsider, it may be too late to recall the harsh words we spoke or undo the damage we did in the heat of the moment.

That's why *the time to prepare for life's disappointments and hurts is in advance*, before they come crashing down upon us. *Now* is the time to build spiritual foundations that won't collapse under the weight of life's reverses; *now* is the time to decide to turn to God and follow His way when troubles come; *now* is the time to strengthen our faith so it won't fail in the midst of a sudden crisis. The Bible says, "Remember your Creator in the days of your youth, *before* the days of trouble come" (Ecclesiastes 12:1, emphasis added).

"I can always tell if a new patient has a strong faith," a hospital chaplain once told me. "If they do, they know from experience what it means to turn to God for strength, and that's what they do. But someone with a weak faith can't do that. They simply don't have the spiritual resources to see them through, and it's too late to get them." Like the foolish man in Jesus' story who built his house on sand, they are defenseless when life's storms come. But, Jesus added, "everyone who hears these words of mine and puts them into practice is like a wise man who built his house on the rock. The rain came down, the streams rose, and the winds blew and beat against that house; yet it did not fall, because it had its foundation on the rock" (Matthew 7:24–25). Some months ago the remnants of a powerful hurricane tore down numerous trees around our home and caused several landslides. But the house itself was untouched, because when it was being built, an architect friend advised us to set it on steel pilings driven down to solid rock, which we did.

How strong is the foundation of your life? And what are you doing to make it stronger? A house's foundation isn't built in a day, nor are our spiritual foundations. Make it your goal to build strong foundations for your life—foundations constructed from prayer and the truths of God's Word. The old hymn says it well: "How firm a foundation, ye saints of the Lord, / Is laid for your faith in His excellent Word!"

Disappointment and Failure

Life turns against us in many ways, but one experience is common to us all: *disappointment*. Sometimes it's only minor: a vacation that had to be canceled, a sudden storm that ruined a picnic. I remember during our courtship Ruth and I frequently wrote each other, and eventually I sent her a letter asking her to marry me. I remember how disappointed I was each day when there was no reply in the mail. (Of course my disappointment turned to joy when her letter of acceptance finally arrived!)

But some disappointments are much harsher: a job that fails to satisfy, a child who becomes rebellious, a marriage that turns sour.

Repeated disappointment almost always triggers a series of other reactions: discouragement, anger, frustration, bitterness, resentment, even depression. Unless we learn to deal with disappointment, it will rob us of joy and poison our souls. We may even end up blaming God, forgetting His promise that "those who hope in me will not be disappointed" (Isaiah 49:23).

Closely related to disappointment is another reality we all experience at some time: *failure*. Just as we all experience disappointment, so we also all experience failure. Like disappointment, failure can run the gamut from mild to almost overwhelming and may trigger a host of reactions, including anxiety, stress, and even despair. It may be the failure to achieve a goal we have set, or failure in a job or relationship. Or it may involve moral or spiritual failure, falling short of what we know God wants of us.

Disappointment and failure aren't identical, but they often occur together, and both can hold us back from God's best for our lives. In some ways, however, failure is the more dangerous, because someone who repeatedly fails may end up becoming a captive to their failures. In other words, *because they failed once, they end up concluding they will always fail.* "Nothing I ever do is right. I've just given up even trying," a young man wrote me. He then confessed that in trying to forget his failures he was on the verge of becoming an alcoholic. Tragically, his belief that he would always be a failure was leading him into a downward spiral of even more failure. His problem wasn't so much that he had failed, but that he had allowed his failures to defeat him. Only with God's help, I told him, could he break this vicious cycle.

Overcoming Disappointment and Failure

Disappointment and failure aren't always wrong; we all experience them, and they are part of life. The Bible says, "We all stumble in many ways" (James 3:2). Nor is every failure or disappointment our responsibility; someone who loses their job because of a corporate downsizing, for example, usually isn't at fault.

But sometimes it *is* our fault, and we always need to examine ourselves honestly and prayerfully to see if this is the case. Sometimes our failure may have been caused by a particular sin—something we allowed to take root in our souls that set us on the path to inevitable disappointment or failure. These also become sin when we allow them to overwhelm us and block God's plan for our lives. Remember: God's desire is for us to become more like Christ—but that can't happen if we allow disappointment and failure to hold us back.

How, then, should we react when disappointment or failure come?

First, remember that God's love for you has not changed. It's easy to believe God loves us when everything is going well; it's harder to believe it when life turns against us. But disappointment or failure are *not* signs that God has forsaken you or stopped loving you. The devil wants you to believe God no longer loves you when you fail—but it isn't true. Sometimes we see God's love most clearly when life is at its darkest.

This doesn't mean God overlooks our sin or is pleased with our disobedience—not at all. But even when we fail Him, God's love for us never fails, and He always stands ready to forgive and restore us to Himself. The people in Jeremiah's time failed God miserably and brought severe judgment upon themselves as a result. But even then, God assured them of His unchanging love: "Because of the LORD's great love we are not consumed, for his compassions never fail. They are new every morning" (Lamentations 3:22–23).

Second, learn to keep your disappointments and failures in perspective. We all know people who get very upset or angry at even the smallest disappointment; you may be one yourself. But overreacting to minor disappointments or failures is just as wrong as pretending they don't exist. Disappointments are part of life; we can't always have our own way, and we need to learn to separate what is significant from what is merely annoying. Getting upset over things that aren't really important (or can't be changed) is useless. Only in heaven will we be free of all disappointments and failures. A friend of mine says that when something minor bothers him, he simply tells himself, "Oh well, a hundred years from now it won't make any difference!"

Not every disappointment or failure is minor, of course; it may have profound implications for our future. It may also point to something deeper in our character or circumstances that needs to be addressed. When that is the case, we need to take heed.

Learning from Our Experience

A third principle for dealing with disappointment or failure is this: Learn from your disappointments and failures, and—with God's help—seek to overcome them.

Could I have done anything to prevent this? Were my hopes or dreams unrealistic, or were my motives wrong? Is there a sin I need to confess or a new path God wants me to explore? What can I learn from this experience—even if it was unavoidable? What is God trying to teach me?

Recently an acquaintance told me about a man who has spent most of his life chasing schemes he was convinced would make him rich. None worked out, however, and now in retirement he has almost nothing. Why had he repeatedly failed, I asked? "He'd never listen to advice or heed his friends' warnings," my acquaintance replied. "Also, he always blamed others for his failures and refused to learn from his experiences." The Bible says, "The way of a fool seems right to him, but a wise man listens to advice" (Proverbs 12:15).

Sometimes God uses life's disappointments to draw us closer to Himself or teach us patience and trust. He also may use them to redirect us toward His will. Don't let failure or disappointment cut you off from God or make you think the future is hopeless. When God closes one door, He often opens another—if we seek it.

The apostle Paul said, "I have learned to be content whatever the circumstances" (Philippians 4:11). He wrote those words while in prison, his plans disrupted and his future uncertain. The reason he could say them, however, was because he had learned to see disappointment and failure from God's perspective, and to trust the future into His hands. May this be true of us. When life turns against you, let the psalmist's prayer become yours: "Show me your ways, O LORD, teach me your paths" (Psalm 25:4).

TWENTY-ONE

WHEN OTHERS DISAPPOINT

*As God's chosen people, holy and dearly loved, clothe yourselves with
compassion, kindness, humility, gentleness and patience.*

—Colossians 3:12

You've heard it many times, and may even have
said it yourself: Life would be great if it weren't for other people.
It's not true, of course; we need others, and without them life is
not great. We weren't meant to live in isolation; God didn't make us
that way. Instead, God put within us a yearning for companionship—
with others and supremely with Himself. When Adam was created,
he lived in the most perfect environment imaginable, but his life was
incomplete. God declared, "It is not good for the man to be alone"
(Genesis 2:18)—and so He created Eve. God knows we need others,
and our greatest joys often come from our relationships.

Nevertheless, no area of human life is so full of difficulties and heartaches as relationships. If you listed everything that upset you during the past week, I suspect most had to do with other people. In a video my wife watches occasionally, the heroine asks her fiancé, "Why is life so difficult?" He ponders a moment and replies with one word: "people." People can be selfless and kind, of course, but they also can be difficult, stubborn, ego-driven, thoughtless, mean, selfish, manipulative—the list could go on and on. Nor is the problem just other people; it's also ourselves.

Why the Conflict?

Why can't we seem to get along with each other?

Some reasons are obvious (at least on the surface). For example, people from different cultures or social backgrounds often clash, because they think everyone should be the way they are. People with contrasting personalities may have a hard time adjusting to each other. Those who think their race or ethnic background is superior will always have problems getting along with others.

Behind these, however, is a deeper problem: *We each want our own way.* "If that person would just do things my way," we say to ourselves, "we could get along!" Unfortunately the other person is probably thinking the same about us—and that leads to conflict. The Bible says, "What causes fights and quarrels among you? Don't they come from your desires that battle within you?" (James 4:1).

This is why simply changing our outward circumstances seldom solves anything. "We thought if we moved to a pleasant part of the country and built a beautiful house we'd be happy," one woman wrote me, "but all we did was take our problems with us. I guess our next stop is the divorce court." Our deepest problems are within ourselves—within our own hearts and minds—and until we confront them and seek God's help to change us, we'll never completely solve them. Jesus said, "Out of the heart come evil thoughts, murder, adultery, sexual immorality, theft, false testimony, slander" (Matthew 15:19). Every sin He lists involves hurting someone else.

Christians aren't immune from these conflicts. As we saw earlier, our old sinful nature still lives within us and constantly tries to assert itself. In addition, Satan will do everything he can to divide Christians and destroy our witness. Only the Holy Spirit can subdue our old nature and overcome it with God's love.

God's Priority: Living in Love

Every year scores of conferences are held on how nations, races, and cultures can get along with each other—without producing lasting results. If you took a survey asking how to solve the world's problems, I'm sure you'd come up with many answers. But most could probably be summarized in one sentence: If we'd just learn to love each other, we wouldn't have so many problems. And they would be right, because you can't love someone and hate them at the same time. The Bible says, "Above all, love each other deeply, because love covers over a multitude of sins" (1 Peter 4:8).

But if the answer is so simple, why doesn't it happen? Let's see what the Bible says.

Remember what we said earlier: God's will is for us to become more like Christ—*and this means becoming more like Him in our character*. The Bible commands us "to put off your old self, which is being corrupted by its deceitful desires; . . . and to put on the new self, created to be like God in true righteousness and holiness" (Ephesians 4:22, 24).

What does it mean "to be like God in true righteousness and holiness"? Is it just avoiding certain habits or ways of living we know are wrong—or is it something deeper? And what does this have to do with getting along with others?

Simply this: *God's will is for us to reflect the character of Christ—and the essence of His character is love.* The Bible says, "God is love. Whoever lives in love lives in God, and God in him" (1 John 4:16). Jesus said, "A new command I give you: Love one another. As I have loved you, so you must love one another. By this all men will know that you are my disciples, if you love one another" (John 13:34–35).

What is love? In English we have only one word—"love"—to express its various meanings, but scholars point out that the Greek language (in which the New Testament was written) uses no less than four different words for love. The first is *eros*, which refers to physical or sexual attraction (our word "erotic" comes from it). A second type of love is *storge*, which refers to family affection, such as love between parents and their children. Another word, *phileo*, describes friendship or brotherly love. (Philadelphia, "the city of brotherly love," gets its name from this.)

The final word, *agape*, has a much broader and deeper meaning and is the most common word for love in the New Testament. *Agape* love is selfless love—love that extends even to those who aren't lovable or even worthy of love. The Bible says this is the kind of love God has for us—and is the kind of love we should have for others.

This kind of love—*agape* love—is more than a warm feeling or an impulsive act of kindness. The love God wants us to have isn't just an emotion, but a conscious act of the *will*—a deliberate decision on our part to put others ahead of ourselves. The Bible says, "Each of you should look not only to your own interests, but also to the interests of others" (Philippians 2:4). This is the kind of love God has for us—a love so deep that it caused Christ to leave heaven's glory and die on the cross for us. The opposite of *agape* love is selfishness, but when Christ's love fills our hearts, it puts selfishness on the run.

What is God's priority for you? *God's priority is that His love would become the hallmark of your life—because it was the hallmark of Christ's life.*

Growing in Love

How does this become a reality? It doesn't happen by accident or by gritting our teeth and hoping that somehow we can make ourselves love others. It happens only as we grow closer to Christ and submit our lives to Him, allowing His Holy Spirit to cleanse and change us. The Bible says, "The fruit of the Spirit is love" (Galatians 5:22).

This happens only gradually, I've discovered, one step at a time. Even now, with most of my life behind me, God is still teaching me what it means to love others the way He does. As we saw earlier, God's plan is to give us *peace*: peace with God, peace in our hearts, and peace with others. Peace with God happens instantly when we come to Christ; the warfare between us and God is over! Peace in our hearts starts growing then also—sometimes rapidly, sometimes slowly. But the third kind of peace—peace with others—takes a lifetime to develop. In fact, it won't be complete until we reach heaven. But this doesn't change God's plan: He wants to put His love within us so we can be at peace with others.

The Bible says, "The goal . . . is love, which comes from a pure heart and a good conscience and a sincere faith" (1 Timothy 1:5). Is this your goal? Ask God today to implant His love within you, and then to help you live according to His love.

Learning to Love

Loving others is essential, but how do we put it into action?

Almost nothing is as complex as the human personality, and no simple formula will ever cover every situation or every relationship.

Library and bookstore shelves are filled with advice—some good, some not—on how to get along with others; radio and television programs on relationships multiply endlessly. In spite of this flood of information, however, we still live in a world of discord and strife. "We're seeing our fourth marriage counselor," one man wrote me, "and we still can't get along."

Where can we turn? People reading the Bible for the first time are often surprised to discover how much human drama it contains. "Before I read it, I assumed the Bible was just a collection of religious sayings," a man told me, "but I discovered it's full of real people. It's more exciting than any novel!" Almost every conceivable human dilemma and conflict is reflected in its pages.

And yet the Bible isn't just another book of advice. The reason is because behind the people in the Bible was another Person: God. This makes all the difference, for He created us, and He loves us and knows all about us. Who can tell us how to get along with each other better than God? Where can we turn for wisdom better than God's Word, the Bible? He alone is "the LORD Almighty, wonderful in counsel and magnificent in wisdom" (Isaiah 28:29). The Bible says, "I have taught you in the way of wisdom; I have led you in right paths" (Proverbs 4:11 NKJV).

Living by God's Principles

The Bible tells us how to put God's love into action, and we need its wisdom and direction. However, it isn't just a book of rules, telling us exactly how to react in every situation. If it did, it would be hundreds of volumes long, because every person and every situation is different.

Instead, the Bible gives us a series of *principles* to guide our relationships. Like lighthouses along a rocky shore, they warn us of dangers and guide us toward safe waters. In the rest of this chapter, we'll examine *seven* of these principles.

The first is this: Make it your goal to live at peace with others. Jesus told His disciples, "Be at peace with each other" (Mark 9:50).

A contentious, belligerent Christian isn't living according to the Spirit but according to the flesh. When we stubbornly insist on our own way and are insensitive to others, peace is not our goal. The Bible says, "Strive for peace with everyone" (Hebrews 12:14 ESV).

Is it possible to be at peace with everyone? Unfortunately it isn't; even our best efforts may not change another person's attitude. Paul wrote, *"If it is possible, as far as it depends on you,* live at peace with everyone" (Romans 12:18, emphasis added). Paul urged us to live in peace, but he also knew it wasn't always possible. On one occasion Paul and Barnabas strongly disagreed over whether or not young Mark should travel with them, and eventually they went their separate ways (Acts 15:36–41). The key is to ask God if we are at fault, and if so confess it and seek His help to overcome it.

The Golden Rule

The Bible's second principle for living in harmony is this: Treat others the way you would want them to treat you. This simple but profound principle is often called the "Golden Rule" and comes from Jesus' words in the Sermon on the Mount: "In everything, do to others what you would have them do to you, for this sums up the Law and the Prophets" (Matthew 7:12).

How different our lives would be if we actually practiced this! Instead of ignoring people or treating them harshly, we'd handle them with respect and kindness. Instead of manipulating them for our own purposes, we'd help them achieve what is best for them. We'd also try to see life through their eyes. Most of all, we'd point them to Christ, for the greatest gift we can offer anyone is His salvation.

A third principle follows from this: Pray not only for your friends but for your enemies. Elsewhere in the Sermon on the Mount Jesus declared, "You have heard that it was said, 'Love your neighbor and hate your enemy.' But I tell you: Love your enemies and pray for those who persecute you" (Matthew 5:43–44). As Jesus was dying on the cross, He looked at those who had crucified Him and prayed, "Father, forgive them, for they do not know what they are doing" (Luke 23:34).

You cannot pray for someone and hate them at the same time. Even if you are asking God to restrain their evil actions, you should also be praying that He will change their hearts. Only eternity will reveal the impact of our prayers on others. Prayer is one way we put the Golden rule into action.

Things to Avoid

Getting along with someone involves not only doing things to strengthen your relationship, but also avoiding things that hurt it. *This leads to a fourth principle: Guard your tongue, and use it for good instead of evil.* The psalmist prayed, "Set a guard over my mouth, O LORD; keep watch over the door of my lips" (Psalm 141:3). How many marriages or friendships have been destroyed because of criticism that spiraled out of control? How many relationships have broken down because of gossip or a word spoken thoughtlessly or in anger? A harsh word can't be taken back; no apology can fully repair its damage.

James was right: "The tongue also is a fire, a world of evil among the parts of the body. It corrupts the whole person, sets the whole course of his life on fire, and is itself set on fire by hell" (James 3:6). Those are strong words, but they are true.

But the tongue can also be used for good—and that should be

our goal! Sometimes it's best to keep silent (as Jesus did before Pilate), particularly if our words will only make things worse. But sometimes God would have us confront someone or try to instruct them, as long as our goal is helping them. The Bible says, "Do not let any unwholesome talk come out of your mouths, but only what is helpful for building others up according to their needs, that it may benefit those who listen" (Ephesians 4:29). How much of your conversation has this as its goal?

Avoiding Revenge

Tragically, history is filled with humanity's thirst for revenge. Countless wars would never have been fought if tribes or nations hadn't lashed out in revenge. The same is true for individuals. Revenge easily descends into an endless cycle of hate and violence.

But the Bible gives us a different principle: Never repay evil with evil. It says, "Do not repay anyone evil for evil. . . . Do not take revenge, my friends, but leave room for God's wrath, for it is written, 'It is mine to avenge; I will repay,' says the Lord" (Romans 12:17, 19).

If someone has harmed us by breaking the law we have the right to bring them to justice, both for our good and the good of society. But hurting someone only because they have hurt us is another matter, and God's people must not fall into that trap. When someone hurts us, our natural instinct is to strike back— but when we do, we not only destroy any possibility of reconciliation, but we also allow anger and hate to control us.

The sixth principle follows from this: Don't only avoid revenge, but don't be a captive to the past.

Recently a woman wrote me a long letter telling why she was so bitter toward her ex-husband. I understood her hurt—but then she mentioned that their divorce had taken place more than twenty years ago. Sadly, she was a captive to the past, poisoned by bitterness all these years. For some, bitterness or anger becomes part of their whole identity, making it even more difficult for them to get rid of it.

We can't change the past; we can only seek God's forgiveness for what we did wrong. But once He has forgotten it, shouldn't we as well? Don't let the past hold you captive any longer, but take your bitterness and resentment and lay them at the foot of the cross. Jesus said, "If the Son sets you free, you will be free indeed" (John 8:36).

The Power of Forgiveness

"It's the hardest thing I've ever done," one man wrote me, "but I feel as if a thousand-pound load has been lifted from my shoulders." *He was talking about the final principle in this list: Practice the transforming power of forgiveness.*

Almost every week someone writes me saying something like this: "I can't forgive. You don't know how deeply I've been hurt." Perhaps this echoes your own thoughts. But nothing releases us from the past or opens the door to reconciliation as completely as forgiveness. Even if the other person refuses to admit any fault or scorns our forgiveness, that must not hold us back.

The Bible is clear: "Bear with each other and forgive whatever grievances you may have against one another. Forgive as the Lord forgave you" (Colossians 3:13). Did you notice that last phrase? God forgave us freely and fully in Christ, and that's how we are to forgive others: freely and fully. Like the man I quoted above, it may be the hardest thing you ever do, but with God's help you can—and you must.

What relationships need strengthening in your life? Don't wait for them to grow cold or bitter, but ask God to help you strengthen them by putting His love into action—beginning today.

TWENTY-TWO

DEALING WITH SUFFERING AND LOSS

Though he brings grief, he will show compassion,
so great is his unfailing love.

—LAMENTATIONS 3:32

NOTHING DEMONSTRATES OUR HUMAN FRAILTY MORE forcefully than pain.

Whether it is the temporary hurt of a bruised thumb or the unendurable agony of an aggressive cancer, pain reminds us that no matter who we are or how healthy we seem, life is fragile and ultimately outside our control. Most of all, pain reminds us that someday our bodies will wear out and die and this life will come to an end. Job said, "Now my life ebbs away; days of suffering grip me" (Job 30:16).

When Pain Overwhelms

As I write this, pain has been my wife's constant companion for years. It may have started when Ruth fell out of a tree many years ago fixing a swing for some of our grandchildren; it may be the result of her genes (for her mother experienced some of the same problems); it may simply be a consequence of growing older. Whatever the reason, over the years the gradual deterioration of the bone structure in her hips and back made it increasingly difficult for her to walk, in spite of a series of hip replacements and other operations. Now she spends her days in her bed or chair, no longer able to walk.

With this has come pain—not just a slight twinge now and then, but steady, unrelenting, at times almost-unbearable pain. During my life I have experienced my share of illness and pain— more than enough to help me understand what Ruth is going through—but I seldom feel more helpless than when watching her clench her teeth while waiting for a pain pill to take effect. I often wish I could somehow take the pain for her.

Yet everyone who knows her will tell you that she never complains, let alone gets angry or depressed over her infirmities. The reason is her strong faith and her conviction that even in the midst of suffering God loves her and is near. If you asked her, she would tell you that she feels closer to God now than at any other time in her life—and she would be telling the truth. She honestly can say with the psalmist, "My times are in your hands" (Psalm 31:15).

Reacting to Pain and Suffering

We all experience pain and suffering, although for millions of people pain is a constant, daily companion. Sometimes it grew gradually—but for others it came suddenly and without warning. As I write this, an able and dedicated woman who has overseen our ministry in Germany for many years lies in pain, virtually paralyzed because of an unexpected fall in her home. Life is uncertain, and the Bible rightly says, "You do not even know what will happen tomorrow" (James 4:14).

By itself pain serves a useful function, of course, alerting us to danger or warning us that something is wrong—and we neglect it at our peril. But when pain persists, it quickly dominates our lives. A president or prime minister may have urgent decisions to make, but if they have a toothache, all they can think about is getting to the dentist.

No one willingly seeks suffering or rejoices in it (although some people pursue physical or emotional pain in a misguided attempt to punish themselves for their sins, not realizing that Jesus took upon Himself the punishment we deserve). But suffering and pain come to us all, and the real question is this: *How should we react?* Let me suggest two steps that have helped me.

First, be on guard against pain's dangers. Whenever we experience any problem, we tend to focus on ourselves—but especially when we don't feel well. When this happens, however, we may be opening the door to all kinds of emotional or spiritual dangers. Many hurting people, for example, become so self-absorbed that they totally ignore the feelings of those around them, even lashing out at those who are trying to help. Others become consumed with self-pity or bitterness. Still others end up in despair or seek relief in alcohol or illicit drugs. And some blame God for their pain; one woman wrote, "If God really loved me, this wouldn't be happening." Another wrote, "I don't know what I've done, but God must be punishing me." Their feelings are understandable—but they are also leading them down a dead-end road.

It's hard to feel good emotionally when we feel bad physically. Most of us can identify with the psalmist when we are stricken with sickness or pain: "My life is consumed by anguish and my years by groaning; my strength fails because of my affliction" (Psalm 31:10). Nevertheless, be alert and ask God to help you overcome pain's pitfalls and dangers.

One way to do this is to pray for others and their needs. Don't just pray for yourself; pray for others also! Some of God's most effective prayer warriors have been men and women who could do little because of disability or illness. But they could pray! You may not be able to do everything you once did, but you can still pray. It takes discipline and perseverance to pray when you don't feel well, but in my experience those who are the weakest physically are often the strongest spiritually through their prayers.

Learning Pain's Lessons

Second, ask God to help you learn pain's lessons. The most remarkable thing about suffering is that God can use it for our good. He may even allow it to happen because of the good He knows will result from it. "I never thought I'd be able to say this," one man wrote me, "but I'm actually glad I had cancer. God used it to get my attention, and I don't think it could have happened any other way." In recent years I experienced two falls, one breaking a hip and the other—just as the hip was almost healed—breaking my pelvis. Both happened in an instant and without warning, yet in the midst of pain, I had a deep sense of God's presence and purpose. God also used them to teach me what it means to depend on Him in *every* situation.

What are some of pain's lessons? Certainly one is that life is fragile and someday it will be over. It's easy to forget this when we're active and feel well—but no matter how healthy we are or how many advances medical science makes, in time our bodies wear out and this life ends. More than anything else, pain reminds us of the brevity of life and the nearness of eternity.

Suffering and pain also should draw us closer to God. When we're healthy, we easily become busy and preoccupied with the present—and end up forgetting God. But when accident or illness set us aside, we have time to reflect on what's really important. Most of all, we have time to examine our relationship with Christ and recommit ourselves and our futures into His loving hands. Throughout the ages suffering Christians have found that the Bible's promise is true: "The LORD is near to all who call on him, to all who call on him in truth" (Psalm 145:18). The Bible also says, "The eternal God is your refuge, and underneath are the everlasting arms" (Deuteronomy 33:27).

When suffering comes, learn to trust each day into God's hands and take it as a gift from Him. In addition, even if you can't concentrate very well, let your lips be filled with prayer and praise. Yes, pray for healing; God is sovereign, and He is able to intervene. But most of all pray for His will to be done in your life—for His will is perfect. Will you love Him any less if He doesn't heal you? May your response instead be like Paul's to his persistent "thorn in the flesh": "But [God] said to me, 'My grace is sufficient for you, for my power is made perfect in weakness.' Therefore I will boast all the more gladly about my weaknesses, so that Christ's power may rest on me" (2 Corinthians 12:9).

Above all, when suffering comes, rejoice in the hope we have of heaven because of Christ. No matter what you are going through, someday it will end and you will be with Christ forever. The Bible says, "Our light and momentary troubles are achieving for us an eternal glory that far outweighs them all" (2 Corinthians 4:17). Earth's troubles fade in the light of heaven's hope.

Loss and Grief

We have already discussed some of life's hurts, but in the rest of this chapter, I want to look at the deepest, most intense pain you and I may ever be called upon to endure: *grief.*

Almost every hurt in life involves some kind of loss—of health, friendship, financial security, inner peace, even hope. With each loss comes sorrow, or even the pain of grief. Few experiences in life, for example, are more painful than a parent's grief over a rebellious child, or the grief we feel if a friend turns against us. Recently a family who lost everything in Hurricane Katrina except the clothes on their backs has come to live in our community; only their faith has kept them from despair.

But nothing is more painful in life than the loss of someone we deeply love, and when it happens, our grief can be almost overwhelming. "It's been two years since my wife died," one man wrote me, "but it feels like yesterday. I know she's in heaven, but that doesn't help me much, and I'm still overcome with grief. Will I ever get over this?"

Ruth and I have now reached the stage in life where we find we have outlived many of our closest friends and near relatives. Even as I wrote this chapter, word came of the death of one of Ruth's dearly loved brothers-in-law. The news of every death always causes us sadness, even when it brings a merciful release from pain or the infirmities of old age. But sometimes it has brought us something much deeper: a profound and enduring sense of sorrow and loss. It has brought us grief.

Some suggest Christians shouldn't grieve when another Christian dies, because we know death is only a transition from the burdens of this life to the glories of heaven. But I cannot agree. Death for the Christian *is* the doorway to heaven's glory. Because of Christ's resurrection we can joyously say with Paul, "Where, O death, is your victory? Where, O death, is your sting?" (1 Corinthians 15:55).

But death is still our final enemy, and when a loved one dies, a great emptiness is still left in our hearts. When that happens, our emotions cross the line from loss and sorrow to something far more intense and lasting: *grief.* The closer we were to someone, the greater will be our emptiness—and the greater too will be our grief. When Jesus came to the tomb of His friend Lazarus, His response was immediate: "Jesus wept" (John 11:35). This is the shortest verse in the Bible, but it poignantly reminds us that Jesus knows what it means to grieve. Christ, the Bible tells us, was "a man of sorrows, and acquainted with grief" (Isaiah 53:3 KJV). The Bible says that as Christians we don't "grieve like the rest of men, who have no hope" (1 Thessalonians 4:13)—but that doesn't mean we won't still grieve. Our hope of heaven tempers our grief, but it doesn't erase it. When we grieve over someone who has died in Christ, we are sorrowing not for them but for ourselves. Our grief isn't a sign of weak faith, but of great love.

Responding to Grief

Recovering from grief, I've come to realize, isn't a single event but a process. Grief grips us suddenly, but lets go of us slowly. Just as our bodies heal only gradually after major surgery, so too do our hearts after the death of someone we loved. But how can we help the process along? How should we respond to our grief?

First, don't be surprised by your grief. "I thought I was prepared for my mother's death," one woman wrote me, "but I was wrong. Her death wasn't a surprise, but knowing I'd never hear her voice again hit me like a ton of bricks."

When a loved one dies, our first response is often numbness and shock. I still recall how stunned I felt when news came that one of my closest friends in high school had been shot down and killed in a fighter plane over Germany. We even may feel guilty, irrationally blaming ourselves for not doing more to prevent their death or not being present when they died. We may even feel angry—toward the doctors or nurses, or toward the loved one for leaving us, or even toward God. One of Lazarus's sisters complained, "Lord, if you had been here, my brother would not have died" (John 11:32). Jesus didn't rebuke her for her feelings; He understood her grief and stayed by her side. He does the same with us.

Second, turn your grief over to God. The psalmist wrote, "Cast your burden on the LORD, And He shall sustain you" (Psalm 55:22 NKJV). Notice that he didn't say, "Cast *some* of your burden on the Lord"; instead, God wants us to cast *all* our burdens on Him— including our burden of grief. Your grief over the death of someone you loved may be the biggest burden you will ever carry. Why carry it alone? Why *not* turn it over to God?

We will only do this when we realize two great truths: *the depth of our weakness and the depth of God's love.* Don't try to carry your grief alone! Instead, turn to your loving heavenly Father and ask Him to lift it from your shoulders—and slowly but surely He will. Remember: He knows what you are going through, and He is truly "the Father of compassion and the God of all comfort, who comforts us in all our troubles" (2 Corinthians 1:3–4).

Third, surround your grief with gratitude. This may sound impossible; how can we be grateful when we lose someone we love? From one point of view this is true: we *aren't* thankful for the loss we have sustained, nor does God expect us to be.

But even in the midst of grief, we can still be thankful, and thankfulness can act like a soothing balm on our hurt. For example, although we mourn the loss of a loved one, we can still thank God for the years we had together and the many ways they enriched our lives. Don't just *recall* the good times you had; *thank God* for them! They were His gracious gift to you.

In addition, we can thank God that our loved one is now beyond all the pain and heartaches of this life and is now safely in heaven forever if they knew Christ. Thank God also that someday you will be reunited with your loved one, and together you will praise and serve God through all eternity. Thank God as well that He is with you right now; He hasn't abandoned you, and He still has a reason for keeping you here. The Bible tells us we should be "always giving thanks to God the Father *for everything*, in the name of our Lord Jesus Christ" (Ephesians 5:20, emphasis added).

Finally, reach out to someone who is also hurting. All around you are people who are experiencing heartache or pain of some kind, and they need your encouragement and help. They need you—and you need them. One of the best things we can do to help ourselves is to help someone else. Grief turns us inward, but compassion turns us outward, and that's what we need when grief threatens to crush us. The Bible says, "Carry each other's burdens" (Galatians 6:2).

When you grieve, ask God to lead you to someone who needs your friendship and encouragement. Pray for them, spend time with them, listen to them, encourage them, share God's love with them. They may be facing illness or some other burden or heartache, and they need your support and kindness. Or they may be walking the same path of grief you are. (Some churches have special "grief groups" for those who have lost loved ones, or God may want you to talk with your pastor about starting one.)

I realize you may not feel like helping someone else; you may think your burden is already too heavy, and you can't imagine taking on someone else's burden also. But a burden shared is a burden halved, and God will encourage you as you encourage others.

As we saw earlier, we will never fully understand this side of heaven why God allows disappointment and suffering and evil. Someday we'll understand, but not now. In Paul's words, "Now I know in part; then I shall know fully" (1 Corinthians 13:12).

But we do know this: God's will is for us to become more like Christ, and *hardship and suffering are part of this process.* A friend of mine says that hard times are the chisel God uses to shape us. This is why the Bible says, "Consider it pure joy, my brothers, whenever you face trials of many kinds, because you know that the testing of your faith develops perseverance. Perseverance must finish its work so that you may be mature and complete, not lacking anything" (James 1:2–4).

In the meantime we live by faith, confident that "neither death nor life, neither angels nor demons, neither the present nor the future, nor any powers, neither height nor depth, nor anything else in all creation, will be able to separate us from the love of God that is in Christ Jesus our Lord" (Romans 8:38–39). Faith isn't blind, nor is it wishful thinking. For the Christian, faith is real—because it's focused not on ourselves or on our circumstances but on Christ. In the midst of life's trials and sorrows, is He the focus of your faith?

SECTION FOUR

STAYING
THE
COURSE

TWENTY-THREE

ONE DAY AT A TIME

*Let us throw off everything that hinders and the sin that so easily
entangles, and let us run with perseverance the race marked out for us.*

—HEBREWS 12:1

WITHOUT FUEL A FIRE GROWS COLD, AND SO DOES
our faith.

As we have seen, many things can disrupt our journey through
life if we aren't careful: destructive emotions, wrong motives, bad
habits, disappointments or failures, difficult relationships, suffering,
and grief. We all experience them, and God wants to help us gain
victory over them.

But for most of us, life isn't a constant stream of major crises or
overwhelming problems. Instead, most of our time is spent in the
routine of daily living: work, family, finances, entertainment, and
so forth. Meals need preparing; trash must be taken out; bills have

to be paid; children require new shoes or help with homework or rides to soccer practice. Even as I write this, an outside drain at our house has clogged, allowing rainwater to seep in and soak the carpet in my study. Life is full of daily challenges and minor annoyances.

And unless we take measures to prevent it, they will smother our faith.

Faith Gone Cold

Although he appears only briefly in the New Testament, Demas was clearly an able and dedicated person. He was probably young and unencumbered with family responsibilities, and twice Paul mentions him as a companion on his travels, enduring the same hardships Paul did while helping him spread the Gospel (Colossians 4:14; Philemon 1:24). Once when Paul was imprisoned for his faith, Demas stayed close at hand to help him, running the risk of being put in prison also.

But his zeal did not last. In one of the Bible's most poignant sentences, Paul wrote, "Demas, in love with this present world, has deserted me" (2 Timothy 4:10 ESV). He was never heard of again.

What happened? We have no way of knowing, of course, but at some point Demas must have decided he had had enough of self-denial; it was time to enjoy life and pursue the things this world has to offer. Paul doesn't say he renounced his faith or became immoral or corrupt; for all we know, he may have gone back to his home church and proudly told them all about his adventures with Paul. But somehow his priorities had shifted, and the things of this world came to mean more to him than the things of Christ. I wonder if he even realized it.

How different was Timothy, another young man who traveled and worked with Paul. He faced the same temptations as Demas, but our last glimpse of him is far different. Timothy also faced numerous challenges and pressures, but the picture that emerges of him in Paul's letters is of a young man determined not to give in to the enticements of this world, but to heed with all his might Paul's injunction to "endure hardship . . . like a good soldier of Christ Jesus" (2 Timothy 2:3). No wonder Paul called him "my dear son" (2 Timothy 1:2).

Demas—or Timothy? Which will you be?

The Pressures

Unfortunately many Christians end up following Demas's path, often without even realizing it. They have committed themselves to Christ, and for a time He is at the center of their lives. But gradually Christ gets pushed to the margins, and other things begin taking His rightful place. Preoccupied with the routines of daily living and pressured by the world's values, they become like the man in Jesus' story who welcomes the Word of God at first, but then "the worries of this life, the deceitfulness of wealth and the desires for other things come in and choke the word, making it unfruitful" (Mark 4:19).

Why does it happen? *There are many reasons, but one is the pressure of time.* Our lives become so hectic that we end up forgetting God. "I pray whenever I think to," one woman told me, "but since the baby came, that's only every few days."

Another reason God gets pushed to the margins is the pressure of the crowd. One man wrote, "I'm a Christian, but I don't want my boss to think I'm an oddball, do I?" A college student confessed, "I was a strong Christian in high school, but now that I'm away from home it's easier to go along with the crowd."

A further problem is unconfessed sin. Small sins grow into big sins, and instead of asking, "What is God's will?" when we're tempted, we say instead, "How much can I get by with and still be a Christian?"

A final reason, however, is often at the heart of the problem: Our spiritual discipline grows lax. Our Bible stays on the shelf; prayer becomes hurried or almost nonexistent; vibrant fellowship with other believers dissolves into passive church attendance; our service to others vanishes. We become self-satisfied and spiritually stagnant instead of yearning to "grow in the grace and knowledge of our Lord and Savior Jesus Christ" (2 Peter 3:18). "God is always there if I need Him," we think to ourselves, "but in the meantime I can just coast along."

Don't forget: Without fuel, a fire grows cold—and without the "fuel" of the Bible, prayer, and Christian fellowship, our faith grows cold. When that happens, Satan has gained victory over us just as surely as if he had trapped us in flagrant sin or blatant unbelief. We have let the routines of daily living smother our faith.

The Basic Principle

What is the solution? The first step, of course, is to realize the problem. "I'm just an ordinary Christian," we say, excusing our spiritual mediocrity and concluding God isn't concerned about it.

But this overlooks a very important principle from the Bible: *Christ wants to extend His authority to every part of our lives.* Nothing is to be omitted, for nothing is outside His concern. Sin has tarnished every area of life, and He wants to erase its stain *everywhere*.

All too often we confine God to one day of the week, assuming the other six belong to us. Or we conclude God is only interested in our souls and isn't concerned about so-called worldly things—our time, money, job, or family. In other words, we divide up our lives and put God into one compartment, while leaving Him out of the others.

But this is a serious error—and one Satan hopes we'll make! If he can persuade us to keep God confined to one day a week, or only one part of our lives, then he has gained a great victory. But someday Satan will be defeated and Christ's Lordship will be reestablished over all creation—and God wants this to begin right now.

What keeps Christ from *every* part of your life? Is it because you want to control it yourself? Or because you've never realized He wants to extend His authority over everything? Is some sin keeping you from His Lordship over your life? Whatever the reason, give yourself without reserve to Christ and submit every area of your life to His control. The Bible says, "Commit your way to the LORD; trust in him and he will do this: He will make your righteousness shine like the dawn" (Psalm 37:5–6).

The Time Trap

It's trite but still true: We all have exactly the same number of minutes in a day. The question is, how will we use them?

Most people today are either too busy—or not busy enough. Either our schedules are so hectic we can't get everything done, or else we are bored and restless, constantly looking for something to amuse us. We are the most frantic generation in history—and also the most entertained. The Bible, however, tells us that both extremes are wrong.

Look at anyone whose life is so busy they never have a spare moment. A businessman asked me once, "What's wrong with being busy all the time? Doesn't the Bible tell us to be diligent and hardworking?" I assured him he was right, up to a point; the Bible *does* say, "Whatever your hand finds to do, do it with all your might" (Ecclesiastes 9:10). It also reminds us, "Lazy hands make a man poor, but diligent hands bring wealth" (Proverbs 10:4).

But sadly, this businessman was a living illustration of the dangers of being too busy. By his own admission he worked sixty or seventy hours a week, leaving little time for his family or rest. His marriage was in shambles; his children had turned against him; his health was shattered. In addition, he constantly felt guilty and depressed because he couldn't get everything done. On the verge of burnout, his life had no joy or peace.

On the other hand, some people have too much spare time. Bored and constantly seeking excitement, they feed their minds on a constant diet of empty entertainment (much of which glorifies violence or promotes immoral behavior), or else they drift into drugs or alcoholism or other kinds of destructive behavior.

We can't always choose how to use our time, of course; sometimes our circumstances control us. My heart always goes out to the single mothers who write me, struggling every day just to survive. Disability, illness, unemployment, or retirement may keep us from doing what we once did and make us feel useless and only "killing time." But even if circumstances control our time, we can still control our attitude—with God's help. He can also help us gain more control over our time and begin to use it in new ways.

Using Time Wisely

How can we use our time wisely? Let me suggest four steps I have found helpful.

First, see each day as a gift from God. Instead of seeing each day as a burden, see it instead as another opportunity God has given you to serve Him. Time isn't inexhaustible, nor can we assume we'll always have more; some day our time on earth will end. The psalmist said, "My times are in your hands" (Psalm 31:15). The first thing we should do when we awake is thank God for the gift of another day.

Second, commit your time to God. God gave it to you for a reason: not to be wasted or mishandled, but to be used for His glory. We are accountable to Him for the way we use our time, and once a minute passes it can never be reclaimed. The Bible says, "Teach us to number our days aright, that we may gain a heart of wisdom" (Psalm 90:12).

How can we put this into action? It may mean asking God to help us schedule our time more wisely and efficiently. It may mean rethinking how we spend our time, and then adjusting it to reflect God's priorities. We may also need to examine why we're so busy (or so bored). Is what we are doing really necessary—or are we simply trying to impress others? We can't do everything, and we need to say "no" if some activity isn't God's will.

Third, set aside time for God and for others. No Christian would say, "I'm too busy for God," but how often have you gone through a whole day without even thinking about Him (let alone praying or reading the Bible)? How often have you ignored someone who needed your encouragement or help?

Why is this? One reason is because we relegate God to our spare time—but end up never having any spare time! In other words, we mentally list everything we have to do and put God at the bottom of the list. But the opposite should be the case. Jesus said, "Seek *first* his kingdom and his righteousness" (Matthew 6:33, emphasis added).

Finally, take time for your own needs. We all need rest and recreation; God made us this way. Some people feel guilty if they take a vacation or even a few hours off, but they shouldn't. In the midst of an incredibly busy schedule, Jesus told His disciples, "Come with me by yourselves to a quiet place and get some rest" (Mark 6:31). If Jesus required times of rest, don't we also? Someone who is chronically exhausted from lack of sleep or improper eating is much more susceptible to Satan's attacks.

With Christ at Work

How we use our time is important, but for most of us a major part of our day is already committed: We are working. This is true not only for those who earn a paycheck; those who stay home often work just as hard (or harder).

Many Christians, however, see little connection between their faith and their daily work, and may even see their work as a burden. After all, they say, didn't God judge Adam by expelling him from the Garden of Eden and decreeing that "by the sweat of your brow you will eat your food" (Genesis 3:19)? But this isn't the whole picture. Work in itself isn't evil; even before the Fall "The LORD God took the man and put him in the Garden of Eden to work it and take care of it" (Genesis 2:15). And in heaven, the Bible tells us, we won't only rest; God also will have work for us to do (Revelation 22:3).

Remember: Christ wants to extend His authority to every part of our lives—*including our work.* Is Christ the Lord of the work you do every day? How can this happen?

First, instead of seeing your job as a burden, see it as a responsibility given you by God. No matter what your work is, if it is legitimate then it has dignity, for it came from God. Our work may seem burdensome and meaningless, but once we realize God gave it to us, our attitude will change. The writer of Ecclesiastes discovered this truth: "A man can do nothing better than to . . . find satisfaction in his work. This too, I see, is from the hand of God" (Ecclesiastes 2:24).

We often speak of someone being "called" by God to the ministry or mission field, but if you know Christ and are in His will, you also have been called to your vocation. (In fact, the word "vocation" comes from a Latin word meaning "to be called.") Does this mean our work will never be dull or hard or tiring? No, of course not. But when we see our work as something God gave us, even the most routine tasks take on significance.

In addition, be faithful in your work. For most of His life, Jesus lived in Nazareth, where Mary and Joseph settled after returning from Egypt. Joseph was a carpenter, and Jesus followed in his steps and became a carpenter also (Mark 6:3).

How good a carpenter do you suppose Jesus was? If you had ordered a cabinet from Him, would you have found the doors didn't fit or the wood was split or He delivered it two months late? Of course not. Should we be any less faithful in our work?

Historians tell us that over half the population of the Roman Empire were slaves. (Some historians say Rome's eventual collapse was caused in part by its support of this morally repugnant institution.) With little chance for freedom, however, Christian slaves in the first century were urged to be faithful workers: "Obey your earthly masters in everything; and do it, not only when their eye is on you and to win their favor, but with sincerity of heart and reverence for the Lord" (Colossians 3:22). Owners also were commanded to be kind and just: "Provide your slaves with what is right and fair, because you know that you also have a Master in heaven" (Colossians 4:1). Over the centuries the seeds of human dignity planted by the Gospel would eventually challenge slavery wherever it existed (although not without many struggles), and slavery of any type today is an offense to God and rightly condemned. But although we live in a much different world, the underlying principle is unchanged: Whether you are an employee or an employer, do your work faithfully and responsibly and with a concern for the welfare of all who are impacted by your work.

Finally, do your work with integrity. Occasionally I receive letters from Christians who are in great turmoil over their work. Their bosses have demanded they do something illegal or deceptive, or they have been subjected to sexual harassment, or they have discovered fraud or some other illegal activity. These situations are often complex and difficult, and sometimes the right course of action isn't easy to discern. But no matter the cost, I tell them, do your work with honesty and integrity, and don't compromise God's moral standards. It may be difficult, but it's far better to do right than to do wrong. God is with you, and He will not abandon you.

The Bible says, "For you were once darkness, but now you are light in the Lord. Live as children of light (for the fruit of the light consists in all goodness, righteousness and truth) and find out what pleases the Lord. Have nothing to do with the fruitless deeds of darkness" (Ephesians 5:8–11). These words apply to every part of your life—including your work.

Don't let life's routines smother your faith, but submit your whole self (including your time and your work) to Christ's authority every day. Then use the "fuel" He has given us to keep your faith's flames alive—the "fuel" of the Bible, prayer, and Christian fellowship.

TWENTY-FOUR

FORKS IN THE ROAD

I will instruct you and teach you in the way you should go;
I will counsel you and watch over you.

—PSALM 32:8

W E CAN'T CHANGE THE PAST, BUT WE CAN CHANGE
the future.

"I'd give anything to be able to undo some of the decisions I've made," a man in prison wrote me not long ago. "I've made one bad decision after another, and now I'm paying the price." His situation may be different from yours, but who of us has never wished we could relive the past and undo the wrong choices we made?

Tragically, many people spend their lives trapped in an endless cycle of bad choices—and bad choices *always* have bad results. The Bible is right: "A man reaps what he sows" (Galatians 6:7). It also warns, "He who sows wickedness reaps trouble" (Proverbs 22:8).

Even Christians aren't immune from making wrong choices. One of life's hardest lessons is that we have to live with the consequences of our decisions—and that's why one of the most important skills we can ever develop in life is the ability to make wise choices.

The journey God has set before us isn't a freeway; we are constantly encountering forks and junctions and crossroads. Which way will we go when we meet them? Life is filled with decisions, and we can't avoid them. Some are minor; we may not even think about them. But others are major (even if we don't realize it at the time) and can literally change our lives. But does God really care about the choices and decisions we make?

Searching for God's Will

For years I prayed that the door might open for us to preach the Gospel in the Communist-dominated countries of Eastern Europe, especially the Soviet Union. When an invitation finally came to preach in Moscow, however, I was thrown into indecision. Had God truly opened the door, or was the devil attempting to lure us into a trap, a trap that could discredit or even destroy our ministry? I have seldom faced a more difficult decision, and I have seldom sought God's guidance more fervently.

The problem was that the invitation came with certain strings attached, including the requirement that I participate in an international peace conference. Such Moscow-sponsored events were usually little more than platforms for Soviet propaganda and often included attacks on the policies of other countries, including my own. Although this particular conference would be under church sponsorship, most observers assumed it would still be controlled behind the scenes by the Soviet government. If I attended, would I become an unwitting tool of Soviet propaganda? Would I be seen

as naive, or as compromising the Gospel? Even some of our organization's board members—men and women whose wisdom I
deeply respected—expressed doubts about my going. The American
vice president called to read a letter from one of our ambassadors
strongly urging me not to attend. Editorials and news stories also
appeared opposing it.

But the more I prayed (and also searched the Scriptures and
sought advice from others), the more convinced I became that God
was leading us to accept the invitation, in spite of the risks. I could,
I discovered, attend the peace conference as an observer instead of
a delegate, thus separating me from its pronouncements. I also
could address the conference on what the Bible says about peace—
including peace with God. I also would be able to preach in two
Moscow churches.

Finally I made the decision to go. Although the trip still caused
controversy, through it all I had a deep sense that God had led us.
Not only was I able to preach the Gospel in Moscow, but God later
opened the door to a much broader ministry in that part of the
world—something I never could have foreseen. Had I refused the
invitation, however, those opportunities never would have developed. I had faced a fork in the road, and God had shown me which
way to go.

Does God Care?

Does God really care about the decisions we make? Does God
have a plan for our lives—a plan we can actually know? Or does He
expect us to make all our decisions on our own?

The Bible's answer is clear: God knows all about us, and He
knows what is best for us. He sees the dangers we face, and He also
knows the joys we could experience. But God not only *knows* what

is best for us, He also *wants* what is best for us. The reason is simple: *He loves us.*

In spite of this, some people have difficulty believing God has a plan for their lives. "He's too busy to bother with me," they conclude. Others never think about God's will, assuming He has left it up to them to decide what to do. Still others have a different problem: They think God is a cruel tyrant who wants to oppress us. Why seek God's will, they think, if it will only make us miserable?

For most of us, however, the greatest barrier to knowing God's will is simply that we want to run our own lives. Our problem is that a battle is going on in our hearts—a battle between our wills and God's will. We may want Him to guide us when we think it's to our advantage—but then we seize control when we think He wants us to do something we don't want to do. "I know that what I'm about to do is wrong," one woman wrote me, "but I'm going to do it anyway. God will forgive me, won't He?"

But these ideas all miss the mark and are spiritually dangerous. They don't take into account who God is and how deeply He cares for us. One of the most important truths I can say about God's will is this: *God's will comes from God's love.* If God didn't love us, He wouldn't care which way we went when we face a decision. But He *does* love us—and that makes all the difference. Because He loves us, we can confidently seek His will, knowing it is always best for us—always. After all, if God loved us enough to send His Son into the world to die for our eternal salvation, doesn't He also love us enough to care about what happens to us tomorrow? The Bible says, "He who did not spare his own Son, but gave him up for us all—how will he not also, along with him, graciously give us all things?" (Romans 8:32).

God loves you—and because He loves you, He has a plan for your life. Don't let anything keep you from seeking it.

The Two Dimensions

How do we discover God's will? Pastors tell me this is the question they are asked most frequently—and with good reason. Could anything be more important than knowing God's will?

We need to realize first of all that God's will actually has *two dimensions* to it. *First, God has what might be called His universal or general will*—that is, His will for every person. This also could be called *His moral will*, because it has to do with our moral and ethical behavior.

God's universal will doesn't change from person to person; it applies to you just as much as it does to me. For example, God's will is for us to commit our lives to Christ and follow Him. God's will also is that we avoid sin; it is never God's will for us to lie or steal or commit sexual immorality or murder or be consumed with covetousness or greed. Do those sound familiar? They should, because they come from the Ten Commandments (which you can find in Exodus 20 and Deuteronomy 5).

Where do we discover God's universal will—His will for every person, including you and me? *We find it in the Bible.* In fact, one reason God gave the Bible to us is so we can know His will: "All Scripture is God-breathed and is useful *for teaching, rebuking, correcting and training in righteousness*" (2 Timothy 3:16, emphasis added). The Bible says, "How can a young man keep his way pure? By living according to your word" (Psalm 119:9).

Sometimes the Bible gives us very specific rules to follow. You don't need to ask God if it's wrong to cheat on your taxes; He has already told us to "Give everyone what you owe him: If you owe taxes, pay taxes; if revenue, then revenue" (Romans 13:7). Or again, you don't need to ask God whether or not it would be wrong to be unfaithful to your spouse; His command is very clear: "Flee

from sexual immorality" (1 Corinthians 6:18). God will never—
never—lead you to do something that is contrary to His written
Word, the Bible.

The Bible not only gives us specific rules, however. It also gives
us more general *moral and spiritual principles* to guide us. When Jesus
was asked to name the most important law in the Old Testament,
He replied with two principles: "'Love the Lord your God with all
your heart and with all your soul and with all your strength and
with all your mind'; and, 'Love your neighbor as yourself'" (Luke
10:27). How different our world would be if only we followed those
principles!

I don't remember when I first heard these words, but I've never
forgotten them: *If you are ignorant of God's Word, you will always be ignorant of God's will.* God has already answered many of our questions
about His will for our lives—but we haven't heard Him, because
we don't know the Bible. When we know God's Word, its principles
and precepts become a "filter" through which we automatically put
every decision, and God uses that inner filter to remove what is
wrong. Make the Bible part of your daily life, and ask God to
engrave its truths on your soul.

God's Individual Will

God, however, not only has a universal will that applies to
everyone. *The will of God also has a second dimension to it: His personal or individual will.* Unlike God's universal will, His personal
will differs from person to person. In other words, God's personal
will for me isn't the same as His personal will for you. God doesn't
sit back and simply watch us live our lives; He knows what is best
for each of us, and life's greatest joy comes from finding His plan
for us—and then doing it.

One of the happiest days of my life was when Ruth said she would be my wife. I could hardly contain my joy! But only a few years before I had faced one of the saddest days of my life, when another fine young woman with whom I thought I would be spending the rest of my life suddenly broke off our relationship. I was brokenhearted, convinced she must be making a mistake—but God knew better. Ruth was God's choice for me (just as I was God's choice for her), and I will always be grateful for His goodness in saving us for each other.

God has a personal, individual plan for each of us. It embraces the big things in life: whom we will marry, what our career will be, where we will live, even when we will die. It also includes the details of our daily lives: decisions about our families, finances, leisure time, friendships, and countless other choices we make. Are you seeking God's will in *everything*? The Bible says, "'For I know the plans I have for you,' declares the LORD, 'plans to prosper you and not to harm you, plans to give you hope and a future'" (Jeremiah 29:11).

Finding God's Will

The practical question, however, is this: How can we discover God's will when we face a major decision? Let me give you *six guidelines* I have found helpful.

First, commit your decision to God. Make it a matter of regular prayer, asking God to guide you and make His will known to you. Ask Him for the wisdom you need, and ask Him also to show you if you are resisting His will. If so, repent of it, and submit your will afresh to the Lordship of Christ. Let the psalmist's prayer become yours: "Teach me your way, O LORD, and I will walk in your truth; give me an undivided heart" (Psalm 86:11).

Unfortunately it's easy to omit this first step. We claim we want God's will—but then we rush off in all directions, frantically trying to decide what to do without ever pausing to ask God to guide us. Or sometimes we assume we already know which way is best—although God may have other plans for us. Don't let this happen to you, but commit *every* decision to Him—not just when it first arises, but throughout the whole process.

Second, search the Scriptures. Does the Bible give any direct guidance about the decision you are facing? Does any principle in the Bible apply to your situation? Did anyone in the Bible ever face a similar decision, and if so, how did they deal with it? (We can even learn from the wrong decisions some of them made.) Remember also what we said above: God never leads us to do anything that is contrary to His written Word.

Third, understand your circumstances. God isn't only working *in* us; He also is working *around* us. Often God guides us through our circumstances.

For example, God made you a unique person, and He wants you to understand your abilities and limitations. God doesn't normally tell us to do something if He hasn't given us the ability to do it. Or God may lead us by opening or closing a door of opportunity as we seek His will. God also expects us to use wisdom as we make decisions. Have we weighed the consequences? Have we investigated the alternatives to the best of our ability?

Fourth, seek godly advice. God has given some people a special gift of wisdom, and when we face a decision, it's often helpful to seek their counsel. The Bible says, "Plans fail for lack of counsel, but with many advisers they succeed" (Proverbs 15:22). Weigh carefully what they say, of course, but God may use them to help you understand your situation. I will always be grateful for the many people God has given me over the years who willingly shared their wisdom and experience with me. Their counsel has been indispensable in helping me discern God's will.

Fifth, trust the Holy Spirit's guidance. When we honestly seek His will, God often gives us an inner conviction or prompting to confirm which way He wants us to go. The Bible says, "Whether you turn to the right or to the left, your ears will hear a voice behind you, saying, 'This is the way; walk in it'" (Isaiah 30:21).

This prompting comes from the Holy Spirit, who lives within us if we know Christ. Jesus said, "When he, the Spirit of truth, comes, he will guide you into all truth" (John 16:13). This inner conviction isn't just a feeling; it is a settled peace that God is leading us in a certain way.

The Holy Spirit doesn't work in isolation, however, and we must guard against confusing our own desires with the Holy Spirit's prompting. We still need to pray, study God's Word, examine our circumstances, and seek godly advice. But God often uses this inner prompting to move us toward a final decision.

Finally, trust God for the outcome. Once God leads you to make a decision, don't draw back. Instead, trust His leading, and believe He goes before you—for He does. Sometimes we'll only be certain God led us *after* we make a decision, but when we truly are seeking His will, He has promised to guide us even if the way is unclear.

One young man I know seems to have thousands of questions about God's will for his life. He talks to everyone about it; he gets advice from everybody he meets; he spends hours talking and wrestling with God's will for his life—but he never reaches a decision.

Don't sit back and wait for some great revelation to come to you while life passes you by. Sometimes it's best to start moving in the direction you think God may want you to go, and then trust Him to lead you—closing doors He doesn't want you to go through and opening up others. The Bible says, "Trust in the LORD with all your heart and lean not on your own understanding; in all your ways acknowledge him, and he will make your paths straight" (Proverbs 3:5–6).

Remember: God loves you, and He *wants* you to know His will. Seek it . . . discover it . . . and then do it. His way is always best.

TWENTY-FIVE

FOR BETTER OR FOR WORSE

*For this reason a man will leave his father and mother and be united
to his wife, and they will become one flesh.*

—GENESIS 2:24

NOTHING BRINGS MORE JOY THAN A GOOD MARRIAGE,
and nothing brings more misery than a bad marriage.

Looking back, I realize that as a young man I thought a great
deal about *getting* married—but I gave much less thought to what it
actually meant to *be* married.

One day a man drove up to the house where I was living during
my last year in college. He was a deacon in a small church nearby and
said the congregation was interested in talking with me about becoming their pastor. During that year I had been preaching in various
churches fairly regularly, and apparently some of them had heard me

speak. After talking with them and praying about it, I accepted their invitation.

The only problem was that Ruth and I were engaged to be married immediately after graduation—and I had completely forgotten to consult her about the decision! It affected her just as much as it did me, and it should have been *our* decision, not just mine. She immediately let me know what she thought of my insensitivity, and I couldn't blame her for being upset. I was beginning to learn—slowly, I'm afraid—that there was a lot more to marriage than simply enjoying each other's company. Over sixty years later I'm still learning.

Marriage: God's Gift

What is marriage? The most important truth we need to know about marriage is that *God gave it to us*. Marriage is God's invention, not ours! Society didn't establish it; God did. Long before sin ever entered the world, God looked down at Adam and declared, "It is not good for the man to be alone. I will make a helper suitable for him" (Genesis 2:18).

Up to that point God had pronounced everything He had made as "good." But now He declared that something was *not* good: Adam's solitary state. Although Adam enjoyed unhindered fellowship with God, that wasn't enough. Adam also needed another person with whom he could share his life—and so God created Eve. The first wedding was performed by God in the Garden of Eden. Marriage is God's gift, meant to bless us and make us complete.

Meant for Each Other

Why did God give marriage to us? The Bible gives several reasons. *For one thing, God gave marriage to us for our companionship.*

God told Adam to search the animal kingdom for a suitable companion, "but for Adam no suitable helper was found" (Genesis 2:20). Adam was made in God's image, and just as love is part of God's nature, so love was part of Adam's nature. He needed someone to love, and He needed to be loved in return. Only another person could take away his loneliness and make him complete.

I'm always encouraged when I hear someone say, "My wife [or husband] is my best friend." Frequently over the years Ruth and I have had to be separated by my travels, sometimes for long periods of time. More than once tears have welled up in my eyes as I left home to catch still another train or airplane. Now that old age is upon us, one of our greatest joys is simply being in each other's presence—wordlessly sitting holding hands, watching television together, praying and sharing the Bible with each other. We are discovering in a deeper way the joy of companionship.

God also established marriage for our mutual help and encouragement. Eve was to be someone who was "suitable" (or "adequate for") Adam—not his slave or servant, but someone who would help him fulfill God's mandate to "be fruitful and increase in number; fill the earth and subdue it" (Genesis 1:28). He could not fulfill God's mandate alone. Adam needed Eve—and Eve needed Adam. One wasn't superior to the other; they needed each other and were dependent on each other. I'm always saddened whenever I see a couple drift apart, each living almost as if their spouse didn't exist. It's also tragic to hear a husband or wife tear down their spouse with criticism or verbal abuse. We need each other's constant encouragement and help.

Designed for Happiness

In addition, God gave us marriage for our mutual happiness and pleasure. You can imagine Adam's delight when God brought Eve to him, and he responded with history's first love poem: "This is now bone of my bones and flesh of my flesh" (Genesis 2:23). (A scholar once told me that this was actually an exclamation, as though Adam were saying, "Hooray!") God wanted them to bring happiness to each other in every way—physically, emotionally, intellectually, spiritually.

Included was God's gift of sex. No gift from God has a greater capacity for joy and happiness, but over the centuries no other gift has been so abused and so twisted by sin. Sex wasn't only given to ensure the continuance of the human race (although that is an important part). Sex was also given by God as an intimate expression of a husband and wife's loving commitment to each other. Because of that, its purpose can only be fulfilled within the commitment of marriage: "For this reason a man will leave his father and mother and be united to his wife, and they will become one flesh" (Genesis 2:24). Sex was to be *a sign* of a couple's unity and *a seal* of their lasting commitment to each other.

God demands sexual purity and faithfulness not because He wants to make us miserable, but because He wants to make us happy. He knows far better than we do that sex outside of marriage *always* falls short of His perfect plan and can bring heartache and mistrust in its wake. If someone has been promiscuous before marriage, what reason will their spouse have for trusting them to be faithful within marriage? When a man and woman simply live together, one thing is always missing: *commitment*. And because they have no lasting commitment to each other, their relationship will always have a measure of instability and insecurity—always. An unbelieving world may say otherwise, but so-called "sexual liberation" is actually sexual slavery—slavery to our own lusts. The Bible warns, "Can a man scoop fire into his lap without his clothes being burned? Can a man walk on hot coals without his feet being scorched? So is he who sleeps with

another man's wife; no one who touches her will go unpunished"
(Proverbs 6:27–29).

Being a Family

A further reason God gave marriage to us was to provide for the well-being of our families. Added to the gift of sex was another divine gift: the gift of children. The Bible says, "Sons are a heritage from the LORD; children a reward from him" (Psalm 127:3).

But children need instruction and love if they are to become responsible, mature adults—and in God's design for the human race, that need was to be fulfilled within the security of the family. God knew that children grow and mature best in a stable, loving family, and this was one reason He gave marriage to us. Husbands and wives weren't just meant to live for themselves; they were also meant to live for the well-being of their children.

Admittedly, in an imperfect and broken world our families often fall far short of this ideal. Divorce, abuse, neglect, poverty, alcoholism, domestic violence, the death of a spouse—these and other problems that affect families are all tragic reminders of our fallen condition.

You may be experiencing some of these in your own life, and if so, you should not hesitate to seek help from people (such as your pastor or a trained counselor) who can assist you. These problems are often complex, and it may be very difficult for you to cope with them or recover from their damaging effects on your own. But never forget: God knows what you are going through, and He wants to surround you with His love and wisdom—and the love and wisdom of other people also. The Bible says, "Many are the sorrows of the wicked, but steadfast love surrounds the one who trusts in the LORD" (Psalm 32:10 ESV). The Bible also promises, "If any of you lacks wisdom, he should ask God, who gives generously to all without finding fault, and it will be given to him" (James 1:5).

Even when circumstances are difficult in our families, however, they must not keep us from striving to do our best. After they rebelled against God and were expelled from Eden, Adam and Eve fell far short of perfection while nurturing their family; one son (Cain) even murdered his brother (Abel). But if they apparently failed with Cain, they still succeeded with Abel, for we are told that "the LORD looked with favor on Abel" (Genesis 4:4). Even when divorce or death or some other problem tears our families apart, we must not give up. God cares about our families even more than we do, and with His help we still can do good things for our children.

Reflecting Christ

God gave marriage to us for a further reason: to reflect Christ. Just as others should see Christ in us as individuals if we are Christians, so they should see Him reflected in our marriages.

Love, joy, peace, patience, kindness, gentleness—these and all the other fruit of the Holy Spirit should be just as evident in the relationship between a Christian husband and wife as they are in our personal character (Galatians 5:22–23). More than that, a couple's unity should be a symbol of Christ's oneness with His people (Ephesians 5:22–33). Do others see Christ in your marriage?

What Goes Wrong?

No one is happier than the devil when a marriage goes wrong, for Satan's goal is always to block God's plan for us. This is why Satan's strongest attacks are often directed at our marriages, for he knows that a strong Christian marriage is a formidable tool in God's hands. Satan's first appearance in the Bible included an attack on a marriage—trying to divide Adam and Eve. His tactics have not changed. He *wants* our marriages to flounder and fail, because he knows that few things will discourage us more thoroughly on the journey God has set before us.

Someone once asked me what problem people write about more than any other in their letters to me, and I replied, "By far, difficulties in marriage." I know of few families today that aren't touched to some extent by the heartache of divorce, including our own. Why do so many marriages go wrong? Can anything be done?

The basic problem behind most marital difficulties can be summed up in one word: conflict. Conflict can take many forms, from couples who simply stop speaking to outright abuse and violence.

But what causes conflict in the first place? The sources are almost endless and aren't always easy to identify. Some conflicts come from problems that people bring into their marriages. They get married from feelings of insecurity or inferiority or from loneliness or from sexual passion or to escape a difficult home situation—any of which can become a source of conflict later on. Someone who comes from a home filled with anger, alcoholism, abuse, infidelity, or some other problem often has serious emotional scars that affect the way they deal with their spouse and lead to conflict. Or a person may be immature and irresponsible, always blaming others for their problems—and this causes conflict. Sometimes spouses have difficulty getting along simply because their personalities clash. If two strong-willed people marry, for example, they will have problems if they don't learn to compromise. Even interfering relatives can be a source of conflict.

Other conflicts are caused by problems that couples create for themselves. Marriage counselors have told me that one of the biggest problems they encounter is conflicts over money. Easy credit and slick advertising cause many couples to become overwhelmed by a sea of debt, which leads to conflict. I often get heartbreaking letters from people whose marriage is being torn apart by unfaithfulness, alcohol, gambling, neglect, or some other destructive sin.

One other source of conflict needs to be mentioned, however, and that is spiritual disharmony. Occasionally I get letters from Christian young people who are in love with a nonbeliever, and their parents oppose the relationship. They are hoping I'll convince their parents to let them get married—but I can't do so in good conscience. The Bible is clear: "Do not be yoked together with unbelievers" (2 Corinthians 6:14). For every letter like this, I receive at least another from an older Christian who ignored God's directive and married an unbeliever—and admits they have paid a painful price in unhappiness, disharmony, mistrust, unfaithfulness, or even divorce. Only occasionally do they tell me their spouse has finally come to Christ, usually after years of prayer and sacrifice.

The Basic Problem

Conflicts in marriage may be caused by many things, but behind almost every one is a more basic cause: selfishness.

Too many husbands and wives enter into marriage with the idea that their spouse exists for one purpose: to make them happy. But building a marriage on such a self-centered goal is building it on sand. If each is only interested in themselves, then neither will be interested in what they can do to make their spouse happy. When that happens, neither is going to feel fulfilled.

True love, however, is not self-centered. Have you ever asked yourself what love really is? To answer that, first ask yourself what the *opposite* of love is. As we noted earlier, the opposite of love isn't just hate, or even indifference, but *selfishness*. That's why love—true love, *agape* love—isn't just a romantic feeling or a physical attraction for someone. Many today confuse sexual attraction or emotional feelings with love, and the media reinforces this idea every day. Far too many people, I'm afraid, get their ideas about love and marriage from the latest celebrity love affair or the most recent film, music video, or talk show. But physical beauty fades, and emotions—while important—come and go. A marriage based *only* on physical attraction or romantic emotions is almost certainly doomed to failure right from the start. Only God—who gave us the capacity to love in the first place—can teach us the meaning of true love.

True Love

What is true love? As we saw earlier in the chapter on relationships, true love is *an act of the will*—a conscious decision *to do what is best for the other person instead of ourselves*. This is why marriage involves *commitment*, the commitment of a man and a woman to each other for as long as they both shall live.

When Ruth and I were married, we stood before our family and friends and said, "I do." By those words we were committing ourselves to each other for the rest of our lives. But we weren't just standing before the congregation; we were also standing before God and declaring our vows to Him. He had brought us together, and now we were vowing to God that we would love each other and be faithful to each other as long as we both would live. Our love was a solemn *commitment*, sealed in God's presence. Over the years when stresses and strains have come our way, Jesus' words have kept us true to each other: "Therefore what God has joined together, let man not separate" (Matthew 19:6).

Love's Portrait

"I want very much to get married," a young woman in college wrote me not long ago, "but I'm not sure I know what love is. I come from a broken home, and I've never seen much of what I'd call true love. Is there such a thing?"

Yes, I assured her, there certainly is such a thing as true love—and with God's help we can discover it. He wants to take away our sin and our selfishness and replace them with His love—the kind of love that makes us concerned not just for ourselves but for others. The Bible puts it this way: "Each of you should look not only to your own interests, but also to the interests of others" (Philippians 2:4).

This is true love—the kind of self-giving, sacrificial love Jesus Christ had for us when "he humbled himself and became obedient to death" (Philippians 2:8). Do you want to know what love is? Look at Jesus Christ, who willingly left heaven's glory to walk amid the sin and corruption of this world, and then made the greatest sacrifice of all—the sacrifice of His life on the cross—so we could be saved. He put us first instead of Himself—and that's what true love does.

Paul's description of self-giving love—what the Bible calls *agape* love—is often quoted at weddings, but quickly forgotten. But it should be engraved on our hearts and minds: "Love is patient, love is kind. It does not envy, it does not boast, it is not proud. It is not rude, it is not self-seeking, it is not easily angered, it keeps no record of wrongs. . . . It always protects, always trusts, always hopes, always perseveres. Love never fails" (1 Corinthians 13:4–5, 7–8).

This is God's road map for lasting love. How different our marriages (and our lives) would be if we followed it!

TWENTY-SIX

KEEPING THE FLAME ALIVE

As for me and my household, we will serve the LORD.

—JOSHUA 24:15

GARDENS DON'T GROW BY THEMSELVES; THEY NEED to be tended and cultivated and weeded. The same is true of a marriage.

Recently I heard about a couple who went to a nice restaurant to celebrate their wedding anniversary. Their server—a woman in her thirties—suspected it must be a special occasion, and when she inquired, they told her they had been married exactly sixteen years.

"Sixteen years!" she exclaimed, then shook her head and added wistfully, "I can't imagine being married to anyone that long." She went on to say that she had already been married twice, and the man with whom she was currently living had made it clear he had no intention of becoming husband number three. Sadly, marriage for her promised little more than a few years of temporary happiness.

I'm afraid this woman's pessimism about marriage could be echoed by many today. Divorce statistics have soared in recent decades, and some young people are even afraid to get married because they fear it won't last. In spite of this, however, almost no one enters into marriage planning for it to fail. Even the Hollywood actress or celebrity pop star walking down the aisle for the fourth or fifth time usually says something like, "I've finally found true love!" Unfortunately, their optimism is often an illusion. But must it always be this way? Is a happy and lasting marriage possible?

Broken Dreams

While this chapter was being written, one of our grandsons got married in the same chapel where Ruth and I said our vows more than sixty years before. As he and his lovely bride visited us, their love for each other and their obvious joy was a delight to see. Like almost every other young couple I've known, they hope theirs will be a perfect, flawless love leading to a lifetime of married happiness.

At the same time, I couldn't help but reflect on all the challenges they'll face in their life together. Like all newlyweds, they come from different backgrounds: different parents, different brothers and sisters, different experiences, even different hopes and dreams. I know they'll need to learn to adjust to each other, which is often difficult. I have great confidence in their maturity and their commitment, but I also know the path ahead will have its share of rough places. Every marriage does—and Satan will do everything he can to exploit them.

Tragically, many couples enter marriage with very romantic ideals, confident their feelings of love and excitement will see them through any difficulty. After all, isn't that what the latest pop songs promise? But then problems arise, and instead of working together to solve them, they begin saying to themselves, "Did I marry the wrong person? He isn't 'Mr. Perfect' after all! Maybe I made a mistake . . . maybe I ought to find someone else."

Divorce has become so common today that we often lose sight of its painful consequences. Some of you know what I'm talking about, because your own life has been scarred by divorce, either that of your parents or your own. Even now you may be struggling with feelings of rejection, bitterness, anger, or failure—all of which often follow in the wake of a divorce. Let me assure you that God understands what you are going through, and He still loves you and wants to comfort and guide you. May you find new hope in Christ as you turn to Him, and may God also bring across your path people who can help and encourage you.

Every divorce represents a broken dream, a shattered hope, a ruined expectation. Every divorce also represents a violation of God's original blueprint for marriage—a blueprint that included the commitment of a husband and wife to each other "as long as we both shall live."

Preventive Medicine

I receive many letters from people whose marriages have ended, and the most frequent phrase they use to describe what happened is something like this: "It just didn't work out."

But divorce isn't something that "just happens," any more than an earthquake "just happens." Some years ago Ruth and I flew to Guatemala immediately after a powerful earthquake hit that country to see how we could help, and I have seldom seen such devastation. Our hosts reminded us that the earthquake had happened because pressures and tensions had been building up beneath the earth's surface for many years, like a tightly wound spring. Finally those subterranean pressures became so intense that they suddenly exploded along a weakness (or fault) in the earth's crust, causing massive destruction. The earthquake didn't just happen; it was the result of years of growing pressure. The same is true when a marriage breaks down. Behind many divorces are pressures that may have taken years to develop.

But there is one important difference between an earthquake and a broken marriage. Nothing can be done to prevent an earthquake—but often much *can* be done to prevent a broken marriage. Every marriage is different, of course, and not every marriage can be saved, despite our best efforts. Sometimes the problems are too deep and tangled. But I am convinced many marriages *could* be salvaged if steps were taken in advance to prevent those destructive pressures from building up—and not only salvaged, but made healthy and strong and fulfilling.

What are these steps? From my own experience and the experience of others (as well as my study of the Bible), let me outline *three cornerstones* for building a stable, fulfilling marriage. We might call them *three steps for keeping the flame alive*. Admittedly they don't cover everything; they are only a starting point, and problems that have taken years to develop won't be solved overnight. Nevertheless, just as a doctor tries to spot problems before they develop, so these steps can be "preventive medicine" for your marriage, heading off problems before they develop.

Commit It to God

The first cornerstone in developing a healthy marriage is also the most important: Commit your marriage to God.

Years ago someone gave me a watch that had been made in Switzerland. For years it kept perfect time, but one day it stopped working. I took it to be repaired, but after examining it, the man shook his head and said, "I'm sorry, you'll have to send it back to the manufacturer. The only person who can fix it is the one who made it." The same is true of marriage.

God designed marriage and gave it to us. Doesn't it make sense, therefore, to follow His instructions for taking care of our marriage? Doesn't it also make sense to turn to Him when something goes wrong? If we disregard God's plan for marriage, our homes will always be in danger. A well-ordered family needs to be founded on a divinely ordered marriage. I have often said that a good marriage requires *three* persons: the husband, the wife—and God. Begin now by committing your marriage (as well as your life) to Christ.

What does it mean to commit your marriage to God? For one thing, it means taking your marriage vows very seriously—vows you made not only to each other but to God. This includes your vow of absolute faithfulness to each other. Hardly a day goes by without at least one heartbreaking letter reaching me from someone whose marriage has been torn apart by adultery.

Our society treats unfaithfulness lightly—but God doesn't, because He knows the pain and devastation it causes. One of the Ten Commandments bluntly declares, "You shall not commit adultery" (Exodus 20:14). One of the few crimes for which the death penalty was mandated in Old Testament times was adultery, indicating how seriously it was taken. The Bible warns, "A man who commits adultery lacks judgment; whoever does so destroys himself" (Proverbs 6:32). Don't wait until temptation comes crashing down upon you to decide whether or not you will keep your marriage vows; by then it's usually too late. Decide that issue *now*, and commit yourself without reserve to faithfulness *now*, so Satan won't be able to gain any advantage over you later.

Committing your marriage to God also means *growing together in your relationship with Christ*. God's will isn't just for us to grow spiritually as individuals, but to grow spiritually together as a couple if we are married. Nothing will bind you together more firmly than learning to walk daily with Christ—praying together, reading God's Word together, going to church together, having fellowship together. One of the cornerstones of a happy home is the spiritual discipline of turning together to God every day.

This isn't always easy with our busy schedules. The devil will always find something that is supposedly more important for you to do! If you have never prayed together before, start by pausing at the beginning of every meal to thank God for the food He has given you. As you become more comfortable praying together, add other concerns to your prayers. In the earlier years of our marriage, when our children were still at home, we had family devotions around the dining table after meals. Now Ruth and I read a passage of Scripture and have prayer together just before going to bed. The key is to find a time that fits your schedule, and then stay with it as much as possible. The Bible says, "Encourage one another and build each other up" (1 Thessalonians 5:11).

Give It Priority

The second step follows from the first: Commit yourself to your marriage.

All sorts of things clamor for our attention today: work, recreation, church, children, television, finances, social obligations—the list is almost endless. If we don't guard against it, our marriage will get crowded out. It may start by taking our spouse for granted, and then gradually drifting apart. But this is not God's plan.

One of the ways we demonstrate our love for God is by demonstrating our love for our spouses. The Bible says, "Husbands, love your wives, just as Christ loved the church and gave himself up for her" (Ephesians 5:25). Christ sacrificed Himself out of love for His people, and a husband should make sacrifices out of love for his wife. When Christ rules a marriage and fills it with His love, the Bible's mandate for wives to submit to (or "fit in with") their husbands and for husbands to love their wives as much as they love themselves becomes easy. A husband who puts Christ first will love and respect his wife, instead of acting like a tyrant (as some have unfortunately misunderstood these words).

What does it mean to commit yourself to your marriage? It means to *give priority to your marriage,* putting its welfare first. That means looking at everything you want to do in terms of its impact on your marriage. It means not seeing your marriage as only one of the many activities, but central to everything else. It means seeing your marriage as a responsibility and not just a privilege.

How important is your marriage to you? What are you doing to strengthen it? *Is it as important to you as it is to God?* Only you can answer these questions, of course—but don't ignore them. Give priority to your marriage, just as God does.

Affection and Respect

A third step in building a strong marriage is to treat each other with affection and respect.

Those may sound like different concepts, but they actually are closely related. Affection without respect means treating someone the way we might treat a pet—enjoying their presence, but looking down on them and denying they have anything important to contribute. On the other hand, respect without affection leads to a cold, unfulfilling relationship.

Mutual affection and respect are *both* essential for a strong marriage. The Bible says, "Each one of you also must love his wife as he loves himself, and the wife must respect her husband" (Ephesians 5:33). The apostle Peter wrote, "Husbands, . . . be considerate as you live with your wives, and treat them with respect" (1 Peter 3:7). Men and women are different from each other—God made us that way—and husbands and wives need to understand and accept those differences (and even delight in them). But one is not "better" than the other. Both the husband and wife are equal in God's eyes, for both bear His image and are equal in mind, conscience, privilege, and responsibility. Abuse of any type has no place in a marriage.

One important way to show respect for your spouse is to learn the art of communicating. This is more than just talking; it also means learning to listen. It means a willingness to share your thoughts with each other, without fearing your spouse will reject you or laugh at you. It means understanding each other on an emotional as well as rational level. In general we men find this harder to do than women, and we need to work on it. I'm sure Ruth has often come to me with a problem of some type, and I've simply given her a quick solution—instead of realizing that what she really needed was my concern and emotional support.

Don't let a day go by without telling your spouse that you love them. Show your affection spontaneously and frequently. A hug, a kiss, a gentle pat or squeeze of the arm, even a glance at each other can say, "I still love you." I vividly remember an elderly white-haired couple who lived in our small community when we first moved there. They had been well-known musicians and teachers, and we'd often see them out walking, holding hands like two love-struck teenagers. They didn't know it, but their example was teaching me something very important as a young husband.

In addition, be courteous, tender, and thoughtful to each other. It always saddens me to hear a husband put down his wife with sarcasm or a cutting remark, or a wife correct her husband or scold him like a little boy, especially in front of others. Think also of special ways you can show you care. When was the last time you surprised your spouse with a favorite dinner or an unexpected gift? Often the *little things* count most. Take care of yourself and your appearance also; by doing so you are treating your spouse with respect (as well as yourself).

I've also discovered humor is important in a marriage—not laughing *at* your spouse but laughing *with* them about life's little quirks. Be an encourager also; the Bible says, "Encourage one another daily" (Hebrews 3:13). Learn to forgive each other as well; my wife often says that "a good marriage consists of two good forgivers." Someone has said that the two most important phrases in a marriage are "I love you" and "please forgive me." Be sensitive also to each other's moods and hurts, and help each other when hard times come. Paul's words in Galatians 6:2 have special meaning for husbands and wives: "Carry each other's burdens, and in this way you will fulfill the law of Christ."

A Word to the Unmarried

Perhaps, however, you are single, either because you have never married or your marriage has been disrupted by divorce or death. Does this mean God considers you a second-class person, or you have somehow missed His plan for your life? No! I am convinced God calls some people to singleness, and they may be better equipped to serve Him as a result. Jesus was unmarried, and so was Paul. Some of God's choicest servants over the centuries have been those who never married. Don't look down on your state, but commit it to Christ and ask Him to fill your life and use you for His glory.

At the same time, don't allow yourself to be drawn into relationships that don't honor God, and avoid sexual impurity of any type (whether heterosexual or homosexual). Those around you may approve of such activities or even aggressively promote them, but if you belong to Christ, you are called to live by a different standard— God's standard. The Bible says, "Do not share in the sins of others. Keep yourself pure" (1 Timothy 5:22).

Or perhaps you are a young person, and you are saying to yourself, "This doesn't apply to me. I'm not even married yet." But someday you probably will be, and *now* is the time to commit your future marriage to God. God is far more concerned about your marriage than you are, and if you are a Christian, you can be sure that He has already chosen the person with whom He wants you to share your life, if it's His will for you to marry. Are you seeking His will for your future marriage? Have you committed this extremely important area of your life to Him? If not, do so *now*.

Avoid falling in love with the wrong person or for the wrong reasons. In our obsession with physical appearance today, we often overlook those inner, lasting qualities that make a spouse truly attractive. The Bible says, "Charm is deceptive, and beauty is fleeting; but a woman who fears the LORD is to be praised" (Proverbs 31:30). The Bible also says, "Your beauty . . . should be that of your inner self, the unfading beauty of a gentle and quiet spirit, which is of great worth in God's sight" (1 Peter 3:3–4).

Whatever your situation, make it your goal to honor God in everything—including your marriage.

TWENTY-SEVEN

PASSING THE BATON

Sons are a heritage from the LORD,
children a reward from him.

—PSALM 127:3

PARENTING IS THE MOST IMPORTANT RESPONSIBILITY most of us will ever face, and none of us does it perfectly.

If I could live life over again, I'd spend less time traveling and more time at home with Ruth and our children. Travel is an essential part of an evangelist's life (although less so with modern communications), but as I look back, I wonder if the countless trips I took were always necessary.

Being separated from my family for extended periods of time was hard—for them and for me. Calling home regularly—something I always tried to do, although it wasn't possible from some parts of the world—was no substitute for actually being there. I missed out on so much as our children were growing—but more important was what they missed by not having their father around. Recent studies suggest a child's character is largely shaped during their first six or eight years. I'm not surprised; almost three thousand years ago the Bible observed, "Train a child in the way he should go, and when he is old he will not turn from it" (Proverbs 22:6).

One summer I was preaching in Europe, and a friend kindly loaned us a house in Switzerland so Ruth and the children could be nearby. I left home some weeks before they did, and when I finally joined them there, I saw a cute toddler wandering around the yard as I drove up. Only after some minutes did I realize he was Ned, our youngest son. He had changed so much during my absence that I didn't recognize him—and he didn't recognize me. The realization of what we both had missed was like a knife in my heart.

Most of the responsibility for raising our five children rested on Ruth's shoulders—a calling she took just as seriously as I took mine as an evangelist. When home I tried to do everything I could to make up for my absences, but I still missed the joy of seeing our children grow and change. I thank God for watching over them during those years and turning them into the fine men and women they have become, but most of the credit goes to Ruth—and to the Lord.

The Gift of Children

We called them "our children," but we always knew they weren't really ours. They were a gift from God, entrusted to us for a few short years until they left to start their own families.

If you have children, never lose sight of the fact that *God gave them to you.* When Esau met his brother Jacob after many years of separation, he asked, "Who are these with you?" Jacob's reply is instructive: "They are the children God has graciously given your servant" (Genesis 33:5). Isaiah, raising his family in a society that had largely forgotten God, boldly declared, "Here am I, and the children the LORD has given me" (Isaiah 8:18). Our children are a gift from God, and someday we must give an account to Him for the way we raised them. For the Christian, family life isn't a detour; it's an important part of our discipleship.

Just as God gave us marriage, so He also gave us the family. Families aren't our invention; they are part of God's design for human society. Family life began with Adam and Eve; when their first child was born, Eve exclaimed, "With the help of the LORD I have brought forth a man" (Genesis 4:1). When Jesus entered the world, it was His Father's will for Him to grow to maturity within a family and experience the love and discipline of earthly parents. Some of the Bible's most alarming words speak of a time when families will break down because "people will be lovers of themselves . . . abusive, disobedient to their parents, ungrateful, unholy, without love" (2 Timothy 3:2–3). When the family is destroyed, society eventually disintegrates. Are we already living in those days?

Why Families?

God gave us our children—but why? *The main reason is so simple we sometimes lose sight of it: God gave us our children so we could prepare them to become adults.* From infancy until the day they finally leave home, our children are moving toward independence— and that is as it should be. If nothing intervenes, life will come full circle: The children we brought into the world will become parents themselves, and the baton will be passed to the next generation. The "empty nest" can be painful for parents, but it's also necessary.

Of course this isn't the whole story. We are to prepare our children for adulthood—but think of all it involves!

For one thing, it means doing all we can *to assure their physical survival*. Nothing is as helpless as a newborn baby—or as demanding. Sometimes young mothers write me saying they thought motherhood would be fun, but instead they're exhausted and overwhelmed. I always try to point out the importance of what they are doing, for children need their constant care if they are to survive. Recently our son Franklin has become deeply involved in the desperate plight of children who have been orphaned because of the AIDS crisis, particularly in Africa. His stories are heartbreaking, with thousands dying each year because they have no one to care for them.

Much of what we do as parents—feeding our children, taking them to the doctor, protecting them, warning them about dangers, and so forth—we do in order to help them survive the perils of youth. It is one of our God-given responsibilities.

Emotional and Mental Development

Our responsibility as parents, however, doesn't stop with providing for our children's physical needs. They may grow into healthy young men and women—but if that's *all* they become, we have failed to prepare them for life. More than that, we have failed to help them become the individuals God wants them to be.

This leads to a second reason why God gives us children: to help them develop mentally and emotionally. Without this, they will enter adulthood ill-prepared and doomed to failure.

To do this we provide for their education and pass on the skills we have learned. We also help them deal with life's hurts and teach them responsibility. In addition, we help them learn to build healthy relationships. While Jesus was with His family, He "grew in wisdom and stature, and in favor with God and men" (Luke 2:52).

We should also help our children develop a healthy and balanced view of themselves. They should know we love them and believe they can make a unique contribution in life. Recently I heard about a woman who taught at one of our major universities. She was widely recognized as a brilliant scholar and was asked to become head of her department. She refused, however, because she had no confidence in herself. She eventually sought help from a counselor, and as they talked, he discovered her father had always belittled her. Instead of complimenting her when she did well, he scolded her for not doing better and told her she must be stupid. Perhaps he thought he was helping her—but is it any wonder she grew up without any confidence in herself?

Emotional and mental development doesn't just happen; it requires deliberate effort on our part. The writer of Proverbs urged, "My son, pay attention to my wisdom, listen well to my words of insight" (Proverbs 5:1). An old Chinese proverb says that a child is like a piece of paper on which every person leaves a mark. This is especially true of parents with their children.

Shaping Character

God has given us our children for another reason, however—one that is of supreme importance: to help shape their moral and spiritual character.

Children may become adults physically, mentally, and emotionally—but if they have no moral and spiritual foundations, they will never know lasting stability. Jesus compared such a person to a man who built his house on sand: "The rain came down, the streams rose, and the winds blew and beat against that house, and it fell with a great crash" (Matthew 7:27). If our children grow up with no understanding of right and wrong . . . no desire to live with integrity . . . no faith in God . . . their souls will be impoverished and they will miss life's highest good. They will be like those "whose own strength is their god" (Habakkuk 1:11).

Moral and spiritual character doesn't just happen, however, any more than physical, mental, and emotional development just happen. Occasionally parents tell me they'll let their children make up their own minds about life and they don't plan to teach them about God or morality. This saddens me, not only because I believe those parents are abdicating their responsibility, but because I know what will probably happen to their children. Like their parents, they will grow up without any moral and spiritual foundations.

This doesn't mean we can "program" moral and spiritual convictions into our children. They aren't computers: They have a will of their own, and as they grow older, they may reject what we taught them. One of life's mysteries is why two children growing up in the same home sometimes take radically different paths—one following Christ, the other rebellious and scornful. Yet it happens.

We can't *make* our children believe as we do—*but we can provide the right environment for their moral and spiritual growth to take place.* Do we teach them what is right and wrong—or are they getting their ideas from the latest movie? Most important, do they see Christ in us? The Bible says, "Show them the way to live and the duties they are to perform" (Exodus 18:20). It also says, "Teach them [God's commandments] to your children, talking about them when you sit at home and when you walk along the road, when you lie down and when you get up" (Deuteronomy 11:19).

Being Wise Parents

Almost nothing is more important than raising our children—or more challenging. Every child is different . . . every family is different . . . and every day is different!

How can we become better parents? Let me suggest *four guidelines* Ruth and I have found helpful.

First, commit your family to God. Raising a family is so difficult—and so important—that we dare not do it alone. We need God's wisdom and help every day. Someone once asked Ruth how she raised our five children, and without hesitation she replied, "On my knees!"

What does it mean to commit your family to God? It means *seeking to follow God's Word* in your family. The Bible isn't a detailed handbook on child rearing; it doesn't tell us exactly what to do in every possible situation. But it does give us principles for raising our children, and we ignore them at our peril. For example, Colossians 3:21 says, "Fathers, do not embitter your children, or they will become discouraged." (Or as another translation says, "If you are too hard to please, they may want to stop trying" [NCV].) Are we following this principle?

Committing our families to the Lord also means *teaching them about God.* When our children were young, we regularly read together from a Bible storybook (usually at bedtime) and always led them in prayer before meals. As they grew older, the children would each take a turn thanking God for our food. Praying with each of them and taking them to church likewise helped them understand God's place in our lives. Most of all, we prayed for them regularly and encouraged them to give their lives to Jesus. Remember: Children learn not only from what we say, but from what we do.

Ruth and I usually had family devotions around the kitchen table after breakfast. We always read a brief Bible passage (sometimes giving each child a verse to read) and then had prayer. Make family devotions interesting—and keep them short! Once I asked a visiting clergyman to lead our family devotions, and his prayer went on and on. Soon our children began squirming, and finally the youngest piped up: "Daddy, that's too long!"

Giving Time

A second guideline is *give priority to your family.* Some parents have difficulty with this, because they are more committed to their careers or social life than their families. "I provide for them, don't I?" more than one busy father has told me, not realizing that what his child really wanted was not more toys, but more of his time. Our children should grow up feeling they are special, but it won't happen if we are too busy. Sometimes we need to stop and ask ourselves, "How will my children remember their childhood? Will their memories be of fun and happiness? Or will they be resentful because I didn't make time for them?"

Children can also learn from their extended family. One of the greatest benefits our children had was being able to spend time with their grandparents, especially Ruth's parents who lived nearby. Many of their happiest memories come from those times with their grandparents.

One reason many families are in trouble is because parents repeat the mistakes their own parents made. But it doesn't need to be that way. One man I knew was raised in a very abusive home, then shuttled from one relative to another. He came to Christ through a caring Sunday school teacher, and later, when he became a parent, he determined he would do better than his parents (and he did). He told me, "You cannot choose the type of family into which you're born, but you can choose the type of family you establish for your children." I wish more parents had his wisdom.

Love at the Center

A third guideline is this: Put love at the center of your family. Love your children—and let them know you love them. God loves them, and so should you. Children who experience love find it far easier to believe God loves them.

Encourage them also. In her private journal (in which she recorded her thoughts and prayers) Ruth once wrote, "Dear Journal, Never let a single day pass without saying an encouraging word to each child. . . . 'More people fail for lack of encouragement,' someone wrote, 'than for any other reason.'"

Love doesn't mean giving our children everything they want. Love sometimes means we say "No" or "Don't"—not because we hate our children, but because we love them and know better than they do what is best for them. Children need our discipline and correction, for whether they like it or not, life is filled with rules and laws. One of the worst things we can do is allow our children to grow up thinking they don't need to keep any rules. A spoiled child becomes a spoiled adult.

I find most children (including adolescents) sense they need guidance and discipline. Even when they are testing the limits, they appreciate a parent who is willing to say, "No—I love you too much to let you do this." The Bible warns, "Discipline your son . . . ; do not be a willing party to his death" (Proverbs 19:18).

By discipline I don't mean constant scolding or lecturing or physical abuse or anger. When a child has to be disciplined, he or she should understand why. Children differ from each other; one of our children usually needed only a disapproving look, while others required stronger measures. Discipline should be firm, fair, sane, and consistent. The Bible says, "A child left to himself disgraces his mother. . . . Discipline your son, and he will give you peace; he will bring delight to your soul" (Proverbs 29:15, 17).

The Open Door

Finally, keep the door open. Someday your children will leave; you can't hold on to them or control them forever, nor should you. But don't let that be the end of your relationship!

Hopefully the relationship has been good, and they will leave with your blessing. Some, however, may be prodigals. Both our sons went through times of rebellion and risky behavior, causing us more than one sleepless night—and much, much prayer. All our children also have gone through periods of discouragement or hurt. But they always knew that we loved them and they were always welcome at home. The Bible's picture of a godly leader also describes the godly home: "A shelter from the wind and a refuge from the storm, like streams of water in the desert and the shadow of a great rock" (Isaiah 32:2). May that be true of your home.

As you have read this chapter, you may have found yourself filled with regret or sorrow—or even anger. Perhaps the family in which you were raised fell far short of what it should have been, or perhaps your own family is now torn by conflict and heartache. Whatever your situation, face it honestly—and then hand it over to Christ. Don't be a slave to the past, but ask God to help your family become everything He wants it to be.

TWENTY-EIGHT

MAKING AN IMPACT

You are the light of the world. . . . Let your light shine before men,
that they may see your good deeds and praise your Father in heaven.
— MATTHEW 5:14, 16

W HY DOESN'T GOD TAKE US TO HEAVEN THE moment we commit our lives to Christ?

After all, since heaven is our ultimate destination, wouldn't it be better if God took us there immediately and spared us all the problems and heartaches of this life? Then we'd never again have to experience worry or sorrow or suffering, and all the burdens and temptations that trouble us now would vanish. *Why doesn't God take us to heaven the minute we commit our lives to Christ?*

The reason is simple: *God still has work for us to do right here.* Heaven is our goal, but until that final moment when He takes us home to Himself, God has a purpose in keeping us here. Earth isn't just heaven's waiting room, where we sit around doing nothing until it's finally time for us to depart. Earth is the stage on which the drama of the ages is being played out—the drama of Christ's victory over sin and death and hell and Satan. And no matter who we are, we have a God-given role to play in that divine drama.

The Divine Purpose

What is this role God has for us? Why does He keep us here?

The Bible gives us the answer: *As long as we are on this earth, God's purpose is for us to bring honor and glory to Him by the way we live.* The Bible says God "chose us in him [Christ] before the creation of the world . . . in order that we, who were the first to hope in Christ, might be for the praise of his glory" (Ephesians 1:4, 12). Jesus told His disciples, "By this my Father is glorified, that you bear much fruit and so prove to be my disciples" (John 15:8 ESV). Is your goal to bring glory to God in everything you do?

But this doesn't fully answer our original question: What is God's reason for keeping us here?

To answer this, imagine what our world would be like if God *did* take us to heaven when we first believed. Without anyone left to demonstrate Christ's compassion and righteousness, what kind of world would it be? Without anyone left to tell others about God's love, how would anyone ever hear about Christ or put their trust in Him? The answer is obvious: Our world would be condemned to live in perpetual spiritual darkness, forever bound by fear and hopelessness and evil.

Why does God keep us here? For one reason: *to tell the world the Good News of Christ.* The Bible says, "You are a chosen people, a royal priesthood, a holy nation, a people belonging to God, *that you may declare the praises of him who called you out of darkness into his wonderful light*" (1 Peter 2:9, emphasis added). Jesus' command to His disciples has never been revoked: "Go into all the world and preach the good news to all creation" (Mark 16:15).

Does this mean we are all supposed to be preachers or evangelists or missionaries? No—although some are. But it does mean we *are* all called to be witnesses for Christ, bringing His love and trans-forming power to a broken and confused world.

One Man's Impact

The story of "The Mutiny on the Bounty" has fascinated read-ers and moviegoers for generations. What happened afterward, however, isn't as well-known—yet is equally fascinating.

For reasons that are still debated, in 1789 the crew of the *HMS Bounty* mutinied against the alleged cruelty of their captain, William Bligh. Bligh and a few others were set adrift in a small boat, but the mutineers stayed with the *Bounty* and eventually landed on an isolated, uninhabited speck of land in the South Pacific called Pitcairn Island. There were only twenty-five of them—nine British sailors and six men and ten women from Tahiti—and shortly after landing they burned the *Bounty* and set about forming a perma-nent settlement.

But their experiment soon turned into a disaster. Conflicts arose between the rough British sailors and the Tahitians, leading to vio-lence and murder. One sailor also discovered a method for distill-ing alcohol from a native plant, turning their tropical paradise into a den of drunkenness, vice, and debauchery. Finally only a hand-ful of the Tahitians and one British sailor, John Adams, survived.

One day Adams discovered the ship's Bible that had been res-cued from the *Bounty* years before, but then forgotten. He began reading, and God used its words to convict Adams of his sin and lead him to faith in Christ. His life was dramatically changed, and almost immediately he began sharing Christ with his fellow exiles. Both Adams's changed life and the Bible's message spoke to them, and they too were converted. When some American sailors stopped by Pitcairn Island in 1808—the first visitors they had ever had—they found a prosperous and harmonious community with no jail, no alcohol, no crime, and no immorality. God had used the witness of one man, John Adams, to transform the entire colony.

All Bottled Up

Far different from John Adams's contagious witness is a letter I received recently from a woman who acknowledged that she and her husband weren't religious and never went to church. Then she added, "Most of our relatives claim to be Christians, and yet none of them ever calls us or invites us over or sends us birthday cards, or even visited me when I was in the hospital. One of them told my cousin that the reason they don't have anything to do with us is because we aren't Christians. If that's the way Christians act, then I don't want anything to do with them."

I urged her to look at Christ, for only He is perfect, and only He will never disappoint us. But her letter sobered me, and I couldn't blame her for feeling the way she did. After all, why should she believe Christ loves her, if those who claim to be His followers don't love her? I don't know if those relatives are actually Christians—but if so, they have completely misunderstood why God keeps them here. Instead of attracting others to Christ, such people turn them away from Him because of their lack of love.

When we come to Christ, God calls us out of this world's sin and confusion. *But then He sends us back into the world*—not to share any longer in its sin and spiritual darkness, but to bear witness to the light of Christ. Jesus said, "As the Father has sent me, I am sending you" (John 20:21). He also prayed concerning His disciples, "I do not ask that you take them out of the world, but that you keep them from the evil one [Satan]" (John 17:15 ESV). The Bible compares us to salt, lamps, yeast, and seed—none of which is of any use as long as it's kept in a closed container. Doing so might preserve them—but that isn't their purpose. Salt was meant to be sprinkled on food to preserve it or make it appetizing; lamps were meant to shine, dispelling the darkness and lighting our way; yeast was meant to leaven the flour so it can be baked and eaten; seed was meant to be sown so crops will grow and bear fruit.

So too with us. How can we remain silent and unconcerned, bottling up the Gospel instead of sharing it with others? To do so is to miss God's purpose in keeping us here. Jesus said, "You are the light of the world. A city on a hill cannot be hidden. Neither do people light a lamp and put it under a bowl. Instead they put it on its stand, and it gives light to everyone in the house" (Matthew 5:14–15). Paul commended the Christians in Rome "because your faith is being reported all over the world" (Romans 1:8). The Christians in Thessalonica faced severe opposition, but Paul could still write that "the Lord's message rang out from you . . . your faith in God has become known everywhere" (1 Thessalonians 1:8).

Reaching Out to a Broken World

Unfortunately, too many Christians are like the relatives of the woman I quoted above: indifferent to the needs of others and unconcerned about their spiritual welfare. Some know they ought to be concerned, but don't know what to do. How can this change? How can we make an impact for Christ on our hurting world?

First, ask God to help you see the world the way He sees it. All around you are people whose lives have been broken and torn apart by the ravages of sin and the harshness of life. For others, life is a constant, unending struggle just to survive. Does God care? Should we?

Someone told me recently about a college student who went on a short-term mission trip to an impoverished country that is constantly torn by war, disease, and famine. She was repulsed by what she saw and couldn't wait to get back to the comfort and security of her own home. One day, however, she cradled a young child in her arms, dying from starvation and too weak to do anything but whimper. Suddenly it hit her: *This child will die without ever once smiling in his entire life—not once.* Immediately she began seeing those around her in a radically different way: through the eyes of Christ. She committed herself to spend the rest of her life in places like that, helping others in His name.

When we look at people from our viewpoint, we value them only in terms of what we think they can do for us. But God looks at people differently—and so should we. Paul wrote, "Christ's love compels us, because . . . . those who live should no longer live for themselves but for him who died and for them was raised again. So from now on we regard no one from a worldly point of view" (2 Corinthians 5:14–16).

Paul hadn't always felt this way; at one time he hated Christians and had little use for people of different races. But God changed his heart, and he became deeply burdened for all who didn't know Christ. God's love filled his soul, and he saw people the way God sees them: as objects of His love. Ask God to make this happen in your life.

Living the Good News

The second essential for making an impact for Christ is to demonstrate Christ's love by the way we live.

One problem many early Christians faced was marriage to an unbeliever. How should they act toward them? Instead of arguing with them, the apostle Peter wrote, they should seek to influence them by the way they live, so they "may be won over without words . . . , when they see the purity and reverence of your lives" (1 Peter 3:1–2). Their lives were to be unspoken sermons, pointing their spouses to Christ. The same principle applies in all our relationships.

However, God also wants us to demonstrate His love in more active ways. *Wherever sin has wreaked its havoc, we should seek to put Christ's transforming love into action.* We will never make this world a perfect place; that will only happen when Christ returns in glory. But we are called to make it a *better* place, doing all we can to alleviate human suffering and combat social injustice. Of all people, Christians should be burdened about the intractable problems that plague the human race, such as poverty, disease, ignorance, famine, environmental damage, racism, violence, and war. God may call you to attack these problems directly, either individually or on a much larger scale. At a minimum, support those who are working to alleviate these problems in Christ's name, both by your prayers and your financial support. By doing so, we demonstrate Christ's compassion for others and also may open the door for the Gospel. Jesus said, "If anyone gives even a cup of cold water to one of these little ones because he is my disciple, I tell you the truth, he will certainly not lose his reward" (Matthew 10:42).

Do others see Christ in the way you live? One woman wrote me, "My friend claims to be a Christian, but she's the worst gossip I've ever seen. Is this the way Christians are supposed to act?" Another wrote, "My cousin says he's a Christian, but he's always complaining and finding fault with everyone. Isn't that wrong?" People are quick to spot the inconsistencies in our lives—and that turns them away from Christ. The old saying is true: What we are often speaks louder than what we say.

Telling the Good News

This leads to a final way you can make an impact for Christ: Learn to share your faith with others.

Simply living a good life isn't enough. People also need to understand what the Gospel is—and they will only understand it if someone tells them. The Gospel has *content*, and it must be communicated in ways people can understand. Paul asked, "How can they believe in the one of whom they have not heard? And how can they hear without someone preaching to them?" (Romans 10:14). Preaching isn't limited to a formal speech or sermon. The word Paul used here means "announcing or communicating a message," and it happens whenever we share Christ with someone—whether in church, across a cup of coffee, in a hospital or dorm room, at summer camp, or even seven miles up in an airplane.

What is the Gospel message someone needs to know? Briefly stated, it consists of *four points*, which I encourage you to memorize so you can tell them to someone else. (I have added some Bible references to each point, which I urge you to memorize also.) First, God created us, and He loves us and wants us to live at peace with Him forever (Genesis 2:7; John 10:10). Second, we have sinned and turned away from God, and as a result we are cut off from Him and subject to His judgment (Romans 3:23; Isaiah 59:2). Third, God still loves us, and He sent His only Son, Jesus Christ, into the world to take the judgment we deserve and bring us back to God (Romans 5:8; Romans 6:23; 1 Peter 3:18). Fourth, we must respond in faith by trusting Jesus Christ as our Savior and committing our lives to Him as Lord (John 3:16; John 1:12; Romans 10:9).

One of the most effective ways to present the Gospel to someone is to tell them what Christ has done for you. They may argue or ask all kinds of questions you may not know how to answer—but they can't deny what Christ has done in your life. Take time to think through your own testimony, and then ask God to help you tell it briefly and clearly whenever He gives you the opportunity. The Bible says, "Always be prepared to give an answer to everyone who asks you to give the reason for the hope that you have" (1 Peter 3:15).

In addition, *pray for those around you who do not know Christ.* You cannot pray consistently for someone to come to Christ but remain indifferent to them. Nor can you pray for their salvation without realizing that God may want to use you to touch their lives. Before prayer changes others, it first changes us.

But prayer is crucial in evangelism for another reason: Only God can change the heart of someone who is in rebellion against Him. No matter how logical our arguments or how fervent our appeals, our words will accomplish nothing unless God's Spirit prepares the way. The Bible says, "The heart is deceitful above all things and beyond cure. Who can understand it? I the LORD search the heart and examine the mind" (Jeremiah 17:9–10).

Only in heaven will we fully understand the mysteries of the human heart and why some people respond to the Gospel while others refuse. But one thing is clear: Prayer is an essential part of evangelism. Sometimes I'm asked to list the most important steps in preparing for an evangelistic mission, and my reply is always the same: prayer . . . prayer . . . and more prayer. Paul urged the Christians in Colossae to "pray for us . . . that God may open a door for our message" (Colossians 4:3).

All around you are people who need Christ: your family, your neighbors, people you work with or go to school with every day. Are you praying for them, asking God to open the door of their hearts to His truth? And are you asking God to use you to tell them about Christ? In addition, God also is calling people to Himself throughout the world, and we need to be praying for them as well. He may put it on your heart to pray for specific missionaries or the people of some particular nation or tribe. You may never meet them in this life—but in heaven you may discover that your prayers had a part in bringing about their eternal salvation.

One of Satan's most effective ways of blocking God's work is to convince us God can't use us to make an impact for Christ. But it isn't true. All around you are people no one else will ever be able to reach with the Gospel. Jesus' words in Luke 10:2 are still true: "The harvest is plentiful, but the workers are few. Ask the Lord of the harvest, therefore, to send out workers into his harvest field"— beginning with you.

TWENTY-NINE

AS LIFE MOVES ON

Even to your old age and gray hairs
I am he, I am he who will sustain you.
I have made you and I will carry you;
I will sustain you and I will rescue you.

—ISAIAH 46:4

IT'S NOT ONLY HOW YOU START A RACE THAT'S IMPOR-tant, but how you finish—and the same is true of the Christian life.

Have you ever had the experience of starting a project but never finishing it? Most of us have. Over time your enthusiasm cooled or you got bored or the project proved too hard, and eventually you simply moved on to something else.

But life's journey isn't like this; we don't have the option of stopping and moving on to something else. Nor do we have the option of finishing it or not finishing it; the journey continues as long as we live. The only question is *how will we finish?*

The Downward Spiral

One of the most tragic stories in all the Bible is that of King Saul, the first ruler of Israel. He was highly gifted; the Bible says he was "an impressive young man without equal" (1 Samuel 9:2). After his coronation he exhibited every quality anyone could ever want in a leader: humility, bravery, charisma, character, administrative skill, strategic brilliance. When word came that an Israelite city was under siege, we read that "the Spirit of God came upon him in power" (1 Samuel 11:6) and the nation rallied around his leadership. The enemy was soundly defeated, and Saul gave God credit for the victory.

But over time Saul changed. His humble dependence on God gave way to arrogance and confidence in himself. When young David single-handedly turned back a powerful Philistine invasion by killing their leader Goliath with his slingshot, Saul—instead of being grateful—became insanely jealous. Insecure and obsessed with his own power, he relentlessly pursued David and sought to kill him. Eventually Saul turned from God to a witch or spirit medium for guidance and ended up committing suicide. Saul's journey started well, but it ended disastrously.

What went wrong? The Bible doesn't give us a detailed answer, but what is clear is that Saul's downward spiral didn't happen all at once. Instead, as the years passed he faced new temptations and challenges, and like a series of falling dominoes one failure led to another.

The Stages of Life

Much of my life as an evangelist has been spent traveling; I've taken far more trips than I can even begin to remember. Although no two journeys were exactly alike, each progressed from one stage to another until its end.

The same is true with life. Each of us is on a journey, inevitably moving from one stage to another until its conclusion. Infancy grows into childhood; childhood blossoms into adolescence; adolescence develops into young adulthood; young adulthood slips into middle age; middle age advances toward the mature years; the mature years give way to old age.

What does this have to do with that other journey God has given us—the journey of the Christian life? Simply this: *Every stage of life has its own temptations and dangers, and Satan will do all he can to exploit them.* As we grow older, we may not face the same temptations we did when we were young—but we will still be tempted. And because they may be different from those we experienced before, they can catch us off guard. In the rest of this chapter, I want to examine some of these latter stages of life and what they may mean to us spiritually. You may not be facing one of them right now—but someday you might, and the time to prepare is now, not when it arrives.

Facing the Empty Nest

As our children were growing, I suspect visitors to our home must have gone away shaking their heads and muttering something about it being a madhouse! Five extremely active children plus assorted dogs and cats were more than enough to guarantee that life was never dull. Since I was often traveling, Ruth bore the brunt of our children's daily struggles, but life with a houseful of children always seemed to keep us in a state of happy chaos.

Then the children were gone. People had told us they would grow up almost before we realized it—and they were right. "I dreaded returning to that now-empty home," Ruth wrote later. We were facing what millions of parents face every year: *the empty nest.* In time God in His goodness filled our lives with new joys (including grandchildren and great-grandchildren), but adjusting to the empty nest was still a challenge for both of us.

People react to this stage of life in different ways. Some approach it with relief, yearning for its peace and freedom. Others (especially single parents) greet it with mixed emotions, thankful a difficult time is behind them but dreading a lonely future. Still others are caught off guard, unexpectedly feeling useless or bored or depressed. Any of these reactions can endanger us spiritually.

What dangers threaten us during this time of change? One is *marital discord.* "We've stayed together for the children's sake," one woman wrote me, "but now that they're gone we can't see any reason to keep on." A husband wrote, "Since our children left, we just don't have anything in common."

Adding to the problem is the fact that middle age often arrives about the same time as the empty nest. Not every person passes through a so-called "midlife crisis," but my mail certainly confirms that many do. "My husband has turned into a different person," one brokenhearted wife wrote me. "Now he's moved in with someone who's young enough to be his daughter and wants a divorce." Another wrote, "My husband is so busy with his career he never pays any attention to me. Now I'm having an affair. You'll probably say it's wrong, but don't I have a right to be happy?" Such letters concern me because I know those paths will never bring lasting happiness and security.

That last letter points out another danger often lurking in the background during this stage of life: *preoccupation with other things.* We realize time is passing, and we may decide to make the most of it—whatever the cost. Some (like this woman's husband) become absorbed in their careers; others try to pack in as many exotic expe-

riences or pleasures as possible. Still others frantically pursue financial security or social position, or try to turn back the clock with
extreme diets or exercise or cosmetic surgery. Life becomes un-
balanced, and *in the process God gets pushed to the fringes*. Instead of staying at the center of our lives, Christ gradually gets relegated to the
shadows. Don't let this happen to you!

Across the Generations

Closely associated with the empty nest is another issue every
parent faces: *relating to our adult children*.

There is no easy answer to this; children differ in their needs
and personalities (just as we do). Parents need much wisdom in
relating to their grown children—and much prayer. Children
likewise have much to learn about relating to their parents as the
years pass.

While every situation is different, the Bible warns us against *two
extremes* in dealing with our adult children. First, it tells us to avoid
trying to control our children once they become adults. "My parents are constantly interfering in our lives," one newlywed wrote
me. "How can we get them to let us alone?"

When children become independent, a major transition takes
place: They are no longer under our authority. This is especially true
once they marry. The Bible says, "For this reason a man *will leave* his
father and mother and be united to his wife" (Genesis 2:24, emphasis added). They become a separate family, and as parents we need to
avoid trying to control them or interfering unwisely in their lives. The
same is true of children who are still single or have gone through the
pain of divorce. That doesn't mean we won't help them or give them
advice—not at all. But we need to be wise in how we do it.

The other extreme is ignoring our adult children. "Our kids

gave us so much trouble," one man said to me, "that I don't care if I ever see them again." His words were harsh, and I was relieved to discover he didn't really mean them—but some parents do. Others simply drift apart from their children. When this happens, we not only weaken our family ties, but we also forfeit opportunities to encourage and help them spiritually.

This is especially true once they have children of their own. Our nineteen grandchildren (and now our great-grandchildren) have brought us great joy over the years, and my heart goes out to grandparents whose contact is limited by distance or divorce. But grandchildren aren't simply a privilege—they are also a responsibility. What will they remember about you? Will they only remember the good times you had together—or will they also remember your joy and your love for Christ?

If God gives you grandchildren, pray regularly for them and do whatever you can to encourage them to live for Christ. Keep contact with them; when you call their parents, talk to them too. Drop them cards and letters and e-mails also, and not just on special occasions. (As I look back, I wish I had been more faithful in doing this.) Most of all, be an example to them. Paul's words to pastors could apply also to grandparents: "In everything set them an example by doing what is good" (Titus 2:7).

As Our Parents Age

As life moves on, another issue may arise: *our aging parents*. At one time they took care of us; now we may have to take care of them. One of the Ten Commandments says, "Honor your father and your mother" (Exodus 20:12)—and this is lifelong. One way we obey this commandment is by helping them as they grow older. It may not be easy (or even possible in some situations) and may involve difficult decisions that require great sensitivity and wisdom. I recall helping my brother and sisters move our aging mother into an apartment because we felt it would be easier for her. But it soon became apparent she would be far happier in her old home, and thankfully we were able to move her back and arrange for a fine person to help her.

If God gives you responsibility for aging parents, seek what is best for them, not what is most convenient for you. And keep contact with them! Often when visiting a nursing home the staff will ask me to greet some of their forgotten residents. "Just saying hello means so much," they'll say. "Their families never visit." How sad! If ever we needed to put the Golden Rule into action, it's with our aging parents.

Retirement: a New Beginning

God wants us to work (whether at home or on the job), but that doesn't mean it's wrong to retire. The Levites (who assisted in Israel's worship) were required to retire at fifty (Numbers 8:24–26), and Moses stepped aside as he grew older, declaring "I am no longer able to lead you" (Deuteronomy 31:2).

Most of us will retire at some stage, but for many retirement turns out to be unexpectedly traumatic. "For years I looked forward to retirement," one man wrote me, "but now that I've actually retired I feel so useless." Another wrote, "I'm about to go out of my mind with boredom." A doctor told me a surprising number of people die within a few years of retirement; he attributed it to their belief life was no longer worthwhile.

Many people, I find, plan financially for retirement—but not spiritually and emotionally. Work isn't only earning a living; work gives us a sense of purpose and worth and opportunities for companionship. But retirement changes this, and many aren't prepared for it. They have never thought through what they'll do with their time, or how they'll find new ways to feel fulfilled.

But listen: *God isn't finished with you when you retire!* When we know Christ, we never retire from His service. If you are facing retirement (or even if it's years away), ask God to show you new ways to serve Him. It may be a part-time job or volunteer work in your community or a new responsibility in your church. Whatever it is, don't look on retirement as a chance to do nothing; think of it instead as a God-given change of career. See your new freedom not just as a chance to travel or pursue your hobbies, but as a fresh opportunity to help others in Christ's name.

As We Grow Older

"I don't like getting old," a friend confessed not long ago, "but I guess I don't have much choice, do I?" I had to agree with him. I never thought I'd live into my late eighties, and I can't say I like the fact that I can't do everything I once did, or that every morning seems to bring with it some new ache or pain—or worse. Ruth and I also don't like the sense of loss we feel as more and more of our contemporaries become disabled or die.

Nevertheless old age has its compensations. More than ever, I find, I see each day as a gift from God—a gift I must not take for granted. It also is a time to reflect back on God's goodness over the years and an opportunity to assure others that God truly is faithful to His promises. Most of all, it's a time to rejoice in our hope of heaven.

It's also, I've discovered, a time to take delight in life's little pleasures—even ones we may have overlooked before. On my doctor's recommendation I have started using a walker to help me keep my balance, and this means I'm constantly looking down at the ground around my feet. Suddenly I'm seeing things I never really noticed before—tiny insects and colorful bits of rock and miniature plants—all reminding me of the beauty and intricacy of God's creation. The Bible says, "Go to the ant . . . consider its ways and be wise!" (Proverbs 6:6). Our memory is also one of God's greatest gifts—to be able as we grow older to relive past events, both mentally and emotionally.

Old age is Satan's last chance to blow us off course, however—and you can be sure he'll try. It's hard not to worry about our health or loneliness or financial situation or any number of other issues we may face as we grow older. It's hard, too, not to feel discouraged as our independence slips away or disabilities grow. We may even wonder if God has abandoned us.

But He hasn't. Jesus' promise is just as true now as at any other stage of life: "I am with you always, to the very end of the age" (Matthew 28:20). The Bible also says that in God's eyes "gray hair is a crown of splendor" (Proverbs 16:31). I can honestly say that I feel closer to God now than at any other time of my life—and this can be true for you. You may not be able to do everything you once did—but you can do something, and God can still use you to bless others. Ask Him to help you reflect Christ as you grow older, instead of turning sour or grumpy.

Devote time to prayer also. A few weeks before his death a Christian friend remarked that if he didn't have the strength to pray aloud, he could still whisper, and if he couldn't whisper, he could still move his lips, and if he couldn't move his lips, he could still pray silently in his mind. A close friend of mine had a list of missionaries he had known over the years, and every morning he would pray for a certain number of them by name. Even as he grew older, he knew he was having a part in their ministry.

Staying the Course

Our later years can be the most fulfilling of our lives—if we commit them to God. But how will we stay the course?

The first step is to be alert to the dangers. You've probably heard the old adage "Forewarned is forearmed"—and it's true. The time to deal with spiritual danger is *before* it happens. How different David's life would have been if he had guarded against the temptations of middle age! Instead, his life became a downward spiral of irresponsibility, adultery, murder, and heartache (2 Samuel 11–12). God forgave him when he confessed his sin and repented—but the damage was done and he never regained his former influence. The Bible says, "Above all else, guard your heart, for it is the wellspring of life" (Proverbs 4:23).

Second, strengthen your commitment to Christ. Don't wait until the storms of old age threaten to blow you off course; *now* is the time to strengthen your faith. The stronger our relationship with Christ, the stronger our defense against the devil's temptations. He will still try to lure us away, but Christ will help us resist. The Bible says, "The man of integrity walks securely" (Proverbs 10:9).

In addition, learn to commit every situation to God, and trust Him for the outcome. God's love for you never changes, no matter what problems you face or how unsettled life becomes. Nothing takes Him by surprise, and He can be trusted to do what is best. Instead of letting fear and anxiety paralyze you, learn to commit everything to God. The Bible says, "Trust in the LORD forever, for the LORD, the LORD, is the Rock eternal" (Isaiah 26:4).

Finally, strengthen the relationships God has already given you. Strengthen your relationship with your spouse . . . your children . . . your friends . . . your fellow believers. When we're isolated or think we don't need others, we become much more vulnerable to temptation and compromise. Satan's fiercest attacks against Jesus came when He was alone (in the desert and in the Garden of Gethsemane). Godly relationships make us accountable to others and fill our lives with joy. I have yet to see Satan overcome a truly joyful Christian.

As his life neared its end, the apostle Paul was left with almost nothing. Imprisoned in Rome because of his faith, he didn't even have a cloak to shield his frail body against the coming winter. His friends had abandoned him or gone elsewhere; only one—Luke—was still with him. Measured by the world's standards his life was a failure.

But not by God's standards! Christ had called Paul to be His disciple, and Paul had been faithful to that calling. As he looked back over his life as a Christian, with all of its hardships and temptations, he could truthfully say, "I have fought the good fight, I have finished the race, I have kept the faith" (2 Timothy 4:7).

Paul finished well. Will you?

THIRTY

———

OUR GLORIOUS HOPE

He will wipe every tear from their eyes. There will be no more death or mourning or crying or pain, for the old order of things has passed away.

—REVELATION 21:4

LIFE IS HARD—BUT GOD IS GOOD, AND HEAVEN IS real.

No one doubts the first part of that sentence: Life *is* hard. Often while writing this chapter my mind has been preoccupied by the death and destruction caused by Hurricane Katrina along the southern coast of the United States. Like the devastating tsunami that struck South Asia only months before, hundreds of thousands were driven from their homes and forced to find shelter elsewhere, often fleeing with nothing more than the clothes on their backs. One family whom a church near us adopted arrived bruised and battered from wading for miles through debris-filled water, a story that could be duplicated thousands of times. Eventually that area will be rebuilt and Katrina may fade from our view, but in the meantime life is hard for those who have been affected—very hard.

Most of us probably will never experience a disaster of this magnitude—but we too know life is hard. Sometimes its harshness comes upon us suddenly and without warning; sometimes it stays with us most of our lives. In this book we have looked at some of life's heartaches and struggles, but no single volume can begin to deal with all of them. Life has its share of joys and laughter—but we also know life's road is often very rough. Temptations assail us; people disappoint us; illness and age weaken us; tragedies and sorrows ambush us; evil and injustice overpower us.

Life is hard—but God is good, and *heaven is real!*

Our Final Destination

One of the Bible's greatest truths is that *we were not meant for this world alone*. Death is not the end of life; it is only the gateway to eternity. We were meant to live forever, and death is only a transition from this life to the next. The question isn't whether or not there is life after death. The only question is where we will spend eternity—either with God in that place of endless joy the Bible calls heaven, or apart from Him in that place of endless despair the Bible calls hell.

Why isn't death the end as it appears to be? Job lamented, "Man born of woman is of few days and full of trouble. He springs up like a flower and withers away; like a fleeting shadow, he does not endure. . . . Man dies and is laid low; he breathes his last and is no more" (Job 14:1–2, 10). Yet Job knew this isn't the whole story. Someday this life will end, but for the Christian death also marks a beginning—the beginning of a new life with God that will last forever. Paul put it this way: "'No eye has seen, no ear has heard, no mind has conceived what God has prepared for those who love him'—but God has revealed it to us by his Spirit" (1 Corinthians 2:9–10). In the midst of life's disappointments and sufferings, heaven is our glorious hope.

How Do We Know?

To many, however, any talk about heaven or eternal life is only wishful thinking. "Heaven is just a myth as far as I'm concerned," one man wrote me. "I'd like to think we'll live forever, but once we're dead, that's the end."

Is he right? How do we know heaven is real?

One reason is because of our inner yearning. Virtually every religion believes in some type of afterlife, and down inside we all sense there must be something beyond this life. This life is incomplete, and we yearn for its fulfillment. Where did this universal yearning come from? The Bible says God implanted it within us: "He has also set eternity in the hearts of men" (Ecclesiastes 3:11). We were made for God, and we yearn to be with Him forever. We can suppress this or convince ourselves it isn't true—but we still hope that life's injustices and evils will be made right someday.

We also know heaven is real because of God's promises. From one end of the Bible to the other, God assures us that we were made to live with Him forever. The psalmist declared, "Surely goodness and love will follow me all the days of my life, and I will dwell in the house of the LORD forever" (Psalm 23:6). Job affirmed, "I know that my Redeemer lives, and that in the end he will stand upon the earth. And after my skin has been destroyed, yet in my flesh I will see God" (Job 19:25–26). Jesus promised, "I am the resurrection and the life. He who believes in me will live, even though he dies"

(John 11:25). Paul taught, "Now we know that if the earthly tent we live in is destroyed, we have a building from God, an eternal house in heaven, not built by human hands" (2 Corinthians 5:1).

There is, however, a third reason why we know heaven is real: because of Christ's death and resurrection for us. Why did Jesus Christ leave heaven's glory and enter this sin-infested world? For one reason: to make our eternal salvation possible. When God created Adam and Eve, His plan was that they would live in perfect harmony with Him forever. But Satan was determined to change that, and with his lies he lured them away from God. When that happened, death came upon the human race, and we are all its victims. Never forget: *Death was Satan's greatest victory.*

But by His death and resurrection, Jesus Christ reversed this. The Bible says Christ came to "free those who all their lives were held in slavery by their fear of death" (Hebrews 2:15). Think of it: *Satan's greatest victory has now been turned into defeat! Death has now been put to death!* No wonder the Bible says, "Where, O death, is your victory? Where, O death, is your sting? . . . Thanks be to God! He gives us the victory through our Lord Jesus Christ" (1 Corinthians 15:55, 57).

Christ's motive in coming to earth was love, and His goal was to destroy death and take us to be with the Father forever. Jesus' resurrection proves beyond all doubt that death is not the end, and ahead of us is heaven. Jesus promised, "In my Father's house are many rooms; if it were not so, I would have told you. I am going there to prepare a place for you" (John 14:2). This is our sure hope.

What Is Heaven Like?

If heaven is real, what is it like? I've never met a Christian who didn't want to know the answer to this question—including me! Even Jesus' disciples wondered; immediately after He taught them about heaven, Thomas protested, "Lord, we don't know where you are going" (John 14:5).

The Bible doesn't answer all our questions about heaven and what it will be like—because heaven is far more glorious than anything we can imagine. Heaven is like the most perfect and beautiful place we can conceive—only more so. Only in heaven will we know exactly what heaven is like. The writer of Revelation, searching for words to describe his glimpse of heaven's splendor, said that "it shone with the glory of God, and its brilliance was like that of a very precious jewel. . . . The great street of the city was of pure gold, like transparent glass" (Revelation 21:11, 21). Paul wrote, "Now we see but a poor reflection as in a mirror; then we shall see face to face. Now I know in part; then I shall know fully" (1 Corinthians 13:12).

Nevertheless, the Bible doesn't leave us in the dark about heaven—and everything it tells us should make us want to go there. Let's look at *four truths* the Bible teaches about heaven and what will happen to us there.

With God Forever

First, the Bible says that in heaven we will be with God. Heaven is many things—but the most important is this: *Heaven is God's dwelling place.* It is the place where God lives! It's true that God is everywhere, but heaven is more than a place. It is a whole different dimension of existence, and God is in its midst, with Christ at His right hand. The Bible says, "We will be with the Lord forever" (1 Thessalonians 4:17).

Think of it: We will be with God forever! And because we will be with Him, we will be absolutely safe from all evil. Sorrow and suffering will never again touch us—never. One of the most moving passages in all the Bible is found in its next to last chapter:

And I heard a loud voice from the throne saying, 'Now the dwelling of God is with men, and he will live with them. They will be his people, and God himself will be with them and be their God. He will wipe every tear from their eyes. There will be no more death or mourning or crying or pain, for the old order of things has passed away. (Revelation 21:3–4)

Home at Last

This leads us to a second great truth about Heaven: We will be home. The word "home" means different things to different people. "I'll never go home again," a young man wrote me after recounting a childhood filled with strife and abuse. Then he added, "But I want it to be different for my children. I want them to have a real home." Down inside he knew home should be a place of happiness and peace, even if his wasn't.

The Bible says this world is not our final home—but we do have one, and that is heaven. The Bible calls us "aliens and strangers on earth" (Hebrews 11:13) and reminds us that "our citizenship is in heaven" (Philippians 3:20). Our heart's cry is like Paul's, who said he "would prefer to be away from the body and at home with the Lord" (2 Corinthians 5:8). From time to time our local newspaper prints obituaries that say the deceased "went to her heavenly home." I always know that person must have been a Christian.

Home is a place of peace and joy—and so is heaven. Home is a place of love and security—and so is heaven. Home is a place of welcome and rest—and so is heaven. The Bible says, "Those who walk uprightly enter into peace; they find rest as they lie in death" (Isaiah 57:2). When we die in Christ, we are at home with Him forever.

As a footnote, sometimes people say to me, "Well, I'm not sure I want to go to heaven. It sounds so boring!" But we won't be bored in heaven, for we will have all eternity to explore God's riches. The Bible also says God will have work for us to do, for we will serve Him and reign with Him—but without the weariness of our work here (Revelation 22:3, 5).

Forever Changed

In addition, the Bible tells us that in heaven we will be like Christ. Someday God's plan to make us more like Christ will be complete, for "we will all be changed—in a flash, in the twinkling of an eye, at the last trumpet" (1 Corinthians 15:51–52).

What does this mean? First, it means we will have new bodies—bodies that will be like Christ's resurrection body. Do I know what we'll look like in heaven? No—but our new bodies will be perfect, beyond the reach of all illness and decay. They also will be recognizable to those we knew on earth. Our present bodies have been corrupted by sin, and we "groan inwardly as we wait eagerly for our adoption as sons, the redemption of our bodies" (Romans 8:23). But someday our wait will be over!

It also means our whole nature will be transformed. Someday we will be like Christ! Now we love imperfectly—but not then. Now our joy and peace are tempered by sorrow and turmoil—but not then. The Bible says, "Dear friends, now we are children of God, and what we will be has not yet been made known. But we know that when he appears, we shall be like him, for we shall see him as he is" (1 John 3:2). What a glorious promise!

All Things New

Finally, in heaven we will be part of a new creation. Sin hasn't only affected our bodies, it has also affected all creation. And just as we will be changed when God's kingdom is fully established, so too will all creation, for *God will reverse every consequence of Adam's rebellion*. In that day "the creation itself will be liberated from its bondage to decay and brought into the glorious freedom of the children of God" (Romans 8:21). Perhaps this is what Isaiah envisioned when he wrote, "The wolf will live with the lamb, the leopard will lie down with the goat, the calf and the lion and the yearling together" (Isaiah 11:6).

When will this take place? The Bible says it will happen when Christ comes again to establish His authority over all creation: "The day of the Lord will come like a thief. The heavens will disappear with a roar; the elements will be destroyed by fire. . . . But in keeping with his promise we are looking forward to a new heaven and a new earth, the home of righteousness" (2 Peter 3:10, 13).

Shortly after his election as the next president, John F. Kennedy asked me to play golf with him in Florida, which I was honored to do. While driving us to the course he stopped the car and asked me if it was true that Jesus would return to earth some day. I was quite surprised at his question, and I was especially surprised he stopped the car to ask it. I assured him it was true, and that all Christian churches (including his own) affirmed it in their creeds. At his funeral only three years later, Cardinal Cushing read from 1 Thessalonians 4:16 about the coming again of Christ: "For the Lord himself will come down from heaven, with a loud command, with the voice of the archangel and with the trumpet call of God, and the dead in Christ will rise first."

Sometimes Christ's promise to return has been overlooked, but Christians have always turned to this great truth during difficult and uncertain times. When I was growing up, the horror of World War I and the despair of the Great Depression sent many Christians (including my mother) back to their Bibles, which led to a new emphasis on prophecy and the hope of Christ's return.

During times of persecution Christians always have found comfort in Christ's promise to come back and destroy all evil. I have seldom spoken in a series of evangelistic meetings without including at least one message on Christ's return.

Christ's second coming reminds us that ultimately our hope is not in this world and its attempts to solve its problems, but in Christ's promise to establish His perfect rule over all the earth. As Jesus ascended into heaven at the end of His time on earth, the angels promised His disciples, "This same Jesus, who has been taken from you into heaven, will come back in the same way you have seen him go into heaven" (Acts 1:11). Jesus warned, "You also must be ready, because the Son of Man will come at an hour when you do not expect him" (Matthew 24:44).

Christ's return can't be separated from another sobering truth, however, and that is the promise of God's judgment. Jesus said, "When the Son of Man comes in his glory, and all the angels with him, he will sit on his throne in heavenly glory. All the nations will be gathered before him, and he will separate the people one from another" (Matthew 25:31-32). Those who have rejected God's offer of salvation, He warned, "will go away to eternal punishment, but the righteous to eternal life" (Matthew 25:46). Paul declared to the pagan philosophers in Athens that God "has set a day when he will judge the world with justice by the man he has appointed. He has given proof of this to all men by raising him from the dead" (Acts 17:31). Their reaction was similar to that of many today whenever God's judgment is mentioned: "Some of them sneered, but others said, 'We want to hear you again on this subject'" (Acts 17:32).

But we ignore God's judgment at our peril. Some day God will judge all those who were responsible for the injustices and evils of this world. Those who have deliberately scorned God and rejected His way of salvation through Jesus Christ will also be judged. And just as God's judgment is a reality, so too is the place the Bible calls hell. Just as heaven is the final destination of all who have trusted Christ for their salvation, so hell (the Bible says) is the final destination of all who reject God's appointed means of salvation through Christ. This is a solemn and sobering truth; a seminary professor I once knew told his students, "Never preach about hell without tears in your eyes." Occasionally someone will write me saying that they look forward to hell, "because all my friends will be there." But the Bible paints a far different picture. It tells us that hell is a place of absolute loneliness and despair, and describes it as a place of "darkness, where there will be weeping and gnashing of teeth" (Matthew 25:30). Most of all, hell is separation from God. Not one word about hell in the Bible would ever make you want to go there.

And the good news is that you don't have to go there! Christ has provided the way of escape—and the reason (as we have seen) is because He endured hell's pain and loneliness in our place. God's promise is true: "Therefore, there is now no condemnation for those who are in Christ Jesus" (Romans 8:1). Don't gamble with your eternal destiny, but make sure of your commitment to Christ today.

Equally devout Bible scholars disagree about some of the details of Christ's return—but one thing is certain: At the end of this present age, Christ *will* come again to establish His kingdom. Someday God's promise will be fulfilled: "I am making everything new!" (Revelation 21:5). Jesus repeatedly promised He would come again, not in the obscurity of Bethlehem but in glory and power over the whole earth. No wonder the Bible calls this "the blessed hope—the glorious appearing of our great God and Savior, Jesus Christ" (Titus 2:13). As she grew older, my mother said she never awakened in the morning without asking herself, "I wonder if this will be the day Jesus returns?" Our constant prayer should be that of John at the end of Revelation: "Come, Lord Jesus" (Revelation 22:20).

In the Meantime

Heaven is real—but what difference does it make right now? Is the old quip true, that Christians are so heavenly minded they aren't any earthly good? Definitely not—and in fact the opposite should be the case.

First, because heaven is real, we have hope: hope for the future, and hope for our lives right now. No matter what happens to us now, we know it won't last forever, and ahead of us is the joy of heaven.

At the beginning of this chapter, I wrote, "Life is hard—but God is good, and heaven is real." I was actually quoting a doctor friend of mine who sometimes tells this to his Christian patients, because he knows how easily we get caught up in our present problems and forget God's promise of heaven. Paul wrote, "If only for this life we have hope in Christ, we are to be pitied more than all men" (1 Corinthians 15:19). But our hope isn't only for this life! In the midst of life's storms, our hope in God's promise of heaven is "an anchor for the soul, firm and secure" (Hebrews 6:19).

In addition, because heaven is real, our lives have meaning and purpose right now. Before he turned to God, the writer of Ecclesiastes concluded, "Everything is meaningless" (Ecclesiastes 1:2). Many today come to the same conclusion. But when we know Christ, we know life *isn't* meaningless, because God has a reason for keeping us here. Every day is a gift from Him and is another opportunity to love Him and serve Him. Heaven doesn't make this life less important; it makes it *more* important.

This leads to a final difference heaven should make: Because heaven is real, we should live every moment for Christ. Life is short; none of us knows how long we have. Live each day as if it were your last—for some day it will be. Peter wrote, "Since everything will be destroyed in this way, what kind of people ought you to be? You ought to live holy and godly lives as you look forward to the day of God and speed its coming" (2 Peter 3:11–12). If you are ever going to live for Christ, it should be now.

Is heaven your goal? Are you looking forward to going there? I know I am, and I pray you are too. What a glorious future God has prepared for us!

Don't let the burdens and hardships of this life distract you or discourage you, but keep your eyes firmly fixed on what God has promised at the end of our journey: heaven itself.

> Therefore we do not lose heart. Though outwardly we are wasting away, yet inwardly we are being renewed day by day. For our light and momentary troubles are achieving for us an eternal glory that far outweighs them all. So we fix our eyes not on what is seen, but on what is unseen. For what is seen is temporary, but what is unseen is eternal. (2 Corinthians 4:16–18)

Praise God for the hope we have in Christ!

A FINAL WORD FROM BILLY GRAHAM

ONE DAY YOUR LIFE'S JOURNEY WILL BE OVER, AND you will enter eternity. But what kind of journey will it have been? At the end of your life, will you look back with sorrow and regret, realizing too late that you had traveled the wrong road? Or perhaps that the road you traveled was the right one—but you had allowed the troubles and temptations of this world to hold you back and keep you from reaching your full potential?

Instead, my prayer is that you would have been on the right road in life—and not only that, but that you would have reached the end of your journey with joy. My prayer is that you would have known God's presence the whole way, and that even in the midst of life's deepest trials you would have found your strength in Him.

If you and I could sit down and talk right now, I'd want to hear about your journey so far. On which road are you traveling? Is it the right road—the road God has set out for you? Or are you still on that broad road of which Jesus spoke—a road that looks deceptively inviting and easy, but in the end leads only to emptiness and sorrow and death?

Now is the time to decide which road you will follow. If you have never done so, I urge you to turn to Christ and by faith invite Him to come into your life today. No matter who you are or what your background has been, God still loves you, and Christ died and rose again so you could be on a new path in life—His path. God's promise is for you: "For God so loved the world that he gave his one and only Son, that whoever believes in him shall not perish but have eternal life" (John 3:16). Make your commitment to Jesus Christ today.

Then make it your goal to follow Him every day. As we have seen in this book, God has given us everything we need to see us through life's problems and hardships and to end our journey well. Don't waste your life, and don't be satisfied with anything less than God's plan.

Some day this life will be over. I look forward to that day, because I know that beyond it is heaven. I pray you do too. But until that day God calls you home, make it your goal to live for Christ.

ACKNOWLEDGMENTS

EVERY AUTHOR IS INDEBTED TO ALL THOSE WHO HAVE influenced their lives, and this is certainly true of me. I can never be grateful enough for all those men and women whom God brought across my path over the years, and the way He used them to enrich me and add to my understanding of the Bible. I am especially thankful for my wife, Ruth; over the years she has been my closest friend and adviser, and without her God-given wisdom and insight, my ministry would not have been possible—including this book.

I also am indebted to those who helped in the preparation of this book for publication, including my executive assistant, Dr. David Bruce; my secretary, Stephanie Wills; and Patricia Lynn, of our Montreat staff. I owe a special word of thanks to my longtime associate Dr. John Akers, whose research and editorial skills enabled him to help me select and recast materials from my writings and messages into a suitable form for this project. Finally, I wish to thank David Moberg and his staff at W Publishing Group for their encouragement and assistance.

You can contact Billy Graham at www.billygraham.org
or The Billy Graham Evangelistic Association
1 Billy Graham Parkway
Charlotte, NC 28201
